S0-BOF-472

FRESHMAN COMPOSITION

FRESHMAN COMPOSITION

BY

HENRY BURROWES LATHROP

Associate Professor of English in the
University of Wisconsin

NEW YORK
THE CENTURY CO.
1921

PE 1408
.L33
1921

Copyright, 1920, by
THE CENTURY CO.

PRINTED IN U. S. A.

DEDICATED
TO
SEVERAL MILLIONS
OF
FRESHMAN THEMES

Apr 21 '33. Dpt. D.C. Zimmerman.

45665

GETTYSBURG COLLEGE
Gettysburg, Pa.
❧ LIBRARY ❧

PREFACE

This book is made up of answers to questions and responses to challenges. For more years than I quite like to see recorded in print I have been trying to show to puzzled freshmen how to do what they are told in Freshman English, and to skeptical freshmen why they are told to do it. There is nothing here which does not grow out of some actual, some constantly recurring situation.

The problems of the teacher and the student as they arise in the progress of the course are detached, incidental, unrelated. The attempt is here made to systematize and codify experience. The purpose of this book is not only to give practical directions, but to bring those directions into relation, to develope an ordered body of guiding principles.

In this respect it departs from the tendency of recent works on the subject, which avowedly follow the rule of thumb. It is the author's belief that for the sake of clearness it is necessary to treat the subject as an organized whole; and that such a treatment need not be false in fact or unliterary in spirit. Moreover, though the treatment of the subject of ''rhetoric''—the theory of composition—ought not to be philosophically complete in such a book, it ought to go to the bottom of the topics which it does consider. Only in this way can conviction and security be attained. ''Is it not best to write as one speaks?''—''Is slang ever justified?''— ''How can I make my sentences better organized?''—

"I know that seems flat; but how can I make it more
vigorous?" The student who frankly puts such questions has a right to be led to see the truth, and to think
with some steadiness about it. The author does not
find freshmen grateful for inadequacy or for easy solu-
tions. He finds them intelligent and sincere. They
may be astonishingly ignorant and crude, scanty in vocabulary, untrained in grammatical analysis, and about
as easy and swift of movement as a set of sack-racers,
but they wish to learn and to understand.

The discarding of systematic treatises on rhetoric was
perfectly natural and necessary. The earlier treatises
on the art of English composition could be little more
than adaptations of Cicero and Quintilian—authors concerned with the art of persuasive oratory. One must
respect a scheme of education which in its very deca-
dence was a vital discipline for such men as Chrysostom
and Augustine. But Greek and Latin rhetoric was far
too narrow as a basis for the theory of modern prose.
It had as its aim the production of a type of character
essentially unscientific and essentially biased in its whole
view of life and letters. The necessity of developing
a facile means of communication for the multiform activities of modern life—the need of a discipline in the
statement of fact, and the explication of ideas for their
own sake in fields of science and technology, and of
journalism, the complexity of modern business, and the
resulting need of a wide-spread command of an accurate and even fairly refined style as a part of general
education, requires the laying of a foundation for writing which does not look to the development of rhetorical
ability in the narrow sense as its directing force. Think
of the entire body of ancient and modern historians, and

see how the rhetorical ideal, not of mere style, but of the whole habit of mind, affects the writing, say of Livy. It was necessary to get totally rid of the system in order to see the problem with a fresh eye. Yet the need of some connected scheme of instruction, of some ordered guidance has constantly been felt, especially in Scotland and in America—in the one because literary English was a somewhat slow and artificial acquisition, in the other because of many influences, among them our large population, using English, indeed, but as a foreign tongue imperfectly mastered.

But teachers of English cannot be permanently satisfied with the method of hitting a head where you happen to see it. This method is wasteful of time, demands too much of the instructor, and tends to leave important matters untouched in the short round of one year of college English. So the author of the present work has taken a new look at the whole subject, and endeavored to treat the art of composition connectedly and respectfully. In this he has gone back to the ancients, not for a system but for principles. The modern theorists, before the recent anarchy, had come to regard their problem too externally, to consider the finished product, to discuss "qualities of style" and the "philosophy of style,"—to lay the foundation for criticism, not for actual practice. The ancients, in cultivating the art of writing, organized their subject systematically, not as a theory, but as an orderly process of exercises—finding material, arranging it, reducing it to connected language, learning the written work by heart, and delivering the speech. The student's work is in this book regarded as a thing which is being made and shaped, plastic under the hand, and the intellectual processes

guiding his work are more considered than the qualities
to be found in the finished product. Some things, indeed, can be brought to form only by revision; they
cannot be planned, but must be done; and with respect
to them it is not possible to give help except by considering what form of expression is satisfactory, and what is
not.

No ordered treatment of the principles of composition in this day can begin except from Professor Wendell's *English Composition*. It is the necessary basis.
At the same time, it seems to the present writer inaccurate in three fundamental respects. The first is the
erection of three apparently coördinate principles of
structure. There is one principle—unity; and to consider unity, coherence, and emphasis as things in any
way independent tends to make students try, as one of
mine put it, to "apply" them successively to their work.
The result is a definite rigidity, a tendency to mechanism
in style. Secondly, Mr. Wendell nowhere recognizes
that language can be spoken, and that emphasis in particular depends upon an appeal to the ear, not to the
eye. To make paragraph breaks, periods, and commas
determine the place of emphasis is to be simply false to
the facts of language. In the third place unity in language or thought is not constructed but evolves through
an act which proceeds in time; and a proper theory and
proper directions as to method must recognize this fact.
Yet Mr. Wendell's clean-cut and sensible simplification of the earlier confusion of miscellaneous rules of
order and method, and his application of his principles
to all units of composition, from the sentence up, was the
beginning of a rational treatment of structure in English composition.

The author has tried to take account of the common-
places of psychology and of philology as laying the necessary foundation for a sound theory of composition. He
owes most to his beloved and venerated teacher, the late
Professor William James; much to the discussion of the
nature of the sentence carried on by Professors Delbrück
and Wundt and others, much to Professor Jesperson, and
to Professor Sweet.   All are at one with what experience
amply shows, that logical relations are mainly communicated by the suggestion of certain effects of sound, quite
adequately analyzed long since by professors of elocution, but not considered effectively in English by theorists of language, so far as the writer knows, until
treated by Professor Sweet, who first deals with word-
grouping and emphasis as a part of grammar. Dr.
Benjamin Rush, *On the Philosophy of the Human Voice,*
as far back as 1827, presented the essential theory of
word-grouping, but the exposition of Dr. S. S. Curry
in *Lessons in Vocal Expression,* 1895, is the clearest with
which the writer is acquainted.

Professor Wendell is the last writer in English who
seems to the writer to have really advanced the theory
of our subject as a whole in a connected book. But
the valuable study of the metaphor by Miss Buck, the
change of Mr. Wendell's term *Mass* to *Emphasis* by
Professor G. R. Carpenter, Dr. Pitkin's use of the term
Intensification as applied to narrative, have been taken
advantage of with gratitude by the writer. Professor
L. A. Sherman's fruitful suggestion of the term *Subordination of Predication* cannot be passed without a
recognition of its fundamental value to those of us who
have striven to clear our minds upon this subject of the
art we teach, however humbly.

If reference has been made to the standard works
which have advanced knowledge in the field of rhetoric,
and to works in subsidiary fields of knowledge, it has
been for the purpose of making the treatment of the subject sound in order that it might be clear and useful.
The purpose of this work is to meet the actual needs
of students as the author finds them in his classes. It
has not been his aim to develop a subject in order to
be complete, or for the gratification of his enthusiasm
for the advance of knowledge. The theory of composition is not a science but a *technë*—a body of principles
with a severely practical end. There are parts of this
book which the average freshman will easily and quickly
grasp—single-mindedness and clearness of order in the
whole composition and the paragraph, for example.
The matter on the sentences will present more difficulty,
because the sentence ought to be the most thoroughly
studied part of the subject, and is in itself the most
difficult. The writer believes that in the analysis of the
sentence here given, there is something both ''new and
useful''—that it ''advances the state of the art.''

An effort has been made to leave room for considerable freedom in the order in which the topics are taken
up, and in the amount of attention which may be given
to each.

The illustrations given are in the main not intended
to be in a highly mannered and individual style.
Though perhaps the illustrations are less salient on this
account, they seem to the author better adapted to develop that normal standard of writing, not marked by
clever eccentricities in any direction, which we ought as
teachers to encourage.

The author takes this opportunity to express his gratitude for assistance given by his colleagues, Professor F. A. Manchester, Professor Warner Taylor, Mr. L. M. Beattie, Miss Hester Coddington, chief Cataloguer, and Mr. L. C. Burke, Assistant Librarian of the University of Wisconsin, and by his former colleague, Mr. W. J. Neidig. Thanks are also due to the holders of various copyrights for permission to use extracts from their books, in particular to Chas. Scribner's Sons, for passages from Stevenson and Henry James; to *McClure's Magazine* for extracts from an article by William James; to the Trustees of the Mark Twain estate for extracts from *Pudd'nhead Wilson;* to the Macmillan Company for passages from W. K. Clifford and others; to Longmans, Green, and Company for a passage from W. H. Hudson; to Little, Brown, and Company for passages from Parkman; to Harper and Brothers for passages from Sir Leslie Stephen and J. R. Green; to Ginn and Company for an extract from Professor W. M. Davis's *Elementary Meteorology;* to Doubleday, Page and Company for passages from various authors; and to the *American Magazine* for an article on Letter Writing.

CONTENTS

CONTENTS

CONTENTS

FRESHMAN COMPOSITION

FRESHMAN COMPOSITION

CHAPTER I

THE WHOLE COMPOSITION

I. UNITY OF PURPOSE

The Principle of Unity.—A composition about to be written may be compared to a road about to be built; the first essential is for the engineer to know exactly where the road begins, and whither it is to lead. How it gets there—its grade, its straightness, the views along the way—all this is important, but less important than that the road shall get there somehow.

It is said of one of our most distinguished public men that he is one who, when he has some practical problem to solve, first discovers some points in the circumference of the circle about it, and by means of these points determines where the center is. Then he tries to break through to that center. If he finds that he cannot make his way through at one point he tries another; but when once he has ascertained the line of attack he drives on steadfastly to the point at which he aims.

The same ideal is in the mind of Professor William James when he says that it is the mark of the superior intellect to perceive the *What 's What* of a given situation. For instance, he suggests, if you were bailing out your boat, and if you had taught your dog to bring down a dipper when you sent him for it, a very clever dog might bring down a tin pail if he could not find the dipper, because the two look alike; but no dog would ever think of bringing down a big coach-sponge. His insight would not be sufficient to show him that a sponge is like a dipper in that it also takes up water. One would have to know the center, the *What's What,* of bailing a boat, as well as of sponges and dippers, for that.

For effective action toward any purpose, the first requisite is insight, making possible concentration on essentials, ''the Napoleon touch,'' bringing all one's force to bear at the one point that counts. To build a road, know where the terminus is, then press on; to master a circle, find the center, then push in; to control a situation, know the *What's What,* then insist on it. To write a composition, set out with a definite conception of the end to be reached, then form every part in obedience to that conception. This is the principle of *Unity.*

Approaching a Subject.—The direction to have and obey a central conception is easily given; it is not so easily followed. No one can have insight at will. The most that a writer can do is to put himself in the way of gaining insight, of understanding his problem, of clearing up his thoughts, and seeing distinctly with the eye of his mind. Generally speaking, a subject in writing must be approached gradually. It looms up at first in a mist, vague and large, almost formless, and to most people alarming as soon as it begins to be questioned. Even well known things appear baffling and painful as subjects of reflection—sometimes the more baffling and painful the better known they are. The mind refuses to hold them before itself, it runs away, it shuts its eyes. People excuse themselves by saying that they can write only when "in the mood," and that they must depend upon "inspiration." Inspiration, however, is a prize granted to the man who wrestles with his subject, and the happy mood is a rare blessing, vouchsafed more and more often as time goes on, to the man of will who has learned that he must work, whatever his mood. In brief, the center can be reached, the *What 's What* seen, the guiding thread or clue found by steadfast energy of thought.

That central definiteness of purpose which contributes to effective writing cannot be attained except by fixing the attention energetically upon some subject of which the writer has a view as a whole, and which he at the same time understands in its parts.

Limiting the Subject.—Commonly the young writer will make the mistake of taking up too large a subject. It may be absurdly large—a topic big enough for a book being thought of for a paper, and one vast enough for a lifetime's study undertaken by a freshman : *Socialism, Woman Suffrage, Sport.* If the subject in itself is not too difficult and complex for the writer's powers of mind, the remedy is to consider what the steps of advance toward the end are, and to be satisfied with taking but one step. Perhaps it will be necessary to divide and to subdivide over and over before a part of the subject manageable within the space and time at the command of the writer is reached. At last a theme small enough to be treated with some fulness within the limits assigned should be found ;—for fulness and interest of treatment are not secured by a broad subject, but by a narrow one. Only by amplitude of treatment, by vivid detail, by lively illustration, by vigorous application, can the life of a subject be given.

For instance, a writer may be well acquainted with the game of lawn-tennis, and may know that he has something interesting to say about it. He is allowed, let us say, one page of manuscript, a hundred and fifty words. He will not write about the history of lawn-tennis; the subject is uninteresting unless it is presented very fully and requires much careful study to be authoritatively dealt with. The general nature or theory of the game is too simple to be worthy of much discussion, though something might be said of the peculiar interest of tennis as distinguished from that of goal games involving team play, such as basket-ball, from that of games with less definite placement, such as volley-ball, and from that of games played on tennis principles, but against a wall, such as court-tennis and handball. The game itself seems likely to afford better material: its mechanical requirements—the court and the tools of the game; its technique—the method of making each stroke; its strategy—the use of the strokes at every contingency and the art of placing. Out of these aspects of the game the writer decides on one; say the tools of the game, or its strategy. These topics are still too broad. Of the tools suppose we take the racket, and determine to give a page of advice to the purchaser of a new racket. Or of strategy we take the use of lobbing, and tell a player who has acquired some expertness in driving but who does not lob at all, why and when to lob. Within the space suggested, even these limited subjects may be found to crowd the writer; and *The Frame of the Racket,* and *When to Lob* may make subjects large enough, especially if a brief illustrative narrative or two be introduced to drive the point of the discussion all the way home.

It is impossible to insist too strongly upon the necessity of limiting the scope of the subject. Consider then a more familiar illustration. Nearly everybody sometimes goes to see the moving-pictures. About them, I say to myself, I have an abundance of impressions, some very vivid; my friends and I have had from first to last a good many thoughts to communicate concerning "film-stars" and "screen-pictures"; but I find that if I try to put down on paper any connected ideas about moving-pictures, all my notions seem to be too scattering and indefinite to be of use to anybody. Perhaps if I examine my mind, I may discover that I have something really central to say about some definite aspect of the vague subject that hovers before me. To do this, I must divide the indistinct total into parts. I must break up the vast confusion in my mind. Perhaps something with reference to which I have already a special interest and some real ideas will quickly come to the surface; perhaps I may have to pass the whole subject patiently in review without discerning any clear line of thought. Perhaps I may sooner or later hit upon some interesting point which I can follow up at another time. I put aside the mechanism of the film and the method of running the biograph. I do not know much about them; and like most people, I am really interested in the result, not in the means. I pass over the advertisements, though some day I might find something to say about newspaper notices, and the posters and photographs in the front of the playhouse. I likewise do not feel interested just now in the theatre building, although

I can see that there are points to be made about the differences between an ordinary theatre and a moving-picture house, and about the arrangements and accommoda-
tions in different moving-picture houses. At this time
I do not care about the incidental music, though I could
say something about the relative advantages of an organ
and a small orchestra, or about the stupidity of the music usually performed, or about the way in which people
chatter even when, as sometimes happens, interesting
and appropriate pieces are played. It is the picture on
the screen itself that I am inclined to think of. That
is the important thing. As I analyze the picture, as I
try to break this total again into parts, I say to myself
that moving-pictures have stories to tell—different kinds
of stories. In telling their stories, they present personages acting; and the personality of the favorite actor
and actress is closely connected with the part which each
plays. The settings, too, of the plays have much to do
with the effect. The plays often teach; and their morals
are worth thinking about. In each aspect of the whole,
also, there are a technique and a method.

These divisions are still too big. Can I go further
with one? Perhaps I say to myself that the way in
which the story is made intelligible, is "put across,"
seems to me curious. The moving pictures have ways
of their own, different from the ways of theatrical per-
formances and of books, and yet related to them. For
one thing, I notice that pictures alone, in connected sequence, are seldom relied on to do all the work. There
is nearly always something more than pantomime. And
now, at last, after long thought, I begin to see my topic,
not yet shaped, but ready to take shape. The letter-
press flashed on the screen seems to me a notable and

somewhat curious part of the story-telling. If I had plenty of room, I might cover the whole of this subject. The title, and the names of the producing staff, and the *dramatis personae,* all decoratively presented with ingenious elegance, are shown, gradually coming closer and closer to the action. After the play itself begins, it is interrupted by passages of narrative explanation and by dialogue, each playing a p   t in the telling of the story, and each having a so   f special technique. For all these topics I have r   ufficient space. I am writing a short theme, and I see in the dialogue of the moving-pictures a manageable, definite, and significant topic. Here is my *subject.*

I observe that at least one of the ways to employ the dialogue is to introduce it at turning-points in order to give the impulse to an advance in the story. On the other hand, dialogue plays a small part at climaxes, in which the mere scene is effective enough to carry the story by itself. Then I test my idea by cases. I think of the purposes in the heroine's or the villain's mind revealed by the dialogue, and of the exceptions to what I have said about climaxes. There seem to be more climaxes with dialogue than I thought; and I wonder if these climaxes would not be stronger without the talk. I think of the times when I have read the words on the lips of the actors. Some actors speak their words very energetically, others lightly. Sometimes I have detected on the lips of the personages speeches different from those on the screen, or even incongruous with them. Now, though my mind may not be made up on all these and other points, I at least see the whole and the parts, and my subject is defined.

Examples of Limited Essay Subjects.—Having begun, I can think of a multitude more of little definite topics. Some of them I jot down:

Bridging Intervals Between Scenes.
Telling a Story by Facial Expression.
Commonplace Gestures and "Registering."
Too much Emphasis on the Star.
Keeping the Subordinate Figures in the Picture.
The Homely Good Character.
The Heroine's Foil. (Freckle-faced, snaggle-toothed, mean-looking, small-eyed, awkward actresses.)
Do Athletic "Stunts" Grow Tiresome?
Characteristics by which the Landscape of Southern California can be detected under any Disguise.
Lighting so as to Accentuate Delicate Points in Acting.
Inappropriate Footgear in the Moving-Pictures.

Each of these topics has been reached in the same way, by the method of dividing a large subject, of subdividing the division, and thus onward until a small, definite theme emerges—until a little, lighted figure appears on the stage of my mind.

Limiting the Subject in a Narrative.—Similarly, if I mean to tell a story, I am likely to think of my jolly camping-trip, or of my long, pleasant summer vacation, full of action and adventure. I try to tell the story of one or the other, and when I try to think out the subject I discover before my mind a confusion of incident; and then if I actually write down a narrative, I am likely to have nothing but a vague, meager list of things that happened, a list of things which sound like the things that happen to everybody. But if I search the memory of the camp or the vacation for particular incidents, I find some that stand out—some in which something definite was done, in which somebody or something did "get to the end of a road," or "break into a center," in which there is a real *What's What*. There was a distinct single thing done when Tom astonished himself and everybody else by hooking a big pickerel, and landing it between the jaws of a mop-handle. There was one event, though it lasted a long time, when the cat got into the fly-paper, had to be washed off with kerosene, and walked about on her forefeet, dolefully mewing, till her hind legs got well. There was something done when the Doctor said the walking fern could not be transplanted, and the Teacher transplanted it. There was a drama begun, continued, and ended, when we did our packing. Something happened when Mr. Brucker showed what kind of man he was by one unlucky answer.

In this way I can note a good many narrative topics:

> The Slip betwixt the Cup and the Lip.
> Under the Tent-Flap to a Dance and Back.
> The Cat that Died of Green Paint.
> The Winning of the Marksmanship Medal.
> Holding One's Own with the Bunch.
> Learning to Swim.
> One Camp Dinner.
> The Midnight Porcupine.

These subjects were thought of just as the subjects connected with the moving-pictures were thought of—by picking out of the large mass of a summer's impressions something definite, single, and complete within small compass.

Limitation Applies to Ideas, not merely to Space or Time.—Observe that the subject itself is made smaller by analysis. Young writers sometimes make the mistake of appearing to divide a subject in time or space, while the matter to be discussed remains as large in idea as ever. *The Principles of My Wireless Telegraphy Mechanism* is practically as much of a subject as *The*

Principles of Wireless Telegraphy. Tariff Legislation To-day may be even more of a subject than *Tariff Legislation,* because it includes, in addition to the general principles of the broader subject, the application of those principles to present circumstances. But *How I Set Up a Hundred-Foot Antenna-Pole,* and *The Tariff on Coffee* are really limited subjects, limited in ideas as well as in space or time.

Simple Aspects of Complex Subjects.—If the subject is in itself too complex and difficult for the writer, some related matter in which he can use his own experience or special knowledge may suggest itself to him. The tariff is a jungle of confusion in detail; the theory of it is a difficult subject of special study; but what the farmers in one county in Iowa thought of the abolition of the duty on potatoes in 1907 or 1927 might happen to be known to him. He might have lived near lead mines and might think he knew about them, and might find out that it was really the lead-mine workers whom he knew, and about whom he could write with interest. Following these clues, he would be likely to reach something capable of being said with energy, clearness, and unity within small space.

Unity Depends on Purpose.—The unity of a composition depends not upon the topic with which it deals, but upon the purpose with which it is written—not upon its subject, but if the expression may be permitted, upon its object. The subject of *coal,* for example, has been much before the mind of everybody in this country for some years; but a writer cannot promise himself that because people are interested in coal, a composition about coal would be interesting. He has first to ask himself, why should I write about coal? What

end is in view in my undertaking this subject? Even
if the writer narrows and limits his subject, even if he
divides it into *Coal in Peace, and Coal in War,* for example, even yet he has not determined his purpose.
But to show how the desire to control coal fields is a
cause of war is a definite purpose, capable indeed of
being limited still further, but in itself definite—a
good subject for a book or an essay. To show how the
possession of an ample supply of coal is a cause of
strength in war, again, is a purpose, involving the consideration of the enormous development and specializa-
tion of the metal industries in war, of the need of manufacturing power and of transportation by land and sea,
and of the activity of the navy. The regulation of the
use of coal in war, involving the restrictions on industry and on the use of coal in domestic heating, the increase of efficiency in the construction and operation of
heating plants, the "tagged shovel," and "heatless
days," is another topic with a purpose. Thus it would
be possible to proceed for a long time, enumerating definite purposes which might cause one to write about coal.
The question is not primarily how big or how small the
purpose, but how definite. Even a small composition
on a little subject may be a mere set of memoranda; it
is possible to jot down mere notes about a hot-air furnace,
as well as about coal, or happiness, or the study of geography. The energy of purpose requisite for efficiency
demands singleness of aim, and singlemindedness in the
pursuit of that aim.

To Get and Give Pleasure a Worthy Purpose.—It
should be said that there is a real purpose in the desire
to tell a story for the amusement of others, or even to
put down an impression for one's own pleasure. A

good story has a point;—it shows off the character of the village gossip, or it makes a reader feel queer about the cellar of a historic old house, or it springs a surprise about an automobile in the road, or it raises a discussion about honesty, or it calls forth respect for the energy of a plucky lad. Likewise, to get into words your own feeling about a concert, or the ways of policemen, or the spray on a rock, just for the fun of it, forgetting other people for the time though later they may be admitted to share your interest, is so difficult, it requires so much concentration of mind as well as so much skill of words, that it deserves to rank as one of the high achievements within the powers of men.

Thinking With the Pen in Hand. Most people think most effectively if they have a pen in hand and write down memoranda. Some, it is true, have the valuable faculty of being able to carry on continuous thinking without such aids, but most people deceive themselves if they pretend to think in an orderly way without making systematic notes. By continuous attention, by repeated attacks, the center is placed, the clue found, the main idea comes before the mind. The story-teller sees his transaction hanging all together and evolving steadily. The debater catches the central meaning, finds the turning-point of his argument. The expositor learns where to place his subject;—what is like it, what is unlike it, what is opposed to it, what it includes, how it is composed. He can turn the difficulty over, see both sides, and smooth out the wrinkles.

Writing Rapidly.—When once the central idea is thus seen, it is best for most people to write out what they have to say rapidly, without delaying on the way or being anxious about the manner of expression. As in-

experienced writers are hasty in thought, they are
dilatory in writing. The result is that they lose the
fresh clearness with which they have seen their subject, and by over-anxious hesitation become stiff and
unnatural in their language. Rapidity in writing itself tends to unity and connectedness, and avoids the
painful hesitation over language which with many
writers makes the act of expression a torture instead
of the normal and healthy act it should be. Impropriety and inadequacy of language can be more effectively
removed by revision than by anxious uncertainty at
the time of composition. Many young writers get into
such a frame of mind about their way of expressing
themselves that they write as if they were afraid of
stepping on an egg every time they put their foot down.
Moreover, the ability to express oneself readily as well
as effectively is an absolute necessity of practical life.
Nothing that is here said should be understood as con-
doning carelessness of thought or negligence of language.
An ideal manner of composition involves thorough preparation, serious meditation, and careful revision, but
a rapidly written first draft.

Even Unity not Always Essential.—This singleness of
purpose and idea is indeed not essential in all pieces of
writing or talk. A pleasant conversation ranges over
many topics; a friendly letter touches upon many separate matters; there are even graceful essays, the interest
of which is that they say a great many pleasant and
desultory things on unrelated topics, without more
unity than a certain personal tone; and whole books,
and delightful ones, which are mere strings of incident
and comment. In these cases, however, there is not mere
confusion, but a sheaf of small units, each having its

own value, and each separate in interest from all the
rest of the units gathered within the one sheaf. The
laws of unity apply to each small single thing in such
collections, as to the larger and more massive units of
works more strenuously one.

Unity of Conception Fundamental.—One cannot
write well, then, because of a gift of speech, or because
of any amount of devotion to language as an art or craft.
First of all, there must be a certain energy in the purpose or idea underlying the whole, with a clear defining
of that purpose or idea, and a resolute effort to take hold
of it firmly.

II. SEQUENCE

A Composition is a Process Composed of Steps.—
Next after determining one's purpose is making one's
way to it, step by step. A composition is a process. It
is a train or course of thought or feeling, so recorded
that a reader can follow and share it. This process,
the train or course of thought or feeling which the
writer went through in the first place, and which the
reader goes through after him, begins, continues, and
ends. It took time to think it out into words; it takes
time to think the words back into thoughts. Moreover,
our minds, as they make their way from one point to
another, do so "as a sparrow flies, not continuously, but
with alternate flyings and perchings," or as a man
crosses a stream on stepping-stones, by successive leaps
from one alighting-place to another, until the shore is
reached. Each flight or step is a complete process,
and at the same time part of a larger total process. So
a composition is made up of stadia of advance, or
sections, each of which is composed of still smaller

stadia; and larger or smaller, each stadium or section possesses a subordinate but real unity.

The Unity of a Simple Sequence.—A composition going by many steps to one goal is one in development; it is one in course as well as one in aim. The simplest movement of this kind is movement of one sequence, like the flight of an arrow. The archer points his shaft, the bowstring snaps, the arrow takes its flight through the air, rises to its highest point, drops down, and strikes home in the target. This process is one in movement as in idea. In it a transaction is complete, a course of events has been finished. So a narrative recording such a transaction rounds out a complete curve, begins definitely at a point of departure, continues in orderly sequence step after step, and ends definitely at a point of attainment.

Simple Narrative.—One event, in such a linear sequence, follows another, like a row of blocks on end, all knocked down by knocking down the first one. Such is the evolution of a direct narrative which moves along a single line of events. Such, for instance, is the report of an experiment in a laboratory, where each step brings on the next. Most anecdotes are of this kind, for example, the following little narrative, from George Borrow's *Bible in Spain.*

We soon arrived at the verge of a deep valley amongst mountains—not those of the chain which we had seen before us, and which we now left to the right, but those of the Teîleno range, just before they unite with that chain. Round the sides of this valley, which exhibited something of the appearance of a horseshoe, wound the road in a circuitous manner; just before us, however, and diverging from the road, lay a foot-path, which seemed, by a gradual descent, to lead across the valley, and to rejoin the road on the other side, at the distance of about a furlong, and into this we struck, in order to avoid the circuit.

We had not gone far before we met two Galicians on their way to cut the harvests of Castile. One of them shouted, "Cavalier (*Caballero*,—as a mode of address in common life, equivalent merely to *sir*), turn back: in a moment you will be amongst precipices, where your horses will break their necks, for we ourselves could scarcely climb them on foot." The other cried, "Cavalier, proceed, but be careful, and your horses, if surefooted, will run no great danger: my comrade is a fool." A violent dispute instantly ensued between the two mountaineers, each supporting his opinion with loud oaths and curses; but without stopping to see the result, I passed on. But the path was now filled with stones and huge slaty rocks, on which my horse was constantly slipping. I likewise heard the sound of water in a deep gorge, which I had hitherto not perceived, and I soon saw that it would be worse than madness to proceed. I turned my horse, and was hastening to regain the path which I had left, when Antonio, my faithful Greek, pointed out to me a meadow by which, he said, we might regain the highroad much lower down than if we returned on our steps. The meadow was brilliant with short green grass, and in the middle there was a small rivulet of water. I spurred my horse on, expecting to be in the highroad in a moment; the horse, however, snorted and stared wildly, and was evidently unwilling to cross the seemingly inviting spot. I thought that the scent of a wolf or some other wild animal might have disturbed him, but was soon undeceived by his sinking up to the knees in a bog. The animal uttered a shrill neigh, and exhibited every sign of the greatest terror, making at the same time great efforts to extricate himself, and plunging forward, but every moment sinking deeper. At last he arrived where a small vein of rock showed itself: on this he placed his forefeet, and with one tremendous exertion freed himself from the deceitful soil, springing over the rivulet and alighting on comparatively firm ground, where he stood panting, his heaving sides covered with a foamy sweat.

Such a narrative records a single transaction, brought about by a series of successive acts. It is a process, made up of successive stages. Even in the arrow shot, the fitting of the arrow to the string, the aiming, the letting go, the flight, the stroke are each distinct steps—not one sweep and steady movement. So, as has been said, the process followed out by a written composition, though it is one, advances by steps in order, each separate from that which precedes and from that which follows, but all going on in orderly line from beginning to end.

Simple Process of Reasoning.—Not only are there processes of events like these; processes of thought go on in the mind, which it is the function of language to record, and which follow one line in continuous sequence. So an argument may march from its first step to its last, in a straight line. Demonstrations in geometry march in this way. Step by step they follow a sequence of reasoning, each advance in which requires all that has preceded and is itself necessary for the advance which is to follow, until the goal is reached. These arguments, it is true, have an introduction and a conclusion, commenting on the work when it is done, just as the bowman might say before shooting, "Now I am going to aim at that target"; and after the arrow had struck, "You see that was a pretty difficult stroke, but I made it." So Euclid begins,—"To prove that the sum of the three interior angles of a triangle is equal to two right angles;" and ends,—"Which was to be proved."

Language is a Simple Sequence.—Such a sequence, direct and single, is the most natural for language to follow. Language itself proceeds in order, sound after sound, syllable after syllable, word after word, phrase after phrase, sentence after sentence, recording idea after idea, conclusion after conclusion, in one line. Language follows a single line,—it cannot record two ideas at once. It keeps going onward, taking for granted all that at any point has gone before. It is possible to reverse the order, to go backward in thought. One might find an arrow stuck in a target, and work back in the order of discovery to the bowman taking his aim. Even a story might be written in that way; but it almost never is. If you were a detective who had investigated the case, you would surely tell the story from the beginning of the action, though you might have discovered it from the end. On the other hand, it is natural to argue in the reverse order, that is from effect back to cause, or from conclusion to premise. Narratives go on, "And then—and then—and then—and then—"; arguments go either way, "Because—because—because—", or, "Therefore—therefore—therefore."

In brief, then, the simplest order proceeds from antecedent to consequent, or the reverse, throughout a transaction or a course of reasoning. The former method is especially characteristic of narrative, the latter of argument. In either case, but especially in argument, an introduction or a conclusion, directing the attention of the reader along the course followed and to the end reached, may be of use.

Sequence with Static Subjects.—A writer may have to deal with more complicated material. There may be, not one string, but half a dozen strings all pulled at once—several processes all going on and combining to make one process, as in the story of some complicated intrigue, or in an argument in which many lines of reasoning converge to one conclusion. The discussion of the problem thus presented is deferred for the present. But there is a question of arrangement almost or quite as difficult; what shall a writer do who has laid upon him the necessity of dealing with a body of things which do not follow in sequence at all, but are all present at once? Suppose a writer had to list the phenomena of the sky at night; where should he begin and end? Or suppose he had to tell of the resources of the United States. The population, the water-power, the agricultural riches, the mines of coal, iron, and copper, the railroads, the business system, the human energy, the factories, and the manufacturing skill are all there together; they have no obvious sequence, and yet they must all be in sequence in a composition.

Sequence from the General to the Particular.—Imagine an explorer, toiling on foot over an unknown country, step by step making his way from ridge to ridge, across streams, and through forests—retracing his steps from impassable places, and after all able only to record the observations on one thin line of progress, and the views a few miles away, supplemented by his own guesses and the natives' reports of things at a distance. Then think of an observer in an aeroplane, rising so high over the same region that he can see it all at once, dimly in detail, but with a clear view of the general outline, the course of the streams, the great trends of surfaces, the patches of forest, and the clear space of open country. Let him come nearer and nearer, developing that first view into its parts, until he approaches near enough to see roads, fences, and houses—even at last to make out the movements of men and animals. How much more clear and intelligent the knowledge, how distinct and firm and sure the grasp of the observer who has gone from the general view progressively to the particular thing, and how much easier his task than that of the toiling pedestrian who has had to create by laborious effort the general view which the flier had with his own eyes from the first. Usually then it is easiest and most clear to proceed when possible from the more general to the less general. In this way the composition takes the form of progressive discovery, and acquires the interest of movement and sequence.

Thus, to return to our problems of arrangement, the general appearance of the starry sky, its dark, velvet, violet depth, with sparkles of light, more or less intense, and vague patches of pale brightness scattered but thinly upon it, precedes any word about particular constellations or individual stars. In the discussion of the resources of the United States, the general mass and character of the resources comes first of all. Next in order follows the division of the resources into great classes—supplies of raw materials, the machinery and equipment for working on the raw material, and human activity, for instance. Then the raw material might be divided int classes—permanent supplies of inanimate material, material produced in annual crops, and so forth. T' is step by step the process of advancing from the general to the particular is carried forward. A survey of the whole is taken at the beginning, a division of the whole mass into large parts or great classes follows; then a survey of the smaller field as it is entered upon is taken anew, a new division following upon that, and so on in order, each stadium being an advance to a definite point, being marked off at its beginning and its end, and being completed before the next stadium is entered upon.

From the Fixed to the Transitory; from Cause to Effect.—Further, there is not only a progress from the more to the less general, but also a progress from the more fixed and more permanent to the less so, and from the more fundamental to the derivative. The trunk of a tree precedes the branches, the branches the twigs, the twigs the leaves. Nebulae precede stars, as being the source from which stars are thought to have their origin. The fixed stars precede the planets, for the fixed stars provide the points of reference by which the places of planets are measured. The planets precede the satellites; the satellites being more fixed and permanent members of the solar system precede the wandering comets. The stable geographical facts about the United States,— its situation, its size, its general climate, its surface,— come first of all in the account of its resources, then follows its mass of mineral supplies within the earth, then comes its soil, and then only its agricultural productions under the hand of man, because the former matters are the more fixed, the latter the more variable, the more caused and conditioned. Again, all these elements precede the industrial activities requiring more proportionately of men's handiwork in each thing produced, and so on.

In brief, the principles that the more general normally precedes the less general, that the more permanent normally precedes the more transitory, and that the causing and conditioning normally precede the caused and conditioned will often be found to be safe guides in cases of difficulty.

III TRANSITION

Marking off the Sections.—A composition proceeding from section to section in orderly sequence should make plain, as each section closes, that that section has reached its end. The next section should start with a well-marked beginning, and the relation between one section and that which follows it should be made plain. For clear connection, nothing more may be necessary than simple straightforwardness,—mere orderly progress. As a composition advances by successive steps, each point where the foot is set down at the end of one stride becomes naturally the point from which the foot steps off for the next stride. That is to say, the conclusion of each section provides the natural ground for the beginning of the section which follows. In this way, one section is naturally and smoothly connected with the following one.

The chapters of novels which have life and action commonly end with definiteness and then begin with a movement forward from the point already reached. Run over Mr. Owen Wister's *The Virginian,* for instance. Chapter I concludes its transaction as the narrator finds the man he has been expecting;—" 'I reckon I am looking for you, seh,' the tall man now observed." Chapter II begins, "We cannot see ourselves as others see us, or I should know what appearance I cast at hearing this from the tall man. I said nothing, feeling uncertain." Another chapter ends, "So I perceived a new example of the old truth, that the letter means nothing until the spirit gives life." The next begins, "It was for several minutes, I suppose, that I stood there, drawing these silent morals." Another ends as the story-teller falls asleep, after a lively evening, and the next begins with his awakening a trifle late the next morning. Thus each chapter concludes definitely, and the chapter following takes its advance from the point just reached.

Stating the Topic of a New Section.—Sometimes, however, the writer must take pains to make a connection between the successive divisions of the composition explicit. To do this, it may be enough for him to indicate at the beginning of each section the topic to be treated in it. Thus Huxley writes in his Autobiography:

I have next to nothing to say about my childhood. . . .
My regular school training was of the briefest. . . .
As I grew older, my great desire was to be a mechanical engineer, but the fates were against this, and, while very young, I commenced the study of medicine under a medical brother-in-law. . . .
Looking back over my *Lehrjahre* (apprenticeship) I am sorry to say that I do not think that any account of my doings as a student would lead to edification. . . .

At times even more than such indications of the topic may be requisite. It may be necessary to make explicit not only the subject of the new division of the work, but also the relation in logic which the new part bears to the old. It may be best to tell the reader that what is to come is a cause, or a refutation, or a result, or a continuation of what has been completed.

Transitional Paragraphs.—The longer the piece, and the more anxious the author to be absolutely clear, the more ample the expressions of transition may be, sometimes reaching the length of an entire paragraph. Thus Newman, in his discussion of the nature of a university, states fully the principle that the highest and most adequate education cannot be obtained by impersonal study but can be given only by personal communication in some place of concourse. He views the principle from several sides, and makes clear that he holds it to be true in every aspect and kind of education; and then he introduces a group of illustrations from analogous fields with the following paragraph:

The principle on which I have been insisting is so obvious, and instances in point are so ready, that I should think it tiresome to proceed with the subject except that one or two illustrations may serve to explain my own language about it, which may not have done justice to the doctrine which it has been intended to enforce.

Sometimes these transitional paragraphs look both backward and forward, as if making a bow to the subject completed, and then introducing the subject to be entered upon. Thus Burke, in his *Speech on the Plan for Economical Reform,* after explaining why reform should on the one hand, from the point of view of the government, be early, and should on the other hand, from the point of view of the people, be temperate, proceeds to lay down with some detail the characteristics of his own plan for economical reform in the British Government.

I am therefore satisfied to act as a fair mediator between government and the people, endeavoring to form a plan which should have both an early and a temperate operation. I mean, that it should be substantial, that it should be systematic, that it should rather strike at the first cause of prodigality and corrupt influences than attempt to follow them in all their effects.

It is to be observed that these transitional expressions are properly part of the sections which they introduce, and not of those over which they cast a retrospect; for the retrospect is intended only to set the foot firm for the next step forward, and would weaken the conclusion of the preceding section if appended to it.

Briefer Transitions.—A transition so long as to fill an entire paragraph is not often needed; even in writing which fully explains a difficult subject a whole sentence is commonly more than enough to make connection. Examples follow.

> We shall be of one mind thus far.   But . . .
> But I do not stop here . . .
> Not only is this the case, but . . .
> I hitherto spoke of . . .

Phrases and parts of sentences are generally sufficient to make an easy and certain transition:

> Turning from the man to his works, . . .
> To illustrate my meaning . . .
> For several ensuing years . . .

Logical Transitions.—The main types of relation, with some of the more common connective expressions, are as follows.

Orderly sequence.

> [Introductory]:   In the first place; To begin with; At the outset; First.
> [Continuing]:   In the second (third, etc.) place; Secondly; Next; Then.
> [Concluding]:   Finally; In conclusion; To conclude.
> [Recapitulating]:   In sum; In brief; In fine; In fact; Briefly; To sum up.

Progress in the same direction.

> And; Now; Further; Moreover; Besides; In addition; Too; Indeed.

Opposition.

> But; Yet; Still; However; On the contrary; On the other hand; For all that; After all.

Concession.

> I admit; I know; I confess; I grant; I must add.

Modification.

> At the same time; Of course.

Inference.

> Hence; Accordingly; Therefore; So; Now; Thus; For this reason; Consequently; In consequence.

Illustration.

> For instance; For example.

IV. EMPHASIS OF STRUCTURE

Emphasis.—One aspect of the problem of placing the parts of a composition is the problem of enforcing the most important parts upon the attention of the reader. Some parts contain the guiding, the dominating ideas, and cannot easily be too much insisted upon. Others are important, but important in sustaining, illustrating, amplifying—helpers, not leaders. Others still take minor places. They are useful, perhaps necessary, but they are not central in the whole composition. How shall these different elements be placed in relation to the whole and to each other?

Conclusions.—It is evident, from the preceding discussion, that of all the sections of a composition the last is the most notable. It is usually that to which all the rest leads; it is the end for which the journey was undertaken. And even when the last part does not contain the object of the whole, it is commonly the part in which all that which precedes finds a fulfillment and a complete expression.

Inexperienced writers often have a difficulty in bringing their compositions to a conclusion. They feel that they have said all they have to say, and yet see that their work is somehow incomplete. The conclusion, like everything else in a composition, does not exist for the

composition in itself, but for the adequate communication of the writer's idea to the reader. Its natural function is to leave with the reader that impression which the author wishes him to carry away from the whole, or in other words to deepen the reader's sense of the purpose directing the whole composition. Undefined and indistinct at the beginning, that purpose should have been gradually revealed by the course of thought through which the composition has progressed.

Significant Last Steps.—Often, perhaps more often than not, a composition requires no conclusion beyond an adequate statement of the last step in the process, or course of thought, which the composition records. Accordingly, a writer who is dissatisfied with the conclusion of a piece of writing should ask himself, first of all, whether the conclusion deals with the right part of the composition. Perhaps something else ought to be put last in order to receive the emphasis which naturally falls upon the concluding element. Perhaps what has been said is presented too briefly or too weakly for its relative importance, or is not so expressed as to bring out its relation to the whole course of the writing.

Was the purpose to tell a story? Then the vital fact in the conclusion is the condition which has been brought about by the progress of a series of incidents from one state of affairs to another state of affairs. The wild horse has been tamed; the untried youth has now proved his manhood; the ways of deceit have once more been proved to be without profit; the disputed territory is clear; the old government has crumbled. The record of the last, the significant step creating the new order of things may be all that is needed in the composition

to bring it to a conclusion; but it must be recorded clearly, energetically and with a sense that it is the final step.

Likewise, it may be quite enough for a satisfactory conclusion if the classification in an exposition be carried through to completeness, or if the last step of reasoning in an argument be distinctly taken.

Concluding Summaries.—Sometimes, it may be well to end with a recapitulation. Especially if the matter has been scattered through a long discussion, it may be well to bring it all together at the end under a single view. Such summarizing conclusions are generally unnecessary with brief and simple pieces of writing. In any event, they should not mark time; that is, they should not record over again, without some impression of advance and progress, that which has once been laid down. For this reason, a summary which repeats in the same words what has already been presented in the introduction produces the effect of formality and sterility of thought. An idea, after it has been examined and considered, is inevitably seen in a somewhat new light from that in which it was seen at first, and the way in which it is stated will manifest that growth and development through which the mind has passed in its reflections. Not infrequently, however, an intelligent summary does make manifest that growth and development, and is an excellent conclusion.

Applications.—But the purpose is often more than to complete a transaction or to follow out a course of analysis or argument. It is to leave with the reader a new point of view, to lead on to a new course of action. The best conclusions look forward, not back. The application and enforcement of the course of thought followed

through the composition is in place in the conclusion. A composition has explained the value of forests to a community, and the effect of forest fires. The conclusion makes the application: is it not a public duty to organize the prevention of forest fires by much more effective means than any hitherto employed?

A composition has explained, as Lowell does in one of his essays, the meaning of democracy—its virtues denied by autocrats, its dangers, overlooked by enthusiasts, its strength, its weaknesses. The conclusion is an appeal to the conscience; it urges that only from a gravely but courageously hopeful temper of individual responsibility can social progress in a democracy result.

A composition argues, as Freeman does, in one of his essays, that the bond of a common language is the first essential of nationality. His conclusion is that the sense of generous sympathy between peoples speaking related languages, though it is fallacious to think of it as really based on any actual kinship, is a justifiable feeling, which legitimately takes its place among the facts with which a statesman must deal.

In brief, if after examination the bare development of the theme in itself proves not to provide a sufficient conclusion, the writer should determine whether there is not some further purpose, some half-conscious or unconscious tendency, which has really directed his writing, and should enforce that purpose briefly in the light of what has preceded. If not, a summary may be in place, so written as not to plod without advance over ground already sufficiently traversed, but to survey the field from the new point of view which has been reached by the previous discussion.

Irrelevant Conclusions.—There are two types of

faulty conclusion very common with inexperienced writers—irrelevant conclusions and afterthoughts. Irrelevant conclusions are such as ignore the point of the composition which they bring to an end. They may deal with something near it, but they do not exactly reach it; they strike the target but they do not hit the bull's-eye. For example, a theme is written on the effects on health of the wartime food restrictions, especially the restrictions on the free use of fats, sugar, and wheat. The conclusion declared that the American people accepted the privations cheerfully, and would accept more severe privations if necessary, because they were bound to win the war. The conclusion is irrelevant; it has to do with *food restrictions,* and not with the *effect* of the food restrictions *on health.* A relevant conclusion would have declared that practically everybody used entirely satisfactory substitutes, so that the restrictions had no effect on health; or it would have been asserted that with care people could maintain their health in spite of the fact that they had to satisfy themselves with less than the normal amount of some of the foods which were placed under restriction; or it would even have admitted that some impairment of the public health was inevitable and must be accepted as necessary. The point is that the conclusion should grow out of and enforce the central idea of the composition, and not be drawn away to something else, near or far from that idea.

Afterthoughts.—Afterthoughts are the result of a lack of adequate preliminary reflection, or of laziness and haste in execution. The writer has about completed his paper when he suddenly thinks of something for which he has not provided; or perhaps he gets tired and treats the last part of the paper inadequately. In either case, he introduces an idea which he does not treat with due proportion to the rest of the composition, and which either produces the effect of a tag hung on to something complete without it, or else of a fragment left annoyingly ragged. A writer describes his room, telling about the impression it makes upon a visitor, about its furnishings and arrangements, and about the view from its windows, and then drops in a sentence,—"But it must be admitted that the arrangements for study are very inadequate," and winds up. A brief paper on football, after a pretty clear account of the American game derived from Rugby football, remarks, "The English have another system of playing football," and drops the subject. A paper on the advantages of studying music treats with due proportion three or four aspects of the development of the powers of a student of music, adds, " There is also the possibility of earning money," and goes no further. In each case, the introduction of the sentence expanded the whole idea of the theme, and made it logically necessary to treat all parts of the expanded theme in proportion. Without the reference to English football, the paper was complete as a discussion of American Rugby. With the sentence on English football it is no longer complete; its subject is Anglo-American football, and this subject is not so treated as to produce the effect of unity. The theme is a mixed number as to American football, and a proper fraction as to the Anglo-American game. The theme about the room was complete about its physical appearance; it becomes a theme on a broader topic when the conveniences for study are introduced, and this broader topic is not realized. The presence of an afterthought, therefore, makes it necessary to consider whether the composition can be considered as complete without it, or whether the conception and working out of the whole essay must be enlarged to new proportions. The new matter might have been left out, but if it enters the composition at all, it must enter with such bulk and weight relatively to the other parts of the composition as justifies its presence along with them.

Beginnings.—Next to the last section, the first is the most conspicuous. It strikes the attention most freshly, and sets the tone and direction of the whole. With reference to the beginning of a composition the advice most commonly needed by young writers is to begin promptly. A beginning is not a thing by itself; it is a part of the whole. Like the end, the beginning should subserve the purpose in the author's mind, and should be special to the composition of which it is an element. Commonly, young writers tend to explain too much and to begin too remotely. An argument on the question whether it is better to go to a large or to a small college should not begin with the benefits of going to college, still less with the benefits of being educated, but with something bearing on the question *immediately* under discussion,—with an examination into the essential differences between the conditions at the two classes of institutions, for example. Young writers often have to write awhile before they really warm to their subject. The introduction has been useful to them, but is of no value to the reader. Cut it off, then, at the point where the composition really begins to attack its subject. In particular, do not begin a composition by advertising the feeling you hope to create by it. Do not begin a description: ''The view from Blue Mounds is a very beautiful one," but place the point of view and begin immediately upon the scene;—"Looking northward from the summit of Blue Mounds, the eye takes in at one sweep the vast valley of the lower Wisconsin River." Do not begin a story about a narrow escape from drowning by recounting all the preparations for the hunting trip in the course of which you went out in a canoe after ducks; and do not say, "I once had a narrow escape from drowning." Begin at the beginning of the transaction which brought you into danger;—"Tom stopped paddling and stared into the mist which seemed to enclose us under a cover, and brought the horizon all round us within a few feet of our canoe." Do not begin to tell how to make a sharpie with the general principles of boat-making, or of carpentry, or with remarks about the difficulty or interest of the task. Tell what a sharpie is;—one of the simplest of safe small boats for an amateur builder, being long, sharp, flat-bottomed, not too heavy to row, and easily rigged with one or two triangular sails. In brief, begin as near to the heart of your subject as you can take your reader with you.

Within the composition, the same principles with reference to the relative importance of the end and the beginning which apply to the whole apply also to each separate section. Each section leads to its minor conclusion, and sets out from its minor beginning. The beginnings and the ends are the points of climax and change, the points of emphasis.

Proportion.—A third means of emphasis broadly affecting the plan of a whole composition is the allotment to the more important matters of a large proportion of the space. Listen to the reports of two participants in the same adventure, for instance of two officers of a

wrecked vessel, one of whom has been in charge of the
crew, the other of the navigation. Each will have something to say of the movements of the ship and of the
behavior of the men, but not in the same proportion.
The one will speak in general terms, hastily, of the listing of the deck and the settling of the hull, but will
expand into ample details upon the courage and discipline of the sailors, with some attention to the few exceptions. The other will recognize in a broad way the
admirable conduct of the men, but will analyze fully
the minute facts which prove just where the ship was
struck, and just what caused the accident.

Or compare the arguments of two advocates on opposite sides. Great Britain and the United States, for
example, at one time were engaged in a controversy
about the hunting of fur-seals. The Americans declared
that in order to save the herds from destruction, they
had a right to prevent sealing in ocean waters entirely;
the British asserted the right of all vessels to hunt freely
on the high seas. The Americans, being anxious to prove
that unless the practice of taking seals in ocean waters
were prevented the seals would cease to exist, expanded
in their arguments upon the life-history and habits of
the animals; the British, desiring to show that the seas
cannot be under the jurisdiction of any one state, dealt
amply with international law and the practice of nations.
Each group of advocates touched but lightly upon the
arguments of the other group, but elaborated their own
arguments, reiterated them, brought them forward from
different points of view, so that the reader almost comes
to wonder whether he is really looking at the two aspects
of the same case.

The greatest stress that can be given to an element

of a composition is to begin with it, to end with it, and to return to it frequently. This is what a story does with its hero and with its principal transaction. *Silas Marner* is Silas Marner's story; if it were Godfrey's story or Nancy's, the beginning and the end and the proportions throughout would be changed. If the battle of Bunker Hill is told from the English point of view, the English preparations will begin the story, the effect of the battle on the English control of the colonies will end the tale, and throughout, the English activity will receive a greater space than the American. If the story is told from the American point of view, the narrative will begin with the importance to the Americans of the conflict, will conclude with the effect of the battle throughout the colonies, and will expatiate throughout on the American actions and personalities,—not on Gage's lethargy, and Burgoyne's artillery service, and Howe's leadership in the field, and the heroism of the British infantry,—but on Warren, and Putnam, and Prescott, the labor of spade and pick, the scantiness of powder and ball, the command, "Don't shoot until you see the whites of their eyes," and the orderly forced retreat under fire which the victorious defeated carried calmly through.

Heightenings of Emphasis; Contrast.—The placing of the important matters at the end and at the beginning, and the allotment to them of a large share of space are general principles of structure. In addition there are means of specially heightening the emphasis on particular things. The first of these is antithesis;—the placing side by side of things which are unlike in some points to which attention is to be called. The things thus contrasted must be of the same class, in order that they may be compared.   If a writer were contrasting two children, one bright and the other dull, he would speak first of the things about which as children they would show intelligence, then about their different ways of acting upon these things; if he were contrasting two bright children, he would speak first of them as intelligent, then about the different characters of their intelligence, one being clever at arithmetic, the other at languages; if he were contrasting two children, both clever at arithmetic, he would speak first of the accuracy and power of analysis possessed by both, then of the quickness of one in mental computations, and of the sureness of the other in following long and difficult problems through to a solution.

In a long story, similarly, the important character is "brought out," as the phrase is, by contrast.   Hamlet in the play is as a prince contrasted with the king in point of nobility, refinement, dignity, honor, and scrupulousness; as a man of thought with Horatio in point of insight, originality, and depth; as a young gentleman with Laertes in point of deliberation, judgment, solidity, fineness, and firmness of character.   The differences between princes are significant as to things concerning princes, between young men as to things important for young men, between men of thought as to characteristics of mind; and the more exactly defined the class to which both contrasted things belong, the more interesting and important the contrast.

Climax.—Another method of heightening emphasis is arranging a number of things in a series of increasing importance or interest—as forming what is called a climax.   The incidents of novels or plays lead sometimes in this way up to culminating points, and then these culminations again lead on up to a higher culmination, until the highest peak of the whole range is reached. The little story of *The Three Bears* leads thus from the tasting of the big bowl and of the middle-sized bowl to the emptying of the little bowl, and then through the sitting in the big chair and the middle-sized chair to the breaking of the little chair, and so forward up to the finding of Silverlocks in the little bed. A climax, like an antithesis, is necessarily confined to the members of one class, and follows along a definite line of progress.

Suspense.—Thirdly, emphasis is sometimes heightened by holding back some particular thing—by suspense. One method of obtaining suspense is to enumerate the characteristics of a thing before naming it. For instance, it is common in political nominating conventions to tell all about a candidate's good qualities before naming him. Thus Colonel Robert G. Ingersoll, in his famous speech nominating Blaine for the Republican candidacy for President in 1876, told how the party wanted a man of large public experience, an ample, varied, and successful experience; a man of character and leadership; a man confident in the determination of the American people to pay their debts, and sure in his knowledge that the means to pay those debts would come from prosperous industry—and only after a long and fervid delineation of the man needed did he name the candidate to whom he had all along pointed. Or sometimes suspense is obtained by recounting a number of effects before the cause which brought them about is stated. This is the method of detective stories. Who was the mysterious Stranger? Where is Sir Mortimer hidden? Poe's tale, *The Murders of the Rue Morgue,* is typical. Two murders have been committed in a house in the *Rue Morgue*—murders not only of the most startling brutality but almost bizarre in nearly all of their circumstances. How account for all these extraordinary things—for the grisly hacking of the victims' throats, for the more than human strength shown in the way the bodies were concealed, for the speech, foreign to every listener, though many of different nationalities had heard it, for the disappearance of the murderer when every avenue of escape seemed to be closed? One fact answers all the questions; it is revealed in time; and the answer comes with the greater effect and interest because of the curiosity aroused about it in the course of the narrative.

The Main Principles of Emphasis.—The chief means of giving distinction to a portion or aspect of a composition, accordingly, are placing it at the end, placing it at the beginning, according to it ample space, and setting it off by contrast, climax, and suspense. The last three all tend to increase even the natural predominance of the concluding parts.

Contrast and Variety.—Most fundamental of all forms of emphasis is contrast—the contrast of the beginning with the silence which precedes it, of the end with the silence which follows it, of every subordinate end and beginning with the pause which has interrupted the continuous onward movement of the composition. Because of the necessity of contrast, every part requires to be set out against every other part by perpetual variety, for monotony of any kind, monotony of form or length or method, weakens the force of the parts and obscures the relationships existing among them. It follows that variety of the parts is essential to unity in the whole, for without distinctness in the parts the whole must lose the definiteness and clearness of progress necessary to unity.   The practical consequence is, that even for clearness, to say nothing of effectiveness of expression, a writer should cultivate an abundance of resource, and learn many ways of framing his language to express his thoughts.

RECAPITULATION

The principles which have been laid down may be included under four heads: energy of conception, orderliness of development, clearness of connection, and appropriateness of relative emphasis.   All are but aspects of one fundamental law—the law of unity.

CHAPTER II

THE PARAGRAPH

I. THE SUBJECT-MATTER OF THE PARAGRAPH

What is a Paragraph?—A paragraph, of course, is one of the "sections," or "divisions," or "stages of progress," each having a minor completeness, through which a composition makes its way in its progress to the attainment of its goal. To be in this way a process made up of smaller processes is in the very nature of a composition, because it is in the nature of the workings of the mind, of which a composition is nothing but the record.

The divisions of a composition do not exist because they are marked off by devices of writing or printing; they are marked off because they exist. Sometimes, indeed, they exist and are important without being marked off at all. In a written argument, the introduction, the statement of the issues, the body of discussion, the conclusion are not indicated by printing, yet they are real units. In every essay, in every chapter of a book, there are unmarked divisions. To single out a step of progress and designate it on the page is to recognize that it possesses some special ground for distinction. The acts and scenes of a play, and the sections, chapters, or volumes of a book are not the only divisions of the whole, but they are those divisions upon which the writer wishes to insist. To mark the divisions by devices of writing or printing, then, is an advertisement to the reader that on his way to the terminus he has reached a station which the writer wishes him to recognize.

The paragraph is that division which the writer wishes the reader to have in his mind as the primary unit of advance. It is the smallest unit in which the feeling is given that a definite space has been traversed. A sentence, to be sure, is an advance, but it is like the advance made by a step or two; a paragraph is the advance made by steps enough to carry the reader to the first place where the writer is willing to have him stop and be conscious that he has got somewhere. On the other hand, it makes its way over as wide a reach as the author feels safe in covering at one rush, without a breathing-spell. It is the biggest amount that can be taken in at one sweep, with a sense that the whole and the parts are together at once before the reader's mind. It contains as little as can produce the sense of continuous progress over a definite ground; it contains as much as can be surveyed with the sense of holding it all at once before the view.

The Length of a Paragraph.—Naturally, then, the length of paragraphs must vary within pretty wide limits. The historian Gibbon covered in one work about fourteen hundred years of human history in the regions from Persia to Spain, and from Egypt to Germany. He was especially anxious to avoid confusion—to prevent the general view from being lost in the mass of detail, necessarily vast in such a work. So he built up enormous paragraphs, devoting one to the manners of the Scythians, and another to a campaign of Belisarius, and another to the description of Germany, and another to the character of the emperor Constantine. He wrote for readers of intellectual grasp and training, desirous of obtaining large general views of history. Even so, it is probable that his paragraphs, two or three thousand words in length, are too long, too difficult to hold in the mind as single advances in the course of thought. Readers, even of disciplined minds, would find his chapters less fatiguing if the present paragraphs were called sections, and were subdivided into smaller paragraphs. Huxley, in his lecture *On a Piece of Chalk,* was addressing untrained listeners, and wished every point to be weighed and well understood before the next was taken up. A point, therefore, was made in every paragraph: "Chalk is to be found beneath where we are;—chalk is to be found north and south of here;—it comes near the surface in a thin curve that traverses England;—it prevails beneath the surface to the southeast of this line;—the chalk of the world is vast in extent;—trace it across the continent of Europe, into Africa, and into Asia." Wishing to delay the mind on each new assertion, he makes short paragraphs—paragraphs too short under ordinary circumstances, though suited to his special purpose. Books enumerating many points of detail all of equal importance, such as catechisms, textbooks of grammar, and those scientific and technical works which communicate much concrete information, have short paragraphs; books of synthesis, such as philosophical and historical works, have long paragraphs. A big book with little paragraphs looks as if it trifled with its subject; a little book with big paragraphs looks clumsy. In brief, short compositions, elementary compositions, compositions accentuating individual points, tend to have short paragraphs; long compositions, intellectually mature compositions, compositions interested in grouping and relationships tend to have long paragraphs.

Experience seems to show about how much of a load the mind of a reader can generally carry away at one load. Ordinary printed books scare away readers if there is not at least one break on practically every page, and if there are not two breaks on most pages,—that is, if paragraphs run over some five hundred words, or average over some two hundred and fifty in length.

Variety in Length.—Moreover, differences in length may give special distinction to special paragraphs. A long paragraph in the midst of short ones gains a certain distinction of momentum,—the emphasis of a rolling drum; a short paragraph in the midst of long ones gains a certain distinction of energy,—the emphasis of a snapping whip. Any monotony becomes tedious and confusing, monotonously long paragraphs heavy, monotonously short paragraphs restless and indistinct. Hence the utmost variety consistent with logic and clearness is desirable.

Too Frequent Paragraphing.—Most inexperienced writers paragraph too often. They are conscious of the effort of thinking out even a small subject and recording the process of their minds, and hence they break their writing into fragments. A little exercise of two or three hundred words is often the better if it is not divided into paragraphs at all.

Dialogue.—Inasmuch as paragraphs express a logical unity, it is natural to paragraph whenever there is a distinct change in the point of view. Hence results the custom of the English language that in written and printed dialogue each speech is usually a paragraph. To express confusion, or a very excited and rapid interchange of speeches, dialogue is sometimes printed solid.

Holding to the Topic.—Paragraphs, of course, like other compositions, should generally speaking follow out a single course of thought in a systematic order. Being short and being parts of larger complete compositions, they cover only a very narrow and very definitely limited field, any departure from which becomes instantly obvious. Hence, for most of the purposes of writing, paragraphs should be held very closely to their exact subjects. In a large work, a digression is easily passed over; the reader slips quickly back from it into the main current of his thought. But in the short space of a paragraph a departure from the topic is too conspicuous and too confusing to be ventured upon except with very good reason.

Irrelevant Introductions.—In the following paragraph from a theme on the good influences of fraternities, the introductory sentence leads the mind of the reader away from the real topic just at the moment under discussion.

The best fraternities are national, and have chapters in most college towns of any importance. Most students are strangers in a college town, coming usually from considerable distances. If they live alone by themselves, they suffer from homesickness; and a homesick student is a poor worker. The same thing is true even if they live in ordinary lodging-houses, perhaps among uncongenial or unfamiliar company. To bring students together in fraternities commonly makes their life more agreeable, and thus tends to overcome loneliness. They find good-fellowship and open-heartedness in their brethren, and they feel at home with them. One result is that they are content with university life, and study all the better.

Digressions.—In the following paragraph from a theme on the advertising campaign of the government during the late war, the italicized sentence, which belongs to the theme but not to the paragraph, greatly weakens the effect of the passage.

Bill-boards all over the country have been covered with printed matter regarding the war. Proclamations and notices and appeals have been posted everywhere. These exciting posters always draw attention, and it makes no difference if they were read before; they are read over and over again. *It is everybody's business to keep informed about the needs of the government;* and the printed posters are among the most effective parts of the government's advertising campaign. Anyone who has not observed the fact will be surprised to find how attentively the public reads a printed notice in fairly large type with an official heading.

Irrelevant Conclusions.—In the following paragraph on the value of football to a soldier the conclusion is irrelevant.

It is apparent that athletics is an important part of a soldier's training, because otherwise the United States and the Allies would not be spending millions of dollars upon giving their soldiers athletic training. Football is especially valuable in preparing men for battle. It enables the muscles to respond freely and easily. By it speed and quickness are developed; speed is important in the advance by rushes, quickness everywhere, but especially in hand-to-hand conflict. Alertness is developed, which plays an important part in trench warfare. Coöperation, and the obedience which is essential to coöperation, are developed, and these are the fundamentals of the soldier's life. *Brains are often pitted against brawn; coaches in previous years wanted brawn, but now they want brains.*

Disproportion of Parts.—Sometimes what is said is not really irrelevant to the topic of the paragraph, but receives so inadequate a proportion of space and development as to seem so. The material introduced expands the idea of the whole, without expanding the treatment to correspond. The sentences in the following paragraphs sound like afterthoughts. They are so hasty and superficial as only to suggest that something ought to be

said about their topics, without saying it. They ought
to be expanded or entirely omitted.

In Milwaukee, as in every large town, visitors have no trouble in finding recreation. *This is true even if you love driving,
though of course horses are now out of fashion.* But it is for
those who like cars that Milwaukee will furnish the greatest
opportunities for pleasure. Long roads, well paved, some of
them with concrete, connect the town with interesting places
all about. I have special reference to the Port Washington
road, the Janesville "plank" road, and the Blue Mound road
leading to a beautiful group of lakes—Lake Nagwicka, Pine
Lake, Lake Okochee, and many more. On each of these one
can roll along for an hour or for a day, in the midst of a
charmingly diversified region, with an undulating surface but
no unreasonably long or steep hills, among prosperous farms,
bright lakes, rich woodlands of oak, lonely marshes and tama-
rack swamps, and quiet stretches of willow-bordered rivers.

In speaking of my association with others, I hope to bring
out especially the training I received in the estimating of character. At —— School I was at first very homesick, and as a
very natural result I could not see that the boys were friendly.
Slowly I began to perceive their good will, and then I began
to understand their character and purpose. I learned to ad-
mire and respect them, and I learned by my relations with them
to some extent how to interpret the actions of others. Last
summer, after my year at this school, I had my first experience
with working for wages. I was employed as inspector of
canned goods by the Colonia Canning Company. *My duties
involved supervising the canning process and directing the men
at their work.* [Certainly something about the knowledge of
men acquired here is called for.] When I came to the University, the question what, if any, fraternity I should join called
for all my knowledge of character for solution. I think I was
helped by my experience in making a decision.

In every occupation, and indeed in every relation in life,
schooling plays a most important part. Of course everybody
knows this is true of a lawyer or a doctor, but even the keeper
of a general store should have not only a general knowledge of
business, but much miscellaneous information and some intellectual training. The first question asked of candidates for
officers' commissions is where and how much they have studied.

Moreover, uneducated men are bores to themselves, and are ill at ease in society. *Examples of literate and illiterate families are found in all cities.* [The point suggested, but not brought out, is the importance of education for healthy family life.]

II.   THE DEVELOPMENT OF THE PARAGRAPH

A good paragraph deals with its limited subject-matter systematically—possesses not only the unity of a definite topic, but the unity of methodical development as well. Paragraphs are, broadly speaking, of two main types,— those which develop from a "topic sentence" and those which do not; that is to say, those in which the central idea is explicitly stated, and those in which it is simply manifested by the course of the paragraph itself, without being put expressly into words.

Paragraphs without Topic Sentences.—Paragraphs which themselves mark the successive advances of continuous progress in a straight line, and which simply include several steps toward the end, do not need formal indications of the ground which they cover.   Narrative paragraphs commonly present as much as makes up a single advance in the action, often with so much description as is required to associate that advance with its necessary conditions.

The narrative parts of the following passage from Washington Irving illustrate the type, the descriptive parts being introduced by topic sentences (see the second and third paragraphs).

[*Rip Van Winkle, called by a voice, and seeing the strange being who had called him, went to help the man.*]

As he was about to descend, he heard a voice from a distance, hallooing, "Rip Van Winkle! Rip Van Winkle!" He looked around, but could see nothing but a crow winging its solitary flight across the mountain. He thought his fancy must have deceived him, and turned to descend, when he heard the same cry ring through the still evening air, "Rip Van Winkle! Rip Van Winkle!" At the same time Wolf bristled up his back, and giving a low growl, skulked to his master's side, looking fearfully down into the glen. Rip felt now a vague apprehension stealing over him. He looked anxiously in the same direction, and perceived a strange figure slowly toiling up the rocks, and bending under the weight of something he carried on his back. He was surprised to see any human being in this lonely and unfrequented place, but, supposing it to be some one of the neighborhood in need of his assistance, he hastened down to yield it.

[*The man, an old fellow in ancient Dutch costume, and Rip together carried a keg of liquor up a rugged gully into a hollow in the mountain, from which a sound like thunder rumbled forth.*]

On nearer approach he was still more surprised by the singularity of the stranger's appearance. He was a short, square-built old fellow, with thick, bushy hair, and a grizzled beard. His dress was of the antique Dutch fashion,—a cloth jerkin strapped round the waist; several pairs of breeches, the outer one of ample volume, decorated with rows of buttons down the sides, and bunches at the knees. He bore on his shoulders a stout keg, that seemed full of liquor, and made signs for Rip to approach and assist him with the load. Though rather shy and distrustful of this new acquaintance, Rip complied with his usual alacrity; and mutually relieving each other, they clambered up a narrow gully, apparently the dry bed of a mountain torrent. As they ascended, Rip every now and then heard long, rolling peals, like distant thunder, that seemed to issue out of a deep ravine, or rather cleft, between lofty rocks, toward which their rugged path conducted. He paused for an instant, but, supposing it to be the muttering of one of those transient thunder-showers which often take place in mountain heights, he proceeded. Passing through the ravine, they came to a hollow, like a small amphitheater, surrounded by perpendicular precipices, over the brinks of which impending trees shot their branches, so that you only caught glimpses of the azure sky and the bright evening cloud. During the whole time, Rip and his companion had labored on in silence; for, though the former marveled greatly what could be the object of carrying a keg of liquor up this wild mountain, yet there was something strange and incomprehensible about the unknown, that inspired awe and checked familiarity.

[*Within the amphitheater was a group of grotesque un-*

earthly beings, in ancient costumes, playing at ninepins.]
On entering the amphitheater, new objects of wonder presented themselves. On a level spot in the center was a company of odd-looking personages playing at ninepins. They were dressed in a quaint, outlandish fashion. Some wore short doublets; others, jerkins, with long knives in their belts; and most of them had enormous breeches, of similar style with that of the guide's. Their visages, too, were peculiar. One had a large head, broad face, and small, piggish eyes. The face of another seemed to consist entirely of nose, and was surmounted by a white sugar-loaf hat, set off with a little red cock's tail. They all had beards, of various shapes and colors. There was one that seemed to be the commander. He was a stout old gentleman, with a weather-beaten countenance. He wore a laced doublet, broad belt and hanger, high-crowned hat and feather, red stockings, and high-heeled shoes with roses in them. The whole group reminded Rip of the figures in an old Flemish painting in the parlor of Dominie Van Schaick, the village parson, and which had been brought over from Holland at the time of the settlement.

[*So silent were they that no sound was heard but that of the rolling balls.*]
What seemed particularly odd to Rip was, that, though these folks were evidently enjoying themselves, yet they maintained the gravest faces, the most mysterious silence, and were, withal, the most melancholy party of pleasure he had ever witnessed. Nothing interrupted the stillness of the scene but the noise of the balls, which, whenever they were rolled, echoed along the mountains like rumbling peals of thunder.

[*Rip, in terror, served them with the liquor from the keg.*]
As Rip and his companion approached them, they suddenly desisted from their play, and stared at him with such fixed, statue-like gaze, and such strange, uncouth, lack-luster countenances, that his heart turned within him, and his knees smote together. His companion now emptied the contents of the keg into large flagons, and made signs to him to wait upon the company. He obeyed with fear and trembling. They quaffed the liquor in profound silence, and then returned to their game.

[*Then, by degrees losing his fear, he drank freely of the liquor, until he was overcome with sleep.*]
By degrees, Rip's awe and apprehension subsided. He even ventured, when no eye was fixed upon him, to taste the beverage, which he found had much of the flavor of excellent Hol-

land's. He was naturally a thirsty soul, and was soon tempted
to repeat the draught. One taste provoked another; and he
reiterated his visits to the flagon so often, that at length his
senses were overpowered, his eyes swam in his head, his head
gradually declined, and he fell into a deep sleep.

[*On waking, and finding that though he had lain down in the
afternoon, it was a bright morning, he bethought himself peni-
tently of all that had taken place the day before.*]

On waking, he found himself on the green knoll whence he
had first seen the old man of the glen. He rubbed his eyes.
It was a bright, sunny morning. The birds were hopping and
twittering in the bushes; and the eagle was wheeling aloft, and
breasting the pure mountain breeze. "Surely," thought Rip,
"I have not slept here all night." He recalled the occurrences
before he fell asleep,—the strange man with a keg of liquor,
the mountain ravine, the wild retreat among the rocks, the woe-
begone party at ninepins, the flagon. "Oh, that wicked
flagon!" thought Rip: "what excuse shall I make to Dame
Van Winkle!"

Each paragraph makes a definite advance, though it
is true that in some cases either smaller or greater advances could easily be insisted upon. The shout could
be separated from Rip's detection of the man who
uttered it; the description of the man from the ascent
of the mountain laden with the keg. Again, the description of the group could be united with the account
of their actions. But there are good reasons for the
present divisions. Rip did not pay so much attention
to the strange being's appearance as he paid to what
he was doing; on the other hand, he was in great terror
and anxiety when he saw the extraordinary aspect of
the players at ninepins. Hence there is a ground for
separating the paragraphs in the one case which does not
hold in the others.

The paragraphs quoted may serve as illustrations of
narrative paragraphs, in which though the paragraphs
are distinct and though the transitions are clearly

marked, yet events follow each other in so continuous and natural a sequence that no special device of organization is necessary; all that is needful is to follow the flight of time. Descriptive paragraphs, as the examples show, tend to be introduced in a more formal manner, but even they often leave their general impression to be inferred. They may present in order the successive experiences of the spectator; they may tell a kind of story of the impressions he receives, as in the following example from Stevenson's *Markheim*.

Time had some score of small voices in that shop, some stately and slow as was becoming to their great age; others garrulous and hurried. All these told out the seconds in an intricate chorus of tickings. Then the passage of a lad's feet, heavily running on the pavement, broke in upon these smaller voices and startled Markheim into the consciousness of his surroundings. He looked about him awfully. The candle stood on the counter, its flame solemnly wagging in a draught; and by that inconsiderable movement, the whole room was filled with noiseless bustle and kept heaving like a sea; the tall shadows nodding, the gross blots of darkness swelling and dwindling as with respiration, the faces of the portraits and the china gods changing and wavering like images in water. The inner door stood ajar, and peered into that leaguer of shadows with a long slit of daylight like a pointing finger.

Paragraphs of thought, as will be seen in a minute, commonly require a more explicit indication of their purpose. Even with such paragraphs, this does not always hold true. To put a topic sentence to the following paragraph from Emerson's *Essay on Wealth* would only tend to make it tame.

Of the two eminent engineers in the recent construction of railways in England, Mr. Brunel went straight from terminus to terminus, through mountains, over streams, crossing highways, cutting ducal estates in two, and shooting through this man's cellar and that man's attic window, and so arriving at

his end, at great pleasure to geometers, but with great cost
to his company. Mr. Stephenson, on the contrary, believing
that the river knows the way, followed his valley, as implicitly
as our Western Railroad follows the Westfield River, and
turned out to be the safest and cheapest engineer. We say
the cows laid out Boston. Well, there are worse surveyors.
Every pedestrian in our pastures has frequent occasion to
thank the cows for cutting the best path through the thicket,
and over the hills; and travellers and Indians know the value
of a buffalo-trail, which is sure to be the easiest possible pass
through the ridge.

Topic Sentences.—The second type of paragraph an-
nounces its topic and then develops it. Through such a
paragraph a continuous train of thought moves, and
moves steadily. But the process is not so much like a
swift arrow-flight as like building a house, laying brick
upon brick. Each brick is lifted; the mortar is spread
for it; it is set in place and perhaps plumbed before the
next is taken up. Or we may recur to our comparison
of the course of our thought to the exploration and map-
ping of a new country; we must work our way to a hill-
top and look about us, we must leave guide-posts on our
road to guide those who follow us, we must put down
the trend of rivers and the slope of hills.

Complete Development of a Topic.—This type of
paragraph, when treated with formal completeness, consists of three parts: an introductory announcement of
the trend of its thought, the discussion of the topic an-
nounced, and a conclusion indicating the new point
reached by this discussion. It is by no means always
necessary to carry out this scheme, the conclusion being
often too obvious to be insisted on.

Macaulay's account of the contrast between the physical weakness and the mental force of William III illustrates the method.

The audacity of his spirit was the more remarkable because his physical organization was unusually delicate. From a child he had been weak and sickly. In the prime of manhood his complaints had been aggravated by a severe attack of small-pox. He was asthmatic and consumptive. His slender frame was shaken by a constant hoarse cough. He could not sleep unless his head was propped by several pillows, and could scarcely draw his breath in any but the purest air. Cruel headaches frequently tortured him. Exertion soon fatigued him. The physicians constantly kept up the hopes of his enemies by fixing some date beyond which, if there were any-thing certain in medical science, it was impossible that his broken constitution could hold out. Yet, through a life that was one long disease, the force of his mind never failed, on any great occasion, to bear up his suffering and languid body.

Illustration.—Any sensible ground of connection may serve as the principle of development in a paragraph of this kind. The foregoing paragraph consists of a general statement developed by a number of illustrative examples, concluding with a restatement of the introductory proposition in the clearer light thrown upon it by the discussion. This is perhaps as common a type as any.

Analysis and Definition.—Sometimes the paragraph is one of analysis and definition. In the following example, Burke is responding to the philosophers who tried to define political freedom in accordance with universal theories. His purpose is to define the nature of political liberty as a practical reality, and as men really think of it.

Civil freedom, gentlemen, is not, as many have endeavored to persuade you, a thing that lies hid in the depth of abstruse science. It is a blessing and a benefit, not an abstract speculation; and all the just reasoning that can be upon it is of so coarse a texture as perfectly to suit the capacities of those who are to enjoy, and of those who are to defend it. Far from any resemblance to those propositions in geometry and metaphysics which admit no medium, but must be true or false in all their latitude, social and civil freedom, like all other things in common life, are variously mixed and modified, enjoyed in very different degrees, and shaped into an infinite diversity of forms, according to the temper and circumstances of every community. The *extreme* of liberty (which is its abstract perfection, but its real fault) obtains nowhere, nor ought to obtain anywhere; because extremes, as we all know, in every point which relates either to our duties or satisfactions in life, are destructive both to virtue and enjoyment. Liberty, too, must be limited in order to be possessed. The degree of restraint it is impossible in any case to settle precisely. But it ought to be the constant aim of every wise public counsel to find out by cautious experiments, and rational, cool endeavors, with how little, not how much, of this restraint the community can subsist: for liberty is a good to be improved, and not an evil to be lessened. It is not only a private blessing of the first order, but the vital spring and energy of the state itself, which has just so much life and vigor as there is liberty in it. But whether liberty be advantageous or not (for I know it is fashionable to decry the very principle), none will dispute that peace is a blessing; and peace must, in the course of human affairs, be frequently bought by some indulgence and toleration at least to liberty: for, as the Sabbath (though of divine institution) was made for man, not man for the Sabbath, government, which can claim no higher origin or authority, in its exercise at least, ought to conform to the exigencies of the time, and the temper and character of the people with whom it is concerned, and not always to attempt violently to bend the people to their theories of subjection. The bulk of mankind, on their part, are not excessively curious concerning any theories whilst they are really happy; and one sure symptom of an ill-conducted state is the propensity of the people to resort to them.

Argument.—In the following paragraph causes are given for the affirmation with which it begins. Carlyle has been insisting on the value of the glorious spiritual gift which Shakespeare had bestowed upon the English. He proceeds:

Nay, apart from spiritualities; and considering him merely as a real, marketable, tangibly-useful possession [*i. e.*, Shakespeare is also practically valuable to the English: the topic sentence]. England, before long, this Island of ours, will hold but a small fraction of the English: in America, in New Holland [Australia], east and west to the very Antipodes, there will be a Saxondom covering great spaces of the Globe. And now, what is it that can keep all these together into virtually one Nation, so that they do not fall-out and fight, but live at peace, in brotherlike intercourse helping one another? This is justly regarded as the greatest practical problem, the thing all manner of sovereignties and governments are here to accomplish: what is it that will accomplish this? Acts of Parliament, administrative prime ministers cannot. America is parted from us, so far as Parliament could part it. Call it not fantastic, for there is much reality in it: Here, I say, is an English King, whom no time or chance, Parliament, or combination of Parliaments, can dethrone! This King, Shakespeare, does not he shine, in crowned sovereignty, over us all, as the noblest, gentlest, yet strongest of rallying-signs; *in*destructible; really more valuable in that point of view than any other means or appliance whatsoever? We can fancy him as radiant aloft over all the Nations of Englishmen, a thousand years hence. From Paramatta, from New York, wheresoever, under what sort of Parish-Constable soever, English men and women are, they will say to one another: "Yes, this Shakespeare is ours; we produced him, we speak and think by him; we are of one blood and kind with him." The most common-sense politician, too, if he pleases, may think of that.

The following passage from Professor William James illustrates the development of a series of paragraphs, all starting out from topic sentences, by specification, by analysis, and by argument.

It is certain, to begin with, that the narrowest trade or professional training does something more for a man than make a skillful practical tool of him—it makes him also a judge of other men's skill. [Topic developed by argument from example.] Whether his trade be pleading at the bar or surgery or plastering or plumbing, it develops a critical sense in him for that sort of occupation. He understands the difference between second-rate and first-rate work in his whole branch of industry; he gets to know a good job in his own line when he sees it; and getting to know this in his own line, he gets a faint sense of what good work may mean anyhow, that may, if circumstances favor, spread into his judgments elsewhere. Sound work, clean work, finished work, feeble work, slack work, sham work—these words express an identical contrast in many departments of activity. In so far forth, then, even the humblest manual trade may beget in one a small degree of power to judge of good work generally.

Now, what is supposed to be the line of us who have the higher college training? [Topic defined.] Is there any broader line—since our education claims primarily not to be "narrow" —in which we also are made good judges between what is first-rate and what is second-rate only? What is especially taught in the colleges has long been known by the name of the "humanities," and these are often identified with Greek and Latin. But it is only as literatures, not as languages, that Greek and Latin have any general humanity value; so that in a broad sense the humanities mean literature primarily, and in a still broader sense the study of masterpieces in almost any field of human endeavor. Literature keeps the primacy; for it not only *consists* of masterpieces, but is largely *about* masterpieces, being little more than an appreciative chronicle of human master-strokes, so far as it takes the form of criticism and history. You can give humanistic value to almost anything by teaching it historically. Geology, economics, mechanics, are humanities when taught with reference to the successive achievements of the geniuses to which these sciences owe their being. Not taught thus, literature remains grammar, art a catalogue, history a list of dates, and natural science a sheet of formulas and weights and measures.

The sifting of human creations!—nothing less than this is what we ought to mean by the humanities. Essentially this means biography; *what our colleges should teach is,* therefore, *biographical history,* not that of politics merely, but *of anything and everything and everything so far as human efforts and conquests are factors that have played their part.* [Topic analyzed.] Studying in this way, we learn what types of activity have stood the test of time; we acquire standards of the excellent and durable. All our arts and sciences and institutions are but so many quests of perfection on the part of men; and when we see how diverse the types of excellence may be, how various the tests, how flexible the adaptations, we gain a richer sense of what the terms "better" and "worse" may signify in general. Our critical sensibilities grow both more acute and less fanatical. We sympathize with men's mistakes even in the act of penetrating them; we feel the pathos of lost causes and misguided epochs even while we applaud what overcame them.

Such words are vague and such ideas are inadequate, but their meaning is unmistakable. *What the colleges*—teaching humanities by examples which may be special, but which must be typical and pregnant—*should at least try to give us, is a general sense of what, under various disguises, superiority has always signified, and may still signify.* [Topic analyzed and defined.] The feeling for a good human job anywhere, the admiration of the really admirable, the dis-esteem for what is cheap and trashy and impermanent—this is what we call the critical sense, the sense for ideal values. It is the better part of what men know as wisdom. Some of us are wise in this way naturally and by genius; some of us never become so. But to have spent one's youth at college, to come in contact with the choice and rare and precious, and yet to be a blind prig or vulgarian, unable to scent out human excellence or to divine it amid its accidents, to know it only when ticketed and labeled and forced on us by others, this is indeed the very calamity and shipwreck of a higher education.

The sense for human superiority ought, then, to be considered our line, as boring subways is the engineer's line and the surgeon's is appendicitis. [Topic defined and applied.] Our colleges ought to have lit up in us a lasting relish for the better kind of man, a loss of appetite for mediocrities, and a disgust for cheapjacks. We ought to smell, as it were, the difference of quality in men and their proposals when we enter the world of affairs about us. Expertness in this might well atone for some of our awkwardness at accounts, and for some of our ignorance of dynamos. The best claim we can make for the higher education, the best single phrase in which we can tell what it ought to do for us, is, then, exactly what I said: it should enable us to *know a good man when we see him*.

Copyright by *McClure's Magazine;* by permission.

III. TRANSITION WITHIN THE PARAGRAPH

Transitions, guide-posts to point the way as the reader proceeds from part to part, are as essential within the paragraph as in compositions on a larger scale. But since the parts of a paragraph are sentences, transitions between them have to do with the arrangement and expression of sentences, and are most conveniently discussed as aspects of the sentence. A method of indicating the relationship of the parts of a paragraph is briefly treated at this point, since it involves the structure not of one sentence only, but of groups of sentences in sequence.

Maintenance of Parallel Form.—One means of effect within the paragraph is not applicable on the large scale of the entire composition: this is indicating parallelism of ideas by beginning the sentences which treat the parallel ideas with the same word or group of words, and keeping the sentences more or less parallel in syntactical form. This form of expression is a natural means of keeping a complicated body of ideas in groups, so that their relations can be easily perceived.

He was the first poet I ever knew. His genius at that time (1798) had angelic wings, and fed on manna. He talked on forever. His thoughts did not seem to come with labour and effort, but as if borne on the gusts of genius, and as if the wings of his imagination lifted him from off his feet. His voice rolled on the ear like the pealing organ, and its sound was the music of thought. His mind was clothed with wings; and, raised on them, he lifted philosophy to heaven. In his descriptions, you then saw the progress of human happiness and liberty in bright and never-ending succession, like the steps of Jacob's Ladder, with airy shapes ascending and descending, and with the voice of God at the top of the ladder. And shall I, who heard him then, listen to him now? Not I! . . . That spell is broken; that time is gone forever; that voice is heard no more; but still the recollection comes rushing by with thoughts of long-past years, and rings in my ears with never-dying sound.   Hazlitt on Coleridge.

IV.   TRANSITION FROM PARAGRAPH TO PARAGRAPH

Either by explicit words of connection or by the natural sequence of the parts, the beginnings and ends of paragraphs should be clearly marked, and the relation between paragraph and paragraph clearly indicated. In the following passage from Cardinal Newman, definite and formal connections are employed.

Thought and speech are inseparable from each other. Matter and expression are parts of one: style is a thinking out into language. This is what I have been laying down, and this is literature; not *things,* not the verbal symbols of things; not on the other hand mere *words;* but thoughts expressed in language. Call to mind, Gentlemen, the meaning of the Greek word which expresses this special prerogative of man over the feeble intelligence of the inferior animals. It is called Logos: what does Logos mean? it stands for both *reason* and for *speech,* and it is difficult to say which it means more properly. It means both at once: why? because really they cannot be divided,—because they are in a true sense one. When we can separate light and illumination, life and motion, the convex and the concave of a curve, then it will be possible for thought to tread speech underfoot, and to hope to do without it —then will it be conceivable that the vigorous and fetile intellect should renounce its own double, its instrument of expression, and the channel of its speculations and emotions.

Critics should consider this view of the subject before they lay down such canons of taste as the writer whose pages I have quoted. [An explicitly transitional sentence.] Such men as he is consider fine writing to be an *addition from without* to the matter treated of,—a sort of ornament super-induced, or a luxury indulged in, by those who have time and inclination for such vanities. They speak as if *one* man could do the thought, and *another* the style. We read in Persian travels of the way in which young gentlemen go to work in the East, when they would engage in correspondence with those who inspire them with hope or fear. They cannot write one sentence themselves; so they betake themselves to the professional letter-writer. They confide to him the object they have in view. They have a point to gain from a superior, a favor to ask, an evil to deprecate; they have to approach a man in power, or to make court to some beautiful lady. The professional man manufactures words for them, as they are wanted, as a stationer sells them paper, or a schoolmaster might cut their pens. Thought and word are, in their conception, two things, and thus there is a division of labor. The man of thought comes to the man of words; and the man of words, duly instructed in the thought, dips the pen of desire into the ink of

devotedness, and proceeds to spread it over the page of desolation. Then the nightingale of affection is heard to warble
to the rose of loveliness, while the breeze of anxiety plays
around the brow of expectation. This is what the Easterns
are said to consider fine writing; and it seems pretty much the
idea of the school of critics to whom I have been referring.

*We have an instance in literary history of this very proceed-
ing nearer home, in a great University, in the latter years of
the last century.* [An explicitly transitional sentence.] I
have referred to it before now in a public lecture elsewhere;
but it is too much in point here to be omitted. A learned
Arabic scholar had to deliver a set of lectures before its doc-
tors and professors on an historical subject in which his reading had lain. A linguist is conversant with science rather than
with literature; but this gentleman felt that his lectures must
not be without a style. Being of the opinion of the Orientals,
with whose writings he was familiar, he determined to buy a
style. He took the step of engaging a person, at a price, to
turn the matter which he had got together into ornamental
English. Observe, he did not wish for mere grammatical
English, but for an elaborate pretentious style. An artist was
found in the person of a country curate, and the job was carried out. His lectures remain to this day, in their own place
in the protracted series of annual Discourses to which they
belong, distinguished amid a number of heavyish compositions
by the rhetorical and ambitious diction for which he went into
the market. This learned divine, indeed, and the author I have
quoted, differ in the estimate they respectively form of literary
composition; but they agree together in this,—in considering
such composition a trick and a trade; they put it on a par
with the gold plate and the flowers and the music of a ban-
quet, which do not make the viands better, but the entertainment more pleasurable; as if language were the hired servant,
the mere mistress of the reason, and not the lawful wife in
her own house.

But can they really think [Explicit transition] that Homer,
or Pindar, or Shakespeare, or Dryden, or Walter Scott, were
accustomed to aim at diction for its own sake, instead of being
inspired with their subject, and pouring forth beautiful words
because they had beautiful thoughts? this is surely too great
a paradox to be borne. Rather, it is the fire within the
author's breast which overflows in the torrent of his burning,
irresistible eloquence; it is the poetry of his inner soul, which
relieves itself in the Ode or the Elegy; and his mental attitude

and bearing, the beauty of his moral countenance, the force and keenness of his logic, are imaged in the tenderness, or energy, or richness of his language. Nay, according to the well-known line, "facit indignatio *versus;*" not the words alone, but even the rhythm, the meter, the verse, will be the contemporaneous offspring of the emotion of imagination which possesses him. "Poeta nascitur, non fit," says the proverb; and this is in numerous instances true of his poems as well as of himself. They are born, not framed; they are a strain rather than a composition; and their perfection is the monument, not so much of his skill as of his power. And this is true of prose as well as of verse in its degree: who will not recognize in the vision of Mirza a delicacy and beauty of style which is very difficult to describe, but which is felt to be in exact correspondence to the ideas of which it is the expression?

Transition by Arrangement of Parts.—Of more importance and interest is the indication of the relations between successive paragraphs by the emphasis resulting from the structure of the paragraphs themselves. The beginning, of course, tends to ground itself upon what has preceded and to point out the direction of the paragraph as a whole; the end has the general function of making clear what the whole paragraph has led up to. The end and the beginning are thus the marked places of emphasis.

The method of connecting by reference forward and backward is illustrated in the following paragraphs by Mark Twain.

Pudd'nhead Wilson had a trifle of money when he arrived, and he bought a small house on the extreme western verge of the town. Between it and Judge Driscoll's house there was only a grassy yard, with a paling fence dividing the properties in the middle. He hired a small office down in the town and hung out a tin sign with these words on it:

DAVID WILSON
ATTORNEY AND COUNSELLOR-AT-LAW
SURVEYING, CONVEYANCING, ETC.

But his deadly remark had ruined his chance—at least in

the law. No clients came. He took down his sign after awhile and put it up on his own house with the law features knocked out of it. It offered his services now in the humble capacities of land-surveyor and expert accountant. Now and then he got a job of surveying to do, and now and then a merchant got him to straighten out his books. With Scotch patience and pluck he resolved to live down his reputation and work his way into the legal field yet. Poor fellow! he could not foresee that it was going to take him *such a long weary time* to do it.

He had a rich *abundance of idle time,* but it never hung *idle* on his hands, for *he interested himself in every new thing that was born into the universe of ideas,* and studied and experimented upon it at his house. One of his pet fads was palmistry. To another he gave no name, neither would he explain to anybody what its purpose was, but merely said it was an amusement. In fact, he had found that his fads added to his reputation as a pudd'nhead; therefore he was growing chary of being too communicative about them. The fad without a name was one which dealt with people's finger-marks. He carried in his coat pocket a shallow box with grooves in it, and in the grooves strips of glass five inches long and three inches wide. Along the lower edge of each strip was pasted a slip of white paper. He asked people to pass their hands through their hair (thus collecting upon them a thin coating of the natural oil) and then make a thumb-mark on a glass strip, following it with the mark of the ball of each finger in succession. Under this row of faint grease-prints he would write a record on the strip of white paper—thus:

JOHN SMITH, *right hand*—

and add the day of the month and the year, then take Smith's left hand on another glass strip, and add name and date and the words "left hand." The strips were now returned to the grooved box, and took their place among what *Wilson called his "records."*

He *often studied his records,* examining and poring over them with absorbing interest until far into the night; but what he found there—if he found anything—he revealed to no one. Sometimes he copied on paper the involved and delicate pattern left by the ball of a finger, and then vastly enlarged it with a pantograph so that he could examine its web of curving lines with ease and convenience.

Copyright; by permission of the Mark Twain Estate; all rights reserved.

V. EMPHASIS OF PARAGRAPH STRUCTURE

Contrast.—Within the paragraph, as in other compositions, contrast may be not only a means of clearness but also of emphasising some particular point. Thus, in the following passage, De Quincey defines the two main functions of literature by the contrast between them, while the literature of power is given peculiar salience. As always, a class of things is first created—functions of literature—between two members of which class—the giving of information and the moving of the genial emotions—a contrast is set up. The second, the more important, is placed last.

Books, therefore, do not suggest an idea co-extensive and interchangeable with the idea of literature; since much literature, scenic, forensic, or didactic (as from lecturers and public orators), may never come into books, and much that does come into books may connect itself with no literary interest. But a far more important correction, applicable to the common vague idea of literature, is to be sought—not so much in a better definition of literature, as in a sharper distinction of the two functions which it fulfils. In that great social organ, which collectively we call literature, there may be distinguished two separate offices that may blend and often *do* so, but capable, severally, of a severe insulation, and naturally fitted for reciprocal repulsion. There is, first the literature of *knowledge;* and, secondly, the literature of *power.* The function of the first is—to *teach;* the function of the second is—to *move*: the first is a rudder; the second, an oar or a sail. The first speaks *to* the more discursive understanding; the second speaks ultimately, it may happen to the higher understanding or reason, but always *through* affections of pleasure and sympathy. Remotely, it may travel towards an object seated in what Lord Bacon calls *dry* light: but proximately, it does and must operate, else it would cease to be a literature of *power,* on and through that *humid* light which clothes itself in the mists and glittering *iris* of human passions, desires, and genial emotions.

Proportion.—The more important an element in a

GETTYSBURG COLLEGE
43665
Gettysburg, Pa.
✠ LIBRARY ✠

paragraph is, the more space is likely to be given it. In the following paragraph from the third of Ruskin's *Lectures on Art,* the author is at the moment chiefly interested in the necessity of sincerity, next in that of sympathy, and distributes his space accordingly. The beginning of the paragraph is a transition from the general theme of the lectures, the principles of art-teaching in the field of drawing, painting, sculpture, and the like, to the theme of the art of language.

And this it was that I called upon you to hear, saying, "listen to me at least now," in the first lecture, namely, that no art-teaching could be of use to you, but would rather be harmful, unless it was grafted on something deeper than all art. For indeed not only with this, of which it is my function to show you the laws, but much more with the art of all men, which you came here chiefly to learn, that of language, the chief vices of education have arisen from the one great fallacy of supposing that noble language is a communicable trick of grammar and accent, instead of simply the careful expression of right thought. All the virtues of language are, in their roots, moral; it becomes accurate if the speaker desires to be true; clear if he speaks with sympathy and a desire to be intelligible; powerful, if he has earnestness; pleasant, if he has sense of rhythm and order. There are no other virtues of language producible by art than these: but let me mark more deeply for an instant the significance of one of them. Language, I said, is only clear when it is sympathetic. You can, in truth, understand a man's word only by understanding his temper. Your own word is also as of an unknown tongue to him unless he understands yours. And it is this which makes the art of language, if any one is to be chosen separately from the rest, that which is fittest to be the instrument of a gentleman's education. To teach the meaning of a word thoroughly, is to teach the nature of the spirit that coined it; the secret of language is the secret of sympathy, and its full charm is possible only to the gentle. And thus the principles of beautiful speech have all been fixed by the principles of sincere and kindly speech. On the laws which have been determined by sincerity, false speech, apparently beautiful, may afterwards be constructed; but all such utterance, whether in oration or poetry, is not only without permanent power, but is destructive of the principles it has usurped. So long as no words are uttered but in faithfulness, so long the art of language goes on exalting itself; but the moment it is shaped and chiselled on external principles, it falls into frivolity, and perishes. And this truth would have been long ago manifest, had it not been that in periods of advanced academical science there is always a tendency to deny the sincerity of the first masters of language. Once learn to write gracefully in the manner of an ancient author, and we are apt to think that he also wrote in the manner of some one else. But no noble or right style was ever yet founded but out of a sincere heart.

Climax.—Climax is a means of emphasis in the paragraph, and is sometimes increased in clearness and effectiveness by the parallel form of successive sentences of increasing significance, and often of somewhat increasing length.

The truth is that there scarcely ever lived a person who had so little claim to this sort of praise as Pitt. He was undoubtedly a great man. But his was not a complete and well-proportioned greatness. The public life of Hampden or of Somers resembles a regular drama, which can be criticised as a whole, and every scene of which is to be viewed in connection with the main action. The public life of Pitt, on the other hand, is a rude though striking piece, a piece abounding in incongruities, a piece without any unity of plan, but redeemed by some noble passages, the effect of which is increased by the tameness or extravagance of what precedes and of what follows. His opinions were unfixed. His conduct at some of the most important conjunctures of his life was evidently determined by pride and resentment. He had one fault, which of all human faults is most rarely found in company with true greatness. He was extremely affected. He was an almost solitary instance of a man of real genius, and of a brave, lofty, and commanding spirit, without simplicity of character. He was an actor in the Closet, an actor at Council, and actor in Parliament; and even in private society he could not lay aside his theatrical tones and attitudes. We know that one of the most distinguished of his partisans often complained that he could never obtain admittance to Lord Chatham's room till everything was ready for the representation, till the dresses and properties were all correctly disposed, till the light was thrown with Rembrandt-like effect on the head of the illustrious performer, till the flannels had been arranged with the air of a Grecian drapery and the crutch placed as gracefully as that of Belisarius or Lear.

Suspense.—Suspense or holding back an idea by the arrangement is a feasible but not a frequent means of emphasis in paragraphs. In the following paragraph, Stevenson keeps the mind alert and the interest excited by the suspense as to the result of the search.

For myself, however, I did but exchange anxieties. I was no sooner out of one fear than I fell upon another; no sooner secure that I should myself make the intended haven, than I began to be convinced that Trent was there before me. I climbed into the rigging, stood on the board, and eagerly scanned that ring of coral reef and bursting breaker, and the blue lagoon which they enclosed. The two islets within began to show plainly—Middle Brooks and Lower Brooks Island, the Directory named them: two low, bush-covered, rolling strips of sand, each with glittering beaches, each perhaps a mile or a mile and a half in length, running east and west, and divided by a narrow channel. Over these, innumerable as maggots, there hovered, chattered, screamed, and clanged, millions of twinkling sea-birds: white and black; the black by far the largest. With singular scintillations, this vortex of winged life swayed to and fro in the strong sunshine, whirled continually through itself, and would now and again burst asunder and scatter as wide as the lagoon: so that I was irresistibly reminded of what I had read of nebular convulsions. A thin cloud overspread the area of the reef and the adjacent sea—the dust, as I could not but fancy, of earlier explosions. And a little apart, there was yet another focus of centrifugal and centripetal flight, where, hard by the deafening line of breakers, her sails (all but the tattered topsail) snugly furled down, and the red rag that marks Old England on the seas beating, union down, at the main—the *Flying Scud,* the fruit of so many toilers, a recollection in so many lives of men, whose tall spars had been mirrored in the remotest corners of the sea—lay stationary at last and forever, in the first stage of naval dissolution. Towards her, the taut *Norah Creina,* vulture-wise, wriggled to windward; come from so far to pick her bones. And, look

as I pleased, there was no other presence of man or of man's
handiwork; no Honolulu schooner lay there crowded with
armed rivals, no smoke rose from the fire at which I fancied
Trent cooking a meal of sea-birds. It seemed, after all, we
were in time, and I drew a mighty breath.

From *The Wrecker;* by permission of C. Scribner's Sons.

RECAPITULATION

In brief, the paragraph has the unity of a definitely
limited theme, severely rejecting inappropriate matter, but adequate in its treatment of what it does
admit. It may or may not explicitly state its
theme, but usually does so with paragraphs of abstract thought. It deals with its material in orderly
sequence, and with clear connection. It often enforces
the parallel relation of its ideas by the syntactical
form of its sentences. It makes use in an even more
marked and obvious way than the whole composition of
devices of order for purposes of emphasis, concentrating the emphasis at the beginning with reference to what
precedes, and still more at the end with reference
to what follows, and usually giving space to ideas in
proportion to their importance. It stresses particular
points by contrast and climax, less often by suspense.
In fact, the principles of paragraph structure are, point
by point, those which govern the structure of all compositions, modified: (1) as the paragraph is brief, (2) as
it is a subordinate part of a larger total, and (3) as its
component parts, namely sentences, are units of grammatical syntax.

CHAPTER III

THE SENTENCE: PREDICATION

I. PREDICATION AND SENTENCE UNITY

Predication.—Under ordinary circumstances, language is intended to express connected thought, or as is commonly said, to "make sense." Language does not usually make sense by merely naming things or stating actions; there is not ordinarily any *sense* in such expressions as "gold," "glitters," "let," "snow." The ideas to which they correspond are not rational by themselves; they are rational only when brought into relation with other ideas by the action of the mind in forming judgments. Thus rational language, language that makes sense, "says something"—says one thing about another something;—"All is not gold that glitters,"—"Where are the snows of yesteryear?" The one something said is a predicate; the other something about which it is said is a subject; and a combination of a subject and a predicate, the expression of a judgment, is called a predication. Hence language, written or spoken, to be rational, must in general be made up of predications.

What is a Sentence?—A predication and nothing less than a predication expresses a complete thought. A sentence may consist of one predication or of several predications, and hence may express one or more complete thoughts; but in a well written sentence, the predications, if there are more than one, are in close connection with each other. Each predication is in a sense a unit; but all the predications taken together make up a more complex unit.

Look at the sentences, for example, in the following passage. They vary in length and in the number of the details introduced into them; some consist of one predication, some of several; yet each sentence is one thing, complete in itself and capable of being taken in as a whole.

It was remarkable; but the taste of Saint Antoine seemed to be decidedly opposed to a rose on the head-dress of Madame Defarge. Two men entered separately, and had been about to order drink, when catching sight of that novelty, they faltered, made a pretence of looking about for some friend who was not there, and went away. Nor, of those who had been there when this visitor entered, was there one left. They had all dropped off. The spy kept his eyes open, but had been able to detect no sign. They had lounged away in a poverty-stricken, purposeless, accidental manner, quite natural and unimpeachable.

Dickens, *A Tale of Two Cities*.

Sentence-Compositions.—Sometimes one sentence is a composition. Nothing is required to complete the adages which contain the treasures of popular wisdom; —"Contentment is better than riches,"—"Put not off till to-morrow that which can be done to-day." The epitaph on the dead at Thermopylae is proudly sufficient in itself;—"Stranger! tell the Lacedaemonians that we lie here in obedience to their commands." Likewise the sayings of Pascal,—"Little things console us because little things afflict us," and of Bacon,—"He who avoids new remedies must expect new evils," are of themselves complete in both thought and expression.

Consecutive Sentences.—These separate sentences,

however, do not represent the normal way of writing. Nearly always a sentence is a subordinate unit in a larger total, like a cell in a living body, independent to some degree, yet not so completely independent that it can perform its functions in separation from the greater whole of which it is a part. Any passage of ordinary connected writing provides examples.

Fractions.—The primary law of sentence-structure is that every sentence, whether a whole composition or part of a larger composition, must be in itself a unit. A thing may fail of unity by being less or by being more than one, by being fractional or by being plural. In the following examples, the clauses beginning *while, though, and that,* are fractions; they are not units which may be parts of a total, but fragments, which must be pieced to the other parts of the unit from which they are broken.

Most of our party went fishing in the afternoon. While three of us took our guns and climbed the mountain in hopes to get a deer.

The currency grew to eighty thousand pounds, trade, building, and inhabitants all the while increasing. Though I now think there are limits, beyond which the quantity may be hurtful.

We are told that the circus parade is to be given up. And that the managers, like the pieman to Simple Simon, will say to the public who wish to see the show, "Show me first your penny."

The fragmentary nature of the separated clauses is evident. In most cases of this kind, the fault may be easily corrected by a change in the punctuation, the dependent members being restored to their proper relations by the change of the period before them to a comma or semicolon.

Mixed Numbers.—As the error of writing fragments for sentences destroys their unity, so does the opposite fault, the inclusion within a sentence of ideas not properly a part of it. Thus reporters sometimes in the effort to produce compactness sweep into one sentence half a dozen pieces of miscellaneous information connected with some topic of the sentence but not a part of its thought. In the following letter, the fact that Governor Davidson had in writing declared himself in favor of irrigation is connected with irrigation, and the Irrigation Congress is connected with irrigation, and the fact that prominent men would speak at the Congress on home-making is connected with the Congress; but the addresses and Governor Davidson have no connection at all.

Governor Davidson has also declared that he is in sympathy with the irrigation movement, in closing a letter to Arthur Hooker, secretary of the board of control of the National Irrigation Congress, which will have its seventeenth session in Spokane, August 9 to 14, when prominent men will discuss problems relating to irrigation, forestry, reclamation of swamp lands, deep waterways, good roads, and home building.

Sometimes the overloading of a sentence occurs in subtle and puzzling ways, requiring skill in adjustment. The unity of a sentence depends upon its point of view and its underlying idea; and these again depend upon the relation of the sentence to the paragraph of which it is a part. An instance is afforded by a sentence in a letter by Alexander Wilson, the ornithologist, written to his publisher in 1810. The writer is describing his journey down the Ohio in a small boat, and describes the "darkness and shadow, obscuring the landscape" in the early morning. He proceeds:

I could only discover when I was passing a clearing by the crowing of cocks, and now and then, in more solitary places, the big-horned owl made a most hideous holloaing, that echoed among the mountains.

Evidently, the difficulty of making out where the clearings were is spoken of in order to illustrate the darkness and obscurity of the landscape. But all these circumstances made Wilson lonely; the owl's hoot made him more lonely; the crow of the cock reinforced the suggestion of the hoot of the owl; and forgetful of the point of view with which he had begun the sentence, he adds to the clause which illustrated the obscurity of the scene a clause about its loneliness. If the writer had from the first been dealing with the loneliness of the morning, the sentence would not have lacked unity; but in the connection in which it appears it obviously contains a digression.

In the following sentence, the effect of the scene, grotesque, solitary, and gloomy, is impressively conveyed by the description, but the details about the feelings of horse and rider on crossing a bridge intrude where they have no right to be present and should be placed apart.

The general features of North Carolina, where I crossed it, are immense, solitary pine savannas, swarming with alligators, dark, sluggish creeks, of the color of brandy, over which are thrown high, wooden bridges, without railings, and so crazy and rotten, as not only to alarm one's horse, but also the rider, and to make it a matter of thanksgiving with both, when they get fairly over without going through; enormous cypress swamps, which, to a stranger, have a striking, desolate, and ruined appearance.

Wilson, Alexander, *Letters*.

Interjectional Expressions.—Although a sentence must always include a predication, it would be a mistake to suppose that every predication must be fully expressed.   A conversation in regular and complete sentences might sound very formal and stiff.   The life and energy of colloquial language sometimes depend in part on speeches broken off, responses in which the predicates are understood, and exclamations in which predicates are taken for granted or never even thought of.

I did but put my head into London on Thursday, and more bad news from America [of the battle of Lexington].
Walpole, H., *Letters.*

The old story: dodging about in a ship for these last five months: indeed during all that time not having lain, I believe for three consecutive Nights in Christian Sheets.
Fitzgerald, E., *Letters.*

"How's things in Boomtown?"
"Oh, same old grind."
"Judge still lyin'?"
"Still at it."
"Major Mullens still swearin' to it?"
Garland, H., *Main Travelled Roads.*

Connective Expressions.—Connective expressions, in which no predications are expressed, may yet sometimes be punctuated as if sentences.

Not that a poet or painter ought to be restrained to the letter of historical truth.
Gentleman's Magazine.

Now for the important part of my note.
Lowell, *Letters.*

II.   INDEPENDENCE AND SUBORDINATION OF PREDICATIONS

A sentence, then, is a unit, a single complete total. But this total is formed of adjusted parts; it is built, as is a house, or a picture, or a motor-car.   A sentence, in other words, is a structure.   A structure may have few parts or many; its parts may be loosely or firmly

fitted together; and they may be simple in their relations or complex, subtle, and elaborate. Thus sentences may be constructed according to many types, each
having peculiar qualities and special uses.

Separate Predications.—Of all forms of sentence, the
least complicated is that which contains but a single
predication, without modifying expressions,—the sentences of a child's primer. For example: "This is a
pretty bird. It has feathers. They are soft feathers.
They are black and white. This bird has a white breast.
It has red on its head. Its bill is very long. It is sharp,
too. This bird pecks wood. It is a woodpecker."

Coördinated Predications.—Next in simplicity are
sentences which contain more than one grammatically
independent predication; for example: "This bird is
pretty; its feathers are soft, its body is black and white,
and its head is red. The bird has a long and sharp bill,
and it pecks wood; the bird is called a woodpecker."

Subordinated Predications.—Still more complicated
are sentences in which one predication is subordinated to
another; as, "This pretty bird, with soft black and
white feathers and a red head, is called a woodpecker,
from its habit of pecking wood with its long, sharp bill."

Degrees of Subordination.—Sentences, then, vary in
the extent to which they subordinate the predications
of which they are made up. At one extreme stand sentences in which every possibly separate idea is predicated; at the other extreme, sentences in which every
predication that can possibly take a dependent place is
subordinated to a single central affirmation; and between the two are sentences in which independent predications are linked one to the other. None of these

typical forms can be uniformly employed. The
simplest writer will sometimes subordinate; the most
complicated will have some simple sentences; but one
type or another will tend to predominate in nearly every
writer's work.

III.   SEPARATE PREDICATIONS

Baby Sentences.—If we turn back to the first sentences about the woodpecker, the most obvious characteristic which we find in them is that they are childish.
They are kindergarten sentences. Each is easily
grasped by an immature mind, and one at a time is all
that a child learning to read can be expected to take in.
But they lack forward-reaching thought, directing purpose, and intellectual grasp. For readers that have got
beyond the primer, such sentences are not merely unsatisfactory, but positively distressing. The details
drip like raindrops from the eaves, monotonously and
disconnectedly. Hence, though these sentences are
separately clear, they are in sequence tedious and confusing. Except, therefore, when reasons exist for making separate affirmations individually distinct without
reference to the connection between them, or for presenting a number of details in rapid succession with
equal emphasis on each of them, the use of a series of
sentences of this form is ineffective.

The Staccato Style.—Some writers affect the habit of
sharply accenting each idea by setting it apart. Their
sentences, having no center of emphasis, are restless;
and having no clear main purpose, are indistinct.

Professor W. P. Ker, in *Craik's English Prose,* speaks
of instances of this fault in Macaulay:

"In Macaulay's prose, the continuity of the narrative or dissertation is frequently sacrificed for the sake of a number of small rhetorical points, which help to stimulate the attention at first, but may easily become monotonous or irritating. The cumulative effect of the story is not always secured; the short sentences, the strings of particulars, interfere with it. Thus the glories of the 'wonderful year' of 1759 are proclaimed in a brisk staccato manner that leaves no clear impression of the significance of the events. 'The year of 1759 opened with the conquest of Goree. Next fell Guadaloupe, then Ticonderoga, then Niagara. The Toulon squadron was completely defeated by Boscawen off Cape Lagos. But the greatest exploit of the year was the achievement of Wolfe on the Heights of Abraham. The news of his glorious death reached London in the very week in which the houses met. All was joy and triumph. Envy and faction were forced to join in the general applause.' Here it is evident that the effect desired is that of variety, and that this variety has broken up a good rhetorical period and dissipated its strength. The ear has not recovered from Ticonderoga and Cape Lagos in time to appreciate the climax of the story at Quebec. It is all confused noise; 'joy and triumph,' 'envy and faction' are discharged at the end in the same loud emphatic monotone as the names of the victories at the beginning."

Immature Over-Predication.—Inexperienced writers, however, though they tend to overpredicate their sentences, do so in a manner which is not so much confusing and restless as weak and immature. Compare, for example, the following extract from a student's theme with the revision of it.

The stage climbed upward. We traveled thus about half an hour. Then we came to a level stretch that ran in a sort of groove in the hills. It was two or three miles long. Suddenly a road-house came into sight. The building was a typical mountain inn. It looked crude but comfortable. A few loungers stirred; but nobody paid us much attention. Our horses were changed. This took ten minutes. Soon we were off, and on our way to the great mountain. We occasionally saw the summit between intervening hills.

After traveling upward for about half an hour we came to a level stretch running for two or three miles in a sort of groove in the hills. Suddenly a road-house came into sight—a typical mountain inn, crude but comfortable, with a group of loungers in front whom our arrival scarcely stirred. After a delay of ten minutes for changing horses, we were once more on our way toward the great mountain, the summit of which we occasionally saw between intervening hills.

IV.   COORDINATED PREDICATIONS

Next in simplicity to sentences consisting of one predication modified slightly or not at all are those composed of two or more independent predications set side by side,—coördinated.

And then rode Melias into an old forest, and therein he rode two days and more. And then he came into a fair meadow, and therein was a fair lodge of boughs. And then he espied in that lodge a chair, wherein was a crown of gold subtily wrought; also there was cloths covered [*i.e.*, set with food] upon the earth, and many delicious meats were thereon. Sir Melias beheld this adventure, and thought it marvelous, but he had no hunger; but in the crown of gold he took much delight. And therewith he stooped down and took it up and rode his way. And anon he saw a knight come riding after him that cried; "Knight, set down that crown that is not yours; and therefore defend you."

Then Sir Melias blessed him self, and said: "Fair Lord of Heaven, help and save thy new-made knight!"

And then they let their horses run as fast as they might, so that the other knight smote Sir Melias through the hauberk and through the left side, that he fell to the earth, nigh dead. And then he took the crown and went his way, and Sir Melias lay still and had no power to stir.

Malory, *Morte D'Arthur.*

Archaic Simplicity.—In this passage the modifying expressions are so closely associated with the words they modify that the modifiers are scarcely regarded as such; they are, moreover, very simple in form, including only a few very short dependent clauses. The effect of the passage is one of archaic simplicity, a simplicity so genuine as to be charming. In the narratives of the Old Testament there are even fewer modifying words, the sentences "hold themselves erect by the sheer strength of substantive and verb" even more completely, and the style has an even greater primitiveness, simplicity, and power.

And when David fought against the Philistines three of the mighty men went down, and came to David in the harvest time unto the cave of Adullam: and the troop of the Philistines pitched in the valley of Rephaim. And David was then in an hold, and the garrison of the Philistines was then in Beth-lehem. And David longed, and said, Oh that one would give me drink of the water of the well of Beth-lehem which is by the gate! And the three mighty men brake through the host of the Philistines, and drew water out of the well of Beth-lehem, that was by the gate, and took it, and brought it to David: nevertheless he would not drink thereof, but poured it out unto the LORD. And he said, Be it far from me, O Lord, that I should do this: is not this the blood of men who went in jeopardy of their lives?

II Samuel 33:13–17.

Unity in Coördinated Predications.—Though the parts of these sentences are not bound very closely by the grammatical structure, they are not brought together at haphazard. They are connected in thought; each sentence is truly a unit and taken as a whole marks a stage in the progress of the narrative. As in the previous sentences so in the following, all the parts taken together make up a whole which it is not possible to include within one clause.

At St. Ives and in the neighboring villages the congregations of Methodists were attacked with cudgels, and everything in the room where they had assembled was shattered to atoms.

Lecky, *England in the Eighteenth Century.*

The road got into more barren heights by the midday, the hills arduous; once or twice we had to wait for horses, and we were still twenty miles from Schaffhausen at sunset; it was past midnight when we reached her closed gates.

Ruskin, *Praeterita.*

Opinions alter, manners change, creeds rise and fall; but the moral law is written on the tablets of eternity.

Froude, *Short Studies on Great Subjects.*

Weak Coördinated Predications.—A special danger of coördinated predications is their tendency in unskilled hands to a weak dragging feebleness, in which the writer, not having the power to concentrate his attention on the most important ideas, diffuses it vaguely over everything of which he treats. Compare the following sentences as originally written and as rewritten.

At the tournament Ivanhoe was seriously injured. The people did not know this, but he fainted at the feet of the Lady Rowena and some of the squires took off his armor, and found his side bleeding. He was then carried out of the lists and placed in one of the tents. Rebecca was at the tourna-

At the tournament Ivanhoe was dangerously wounded. The injury, however, was not discovered until, as Ivanhoe fell fainting at the feet of the Lady Rowena, one of the squires removed the knight's body armor and found his side bleeding. The unconscious man was carried out of the lists and

ment with her father, and she saw that Ivanhoe was wounded and offered her litter to carry him to some place where his wound could be dressed. Some of the men then placed him in the litter and the party then drove off toward Rebecca's home.

They arrived there, and then Rebecca dressed Ivanhoe's wounds and then let him sleep, for he needed rest and he had not yet regained consciousness. After a time Ivanhoe awoke, and he saw Rebecca bending over him fixing the bandage. Ivanhoe asked where he was and how he reached there. Rebecca told him that he was wounded at the tournament and she brought him to her home until his wounds should be healed.

laid in one of the tents. Rebecca, who was at the tournament with her father, offered her litter to carry the wounded Ivanhoe to some place where his hurt could be treated. She had him taken to her house, dressed his wound, and left him to his needed repose. After some hours, he awoke, and saw Rebecca bending over him and adjusting the bandage. When he asked where he was and in what way he had reached there, Rebecca told him how he had been wounded and how she had brought him to her home to be healed.

V. SUBORDINATED PREDICATIONS

The third type of sentence is that in which one predication is subordinated to another. In sentences of this type a whole body of ideas is brought under one dominant predication. In the following sentence, for example, there are two main predications, each with many predications subordinated to it.

If then the power of speech is as great as any that can be named,—if the origin of language is by many philosophers even considered to be nothing short of divine,—if by means of words the secrets of the heart are brought to light, pain of soul is relieved, hidden grief is carried off, sympathy conveyed, counsel imparted, experience recorded, and wisdom perpetuated,—if by great authors the many are drawn up into unity, national character is fixed, a people speaks, the past and the future, the East and the West are brought into communication with each other,—if such men are in a word the spokesmen and prophets of the human family,—*it will not answer to make light of Literature or to neglect its study; rather we may be sure* that, in proportion as we master it in whatever language, and imbibe its spirit, we shall ourselves become in our own measure the ministers of like benefits to others, be they many or few, be they in the obscurer or the more distinguished walks of life,—who are united to us by social ties, and are within the sphere of our personal influence.

Newman, Idea of a University.

Predications Reduced to: (1) Clauses; (2) Phrases; (3) Words.—There are several degrees to which the subordination of predication can be carried. The first is the reduction of independent to dependent predications, which retain their verbs and become subordinate clauses; for example, *"If a man will not work,* neither shall he eat."* The second is the change of the clause to a phrase;—*"In the sweat of thy brow* shalt thou eat bread."* The third step is to reduce the clause to a word;—"The *idle* man shall go hungry."* The following sentences illustrate the three forms of subordination employed side by side.

A huge and dripping Brahminee bull shouldered his way under the tree. The flashes revealed the trident mark of Shiva on his flank, [modifying phrase], the insolence of head and hump [predicative word, noun], the luminous stag-like eyes [predicative words, adjectives], the brow crowned with a wreath of sodden marigold blooms [predicative word, participle], and ⁺he silky dewlap that almost swept the ground [subordinate clause].

Kipling, The Day's Work.

It was one *wild dreary* day in the spring; a day *of furious wind* and *cutting rain;* a day *when . . . the ships creaked and groaned* at the wharfs and *the harbor was* a *sheet* of wind-driven foam, and *the domain was strewn* with broken boughs.

Kingsley, H., Geoffrey Hamlin.

Loose and Close Attachment of Subordinate Elements.—There are then three degrees to which predications may be subordinated. Subordinate predications may be clauses, phrases, or words. There are also degrees in the closeness with which the subordinate element, whether clause, phrase, or word, is attached to the context. At one extreme, the subordinate element is almost independent of the context, supplementing or explaining it. At the other extreme, the subordinate element is amalgamated with the context, melted into it, so as to be an inseparable part of the whole; and there are many intermediate degrees between the extremes.

Supplementary Expressions.—Some subordinated expressions supplement the context, almost like independent clauses.

Clauses.—Some relative clauses in effect add ideas to the main clause.

Another of the Cavidae is the Agouti, which [and the animal, it may be added] is an inhabitant of the Antilles.

> They lowered him with the sound
>   Of requiems to repose,
> When [and just then] from the throngs around
>   A solemn voice arose.

I prayed him to finish the window; which ⌜and this⌝ he did with perfect success.

Phrases.

The gangs poured by in the dusk; men stopping to knit a loin-cloth or fasten a sandal; gang-foremen shouting to their subordinates as they ran or passed by the tool-issue sheds for bars and mattocks; locomotives creeping down their tracks wheel-deep in the crowd; . . .

Kipling, The Day's Work.

And so we talked for half an hour, . . . the green with-
drawing wave growing smoother by degrees, but farther out
we could see it still rough with big rollers, foam-crested; the
little ringed dotterels and the large grey plover running about
on the sand and feeding unconcerned near us; the big patient
horses standing with masses of wet seaweed glistening at their
feet.

Hudson, W. H., Nature in Downland.

Words.

"I am sure of it; absolutely."

"Let me have a pair of kid gloves,—black."

Nonessential Elements.—The subordinate elements
may somewhat loosely modify the whole or a part of a
clause.   They affect that which they modify, but are not
essential to the meaning of the whole.   Such nonessential elements should be set off by punctuation.

Examples of nonessential (non-restrictive) elements:
Clauses.

We are all made of the same clay, though some of the
lumps are a little finer, and some a little coarser.

Chesterfield, Letters.

You're not in a fit state to come here, if you can't come here
without spluttering like a bad pen.

Dickens, Great Expectations.

And, since the thoughts and reasonings of a great author
have, as I have said, a personal character, no wonder that his
style is not only the image of his subject, but of the mind.

Newman, Idea of a University.

Socrates took away all ignominy from the place, which
could not be a prison whilst he was there.

He will look on the world, wheresoever he can get a
glimpse of it, with eager curiosity.

Carlyle, Johnson.

When I look upon the tombs of the Great, every emotion of
envy dies in me; when I read the epitaphs of the Beautiful,
every inordinate desire goes out; when I meet with the grief

of Parents themselves, I consider the vanity of grieving for those whom we must quickly follow: when I see Kings lying by those who deposed them, when I consider rival wits placed side by side, or the holy men that divided the world with their contests and disputes, I reflect with sorrow and astonishment on the competitions, factions and debates of mankind.

Addison, Spectator.

Phrases.

Another man, *with a piece of crumpled paper in his hand,* said that the yard-master said that if the other man said anything, he (the other man) was to shut his head.

Kipling, The Day's Work.

I read an epitaph or two, *with a faint cry of love and grief echoing through the stilted phraseology of the tomb,* and then I went to the altar.

Benson, A. C., The Upton Letters.

> . . . This my hand will rather
> The multitudinous seas incarnadine,
> *Making the green one red.*

Shakespeare, Macbeth.

We were now standing at a great altitude between two bays; *the wilderness of waters before us.*

Borrow, G., The Bible in Spain.

> *Thus done the tales,* to bed they creep,
> By whispering winds soon lull's asleep,

Milton, L'Allegro.

Every calculation made of these valuables, Mrs. Rebecca found . . . that she might reckon on six or seven hundred pounds.

Thackeray, Vanity Fair.

This meal over, she resumed honest Rawdon's calculations of the night previous, and surveyed her position.

Ibid.

"Thank Heaven that is over," George thought, bounding down the stair, *his sword under his arm,* as he ran swiftly to the alarm ground.

Ibid.

Words.

If you lay your ear to the side of the cabin, the next time you are in a steamer, you will hear hundreds of little voices in every direction, *thrilling* and *buzzing,* and *whispering* and *popping,* and *gurgling* and *sobbing* and *squeaking* exactly like a telephone in a thunder-storm.

Kipling, The Day's Work.

An incessant lightning, *forked and blue,* showed all that there was to be seen.

Ibid.

Yesterday we had a man of a very different sort; *earnest* enough and *high-minded,* I am sure, but he seemed to have forgotten, if he had ever known, what a boy's heart and mind are like.

Benson, The Upton Letters.

And looked aloft to the hall-roof, *high up* and *grey* as the cloud.

Morris, W., The Fall of the Niblungs.

Essential Elements.—At times the subordinate element is *essential* to the meaning of its context, so that the two communicate one complex idea. Such expressions, on account of the closeness of their connection with the rest of the sentence, should not be set off by punctuation.

Examples of essential (mainly restrictive) elements:

Clauses.

An ideal democracy is a society *in which good manners are universal.*

Crothers, S. M., The Gentle Reader.

Let them show me a cottage *where there are not the same vices of which they accuse courts.*

Chesterfield, Letters.

[They] laid down their young lives for thee, O Mother England! as willingly—poured out their noble blood as cheerfully—*as ever, after a long day's sport, when infants, they*

*had rested their wearied heads upon their mother's knee, or
had sunk to sleep in her arms.*

De Quincey, *The English Mail Coach.*

So absolutely was fear swallowed up in joy *that in the
mere simplicity of her fervent nature, the poor woman threw
her arms round my neck, as she thought of her son, and gave
to me the kiss which was secretly meant for him.*

Ibid.

My punishment is greater *than I can bear.*

Gen. 4:13.

Phrases.

The devil take Henry *of Lancaster.*

Shakespeare, R. II 55.

It is this lust *for doing something tangible, for sitting down
quickly and writing fitly, for having some definite result to
show,* which is the ruin of me and many others.

Benson, *Upton Letters.*

I wonder whether those little silver pencil-cases *with a
movable almanack at the butt end* are still favorites with boys,
and whether pedlars still hawk them about the country.

Thackeray, *Roundabout Papers.*

Words.

To be nameless in *worthy* deeds exceeds an *infamous* history. The Canaanitish woman lives more happily without a
name than Herodias with one; and who would not rather be
the *good* thief than Pilate?

Browne, Sir T., *Urn Burial.*

The plain fact is that the new lines of *scientific* and *historical* inquiry which have been opened in modern times have
had a distinct and deep effect upon the politics of the age.

Freeman, E. A., *On Race and Language.*

Examples of Subordinated Predications.—The following passages illustrate various types of subordinated
predications. In the first, a skilful newspaper report,

brevity and rapidity are secured by subordinating details without omitting them.

Atlanta, Ga., March 16th.—Awakening from a sleep in which he had dreamed that a near-by railroad trestle on the Southern Railroad had been washed away, O. T. Kitchens, a section foreman, although suffering from illness, arose from his bed and went to South River, six miles from here, before dawn yesterday morning, to discover that his dream was a reality. The foreman found that the stream, swollen by heavy rains, had carried away a trestle spanning a 65-foot chasm. He knew that a passenger train en route from Atlanta to Columbus, Ga., soon was due to arrive on the opposite side, but he had no means of reaching that point to warn the engineer of the danger, and the river is three-quarters of a mile wide. Standing on the bank, the man put his hands to his lips and repeatedly hallooed for half-an-hour. Finally he heard an answering shout, and called out a warning to J. E. Daniel, the man who had heard him. Daniel flagged the train just as it neared the brink of the stream.

The Illustrated London News 50 :652.

In the following passage, the writer has striven to make language do the work of a pictorial sketch,—to unite many delicately but vividly observed details in a single impression. The effect is interesting, but too conscious and artificial, and too exacting in its demands upon the reader's alertness to be regarded as thoroughly sound in style.

Mrs. Stringham was never to forget—for the moment had not faded, nor the infinitely fine vibrations it set up in any way ceased—her own first sight of the striking apparition, then unheralded and unexplained: the slim, constantly pale, delicately haggard, anomalously, agreeably angular young person of not more than two and twenty in spite of her marks, whose hair was somehow exceptionally red even for the real thing which it innocently confessed to being, and whose clothes were remarkably black even for robes of mourning.

James, H., *The Wings of the Dove;* by permission of C. Scribner's Sons.

The following extract represents more truly than either of these a normal English style, in which the subordination of the predications is carried far enough to give the units of thought substance, but is not excessive.

At the renewal of the battle, Captain Ball, though his ship was on fire in three different parts, laid her alongside a French eighty-four; and a second longer obstinate contest began. The firing on the part of the French ship having at length for some time slackened, and then altogether ceased, and yet no sign given of surrender, the first lieutenant came to Captain Ball and informed him that the hearts of his men were as good as ever, but that they were so completely exhausted, that they were scarcely capable of lifting an arm. He asked, therefore, whether, as the enemy had now ceased firing, the men might be permitted to lie down by their guns for a short time. After some reflection, Sir Alexander acceded to the proposal, taking of course the proper precautions to rouse them again at the moment he thought requisite. Accordingly, with the exception of himself, his officers, and the appointed watch, the ship's crew lay down, each in the place to which he was stationed; and slept for twenty minutes. They were then roused; and started up, as Sir Alexander expressed it, more like men from an ambush than from sleep, so co-instantaneously did they all obey the summons! They recommenced their fire, and in a few minutes the enemy surrendered; and it was soon after discovered, that during that interval, and almost immediately after the French ship had first ceased firing, the crew had sunk down by their guns, and there slept, almost by the side, as it were, of their sleeping enemy.

Coleridge, *The Friend*.

RECAPITULATION

An expression which makes "complete sense" is called a predication; a sentence may contain one or more predications, but not less than one. In not a few cases, however, especially in exclamatory or transitional expressions, the predication is implied or suggested. A good sentence does not admit matter foreign to its central idea. Sentences (1) may present predications independently, (2) may coördinate them, or (3) may subordinate them. The tendency of inexperienced writers is to over-predicate, and to employ excessive coördination. Subordinated predications may be reduced (1) to subordinate clauses, (2) to phrases, or (3) to single words. Such subordinate elements, whether clauses, phrases, or words, may be loosely or closely attached to the context in which they appear. The most loosely attached expressions are supplementary to the context; somewhat closer in connection are nonessential modifiers; still closer are essential modifiers.

CHAPTER IV

THE SENTENCE: COÖRDINATE ELEMENTS

I. CONSISTENCY OF THOUGHT AND FORM

Maintaining the Point of View.—A sentence in a student's exercise reads, "I was a freshman,—young, green, and just coming out of chapel." Why is the sentence absurd? Because the three descriptive elements are inconsistent; youth and greenness are more or less lasting qualities; coming out of chapel is a temporary action. A class is formed of things which are not of the same kind. The point of view is changed. Another sentence is as follows, "There are instances of students arriving on the grounds with less than fifty cents and a complete stranger." Here the ideas are consistent; lack of money and lack of acquaintances belong genuinely to one class of things. But the syntactical form in which the two ideas are expressed is not consistent; *fifty cents* and *a complete stranger* are not what the student was *with*. To have true unity, the sentence should show the classification of ideas by the form;—"almost without money and entirely without acquaintances,"—"strangers and all but penniless strangers." Thus to secure unity, the point of view should be so maintained as to produce consistency alike in the thought and the form of the parts. Elements coördinate in form should be coördinate in idea; elements coördinate in idea should be coördinate in form.

The following examples illustrate the scope of the principle.

Inconsistent parts.	*Consistent parts.*
The gentlemen *suggested* that I *wait* till the first of the month.	The gentlemen *suggested* that I *should wait* till the first of the month. [Past point of view.]
Then comes *a* Siwash, as *the* Indian is commonly called.	Then comes *a* Siwash, as *an* Indian is commonly called. [Single examples of a class.]
The wind blows here for three hundred and sixty-five days *in the* year, and twenty-four hours *per* day.	The wind blows here for three hundred and sixty-five days *in the* year, and twenty-four hours *in the* day. [Equal ratios.]
Many people *shrink* from the undertaking of building a house, *dislike* to run the gauntlet of dishonest contractors, besides *realizing* the difficulty of finding a desirable lot.	Many people not only *shrink* from the undertaking of building a house, and *dislike* to run the gauntlet of dishonest contractors, but are *discouraged* at the outset by the difficulty of finding desirable lot. [Classes of hesitations.]
Determining to buy a bicycle, I set out on a tour of *inspection* and *information.*	Determining to buy a bicycle, I set out on a tour of *inspection* and *investigation.* [Actions performed by the subject.]

Further examples of inconsistency will set the principle in still clearer light.

The object is to make the skin tender and even crack.

All which were imps she cherished with her blood,
To make her charms succeed and good.
Otway, *The Poet's Complaint.*

It was some distance from home, and my first going away alone.

It was in the mountains, and a country thickly overgrown
with trees.

Being connected . . . with a great and extensive project,
that required the whole man to execute, and *which* an unforeseen succession of employs prevented my attending to, it has
hitherto remained unfinished.

Franklin, *Autobiography.*

He told *of* his music-lessons under Beethoven, and *how*
Beethoven had recognized his talent.

Walking affords relaxation to the *mind,* and especially to
the *student,* who spends hours in his room with his books.

Coördinate Independent Clauses.—The least subordinated parts of which a sentence can be composed are
independent clauses. In a sentence composed of such
clauses, the principle of consistency requires that the
point of view shall be maintained throughout all the
clauses. For instance, in the following sentence, the
second clause is concerned with the contrast between
the old man's usual loquacity and his refusal to tell
what the inquirer wished to know about; but the first
clause is concerned with the general description of the
old man, of which loquacity is but one element.

He was a grey-bearded old fellow, good-natured and talkative, but I could not get him to tell me why he lived the life
of a hermit.

The underlying unity of the sentence may be manifested by rewriting it; thus:

The grey-bearded old fellow was good-natured and talkative,
but I could not get him to tell me why he lived the life of a
hermit.

Keeping the Grammatical Subject.—The unity of
idea in a sentence of the kind just quoted, a sentence

composed of coördinate predications, is often obscured by changing the subject in successive clauses, and may be manifested by keeping the subject unchanged. In many cases, a little care will thus give a natural center to a sentence which at first sight seems to be without true unity.

Last year I attended a normal school, and the zoölogy teacher took a great interest in obtaining specimens for the museum.

Last year I attended a normal school, and was under the instruction of a zoölogy teacher who took a great interest in obtaining specimens for the museum. [The point of the sentence was to explain why the writer still kept collecting specimens.]

The Coast Range and the Sierra Nevada Mountains follow nearly parallel courses through the greater part of the state of California, leaving a trough-like depression between them; but about three hundred miles from the southern end of the state, an elevation of land crosses this depression, joining the two ranges.

Through the greater part of the state of California, the Coast Range and the Sierra Nevada Mountains follow nearly parallel courses, leaving between them a trough-like depression; but about three hundred miles from the southern end of the state, the two ranges are connected by an elevation of land, which crosses the long, narrow valley.

The ceiling has medallion portraits of President Washington's cabinet, painted by the French artist Bernand, and the walls he painted with fruits and flowers.

The French artist Bernand decorated the walls with fruits and flowers, and the ceiling with medallion portraits of President Washington's cabinet.

Keeping the Voice Unchanged.—An unnecessary change to the passive voice sometimes alters the point of view in a sentence.

We boys gathered some cattails; some were [*better:* we] tacked on the walls for ornaments, and the rest we piled in a corner.

With practice, one can tell at a glance whether the cake is baking properly, and if not what the difficulty is; and the heat can generally be regulated [*better:* can generally regulate the heat] before any harm is done.

The Parts of Clauses.—So much for the principle of consistency of coördinate parts when those parts are independent clauses; let us now consider the application of the principle to the parts into which clauses are divided. Every clause, of course, consists first of all of two parts: that which taken all together makes up the subject in the largest sense, and that which similarly makes up the predicate, perhaps including an object. These main parts always contain some central expression, sometimes modified, sometimes unmodified. The subjects and objects are in function substantives,—that is, nouns or pronouns; their modifiers are adjectives. The predicate has as its central part a verb; the modifying elements of the predicate have an adverbial function. Thus, there are only four kinds of expressions, substantival, adjectival, adverbial, and verbal, which communicate a kind of meaning in themselves; and such expressions may be single words or groups of words. Some words,—*in, the, and,*—communicate only meanings of relation, and enter into combination with other words to make or connect expressions which have full meaning. Clauses, then, are divided into members fulfilling functions of syntax within them. The functions of these members are: (1) verbal; (2) substantival— having the effect of nouns and pronouns; (3) adjectival —used to modify substantives; (4) adverbial—used to modify verbs, adjectives, and other adverbs. Verbal expressions may be single words or phrases (combinations of words which have a single syntactic function, and which include no definite and complete predication). Substantives, adjectives, and adverbs may be words, phrases, or clauses (combinations of words including a definite and complete predication).

Concrete Coördinate Substantive Expressions.— Substantive expressions, of course, are either concrete or abstract. Concrete substantive expressions, whatever their form, whether words, phrases, or clauses, may be freely coördinated. "Peter [proper noun], and I [pronoun], and some other ambitious lads [phrase; common noun], and outlaws, and debtors [words; common nouns], and the dissatisfied [participial phrase, common noun], and the unhappy [adjectival phrase; common noun], and whoever hoped to find in the new regions the opportunities denied to him or neglected by him in the region where he was born [clause; common noun] were in the great throng that toiled up the pass."

Abstract Substantives.—The case is different with abstract expressions. In the English language there are four principal kinds of abstract expressions: ordinary non-verbal nouns (*fear* is an evil); verbal nouns in *ing* (*fearing* is evil); infinitive phrases (*to fear* is an evil); and noun clauses (*that a man should fear* is an evil). Speaking broadly, the English idiom at most only tolerates the combination of non-verbal with verbal nouns, and practically forbids all other combinations of any of these forms with any other.

Word-Nouns and Clauses Inconsistent.—Thus in the following sentences the non-verbal noun and the clause are inconsistent in form as objects of *suspect*.

Common modesty should, on this occasion, make a man suspect his own judgment, and that he misapplies the rules of his art, when he finds himself singular in the applause which he bestows on his own writings.

Addison, *Guardian*.

The coördination of the two constructions here, as often, causes the word with which they are both connected to be used in two senses; to *suspect one's judgment* means to *regard it with suspicion;* to *suspect that one misapplies rules* means to *believe it possible* that one does so; hence to make the parts of the sentence consistent it is necessary to express these two coördinate but distinct ideas with clearness.

The following sentence provides an example of a similar combination, less awkward that the last, however.

These trophies have largely inscribed on them the merits of the cause, a full impartial account of such a battle, and how the victory fell clearly to the party that set them up.

Swift, *Battle of the Books*.

In the next illustration the coördination of the noun *accounts* with the that-clause as objects of *heard* is exceedingly harsh, partly because the enthusiasm of *glowing* is confined to the *accounts*.

We had heard glowing accounts of a wide grassy plateau with a river running through it, and that beyond this level stretch were the woods, the mountains, and Lassen's Butte.

Infinitives and Substantive Clauses Inconsistent.— The combination of the infinitive and the clause produces a very incongruous effect. For example:

He commanded me to bear this shield to the court of King Arthur, requiring and praying some good knight *to* take this shield, and *that* he would fulfil the quest that he was in.

Malory, *La Cote Mal Taile*.

Inconsistent: Four girls decided to spend some time on the beach, and that they would camp by themselves.

Consistent: to spend, and *to camp;* or *that they would spend,* and *would camp.*

Inconsistent: They cared more to see the battle than who won.

Consistent: than *to know* who won.

In the following sentence the presence of a subject for the infinitive, and the length of the members obscures the inconsistent coördination, and makes the sentence sound less awkward than the preceding examples:

Five hundred monks of Mount Nitria, imagining the life of their chief to be in danger, and that their religion was threatened at his fall, flew into the city with ungovernable rage.

Goldsmith, Bee.

A brief practical rule with regard to consistency of form in the coördination of substantives is: be careful of abstract expressions differing in syntactical form.

Adjectives, Adherent, Appositive, and Predicative.— Adjectives, like substantives, may be words, phrases, or clauses. Moreover, like substantives, adjectives of different types can sometimes be coördinated without inconsistency, and at other times cannot be so. The principle governing the coördination of adjectives depends upon the degree of closeness with which the adjective is connected with the substantive which it modifies. In the closest connection of adjective and substantive, the two make up one complex idea. In such a case the adjective is what is called *adherent.* All adjectives between the article and the noun are adherent;—"the busy bee," "the whirling top," "a fine breeze,"— though the presence of the article of course is not necessary to this close relation: "whirling tops," "O happy day!" Next in closeness is the relation of the adjective to the noun in which the adjective is what is called *appositive,*—supplementary to the noun, adding a new idea to it, instead of being amalgamated with it in one complex idea: "The bees, busy in the morning, are now at rest." The appositive adjective usually follows the noun, but may precede it: "Busy in the morning, the bees go to rest before dark." This kind of adjective, however, cannot come between article and noun. Thirdly, an adjective, like a substantive, may be definitely predicated of a substantive: "The bees are busy."

Adherent Adjectives.—Single words and certain short groups of words may be adherent adjectives. Typical examples of such groups are: *an out-and-out rascal, an up-and-down manner; an easy-going fellow; a turn-down collar; a thoroughly well-disposed native; a very fortunately situated station; a three-year-old horse; a twenty-foot pole; one soon-to-be-forgotten remark.* Such complicated attributive modifiers as the following are hardly conceivable except in jest.

> The very devil has feelings, and if you prick him, will roar, whereby you, at all events, gain the *not-every-day-of-the-week-to-be-attained* benefit of finding out where he is.
>
> Kingsley, *Alton Locke.*

It follows that only very short phrases may be co-ordinated with words in the adherent position;—*a pleasant and easy-going companion; a healthy and advantageously situated military post.*

Appositive and Predicate Adjectives.—In the appositive and predicate relations, however, word and phrase adjectives of all types may be freely used and freely co-ordinated, if they fall naturally into a single class.

Ceres herself, who, *in graceful Italian dress,* [prepositional phrase] and *decked airily with fruit and corn,* [participial phrase] steps across a country of cut sheaves. . . .

Even appositive or predicative substantives may be coördinated with adjectives; and this is true of participles as well as of ordinary adjectives.

I am told that [some such men] have been made bishops: persons *not to be suspected* [infinitive] of any sort of Christian superstition, *fit colleagues* [noun] to the holy prelate of Autun, and *bred* [participle] at the feet of that Gamaliel.
    Burke, *Letters to a Member of the National Assembly.*

Every man is not *a proper champion* [predicate noun] for truth, nor *fit* [predicate adjective] to take up the gauntlet in the cause of verity. *Ibid.*

The adjective clause gives rise to difficulty. It is not used in the predicate; and although it appears in good writers in the appositive relation, after the noun, in co-ordination with the adjective word and phrase, the effect is usually awkward. Some examples follow.

These we can spare to France, to fill the new episcopal thrones: men *well versed* in swearing; and *who will scruple* no oath which the fertile brains of your reformers can devise.
    Burke, *op. cit.*

For the people of Attica, he comes from Boeotia, a country *of northern marsh and mist,* but *from whose* sombre and black marble *towns came* also the vine, the musical reed cut from its sedges and the worship of the Graces, always so closely associated with the religion of Dionysus.
    Pater, *Greek Studies, A Study of Dionysus.*

It is probably best for inexperienced writers to avoid such sentences altogether, but in any event the adjective members coördinated should be really capable of being put into one class, and should not, as in the following sentence, be essentially inconsistent in idea.

The young girl, about seventeen years of age, and who wore a shabby black hat and suit, was oddly out of place among the massive pieces of antique furniture.

Predicate Adjectives not Coördinate with Part of Verb.—A common type of inconsistent structure occurs when a predicate adjective, whether a word or a phrase, is coördinated with a part of a verb; for example: ''My companion was very large indeed, and enveloped in a green shawl which made her look larger still.'' Here the descriptive adjective *large* and the word *enveloped*, not descriptive but a part of the passive voice, are placed in the same category; the auxiliary verb should be repeated,—''and *was* enveloped.'' Other examples follow.

The right bank was abrupt, and [was] profusely covered with blackberry vines.

He was in this state one morning, and [was] sitting on the porch in front of a store when a lawyer passed by.

The people were soon out of all the cars but one, and very few [were] hurt.

The leaves are thick and succulent, and the edges [are] covered with fine soft hairs.

Adverbs of All Kinds May be Coördinate.—All adverbial forms may be freely combined, if they are coördinate in sense.

I will stay *here* [word], or *at the hotel* [phrase], or *where you please* [clause].

Verbs: Sequence of Tenses.—As to the combination of verbs, the only consideration to be observed is that the point of view in the tenses, whether past, present, or future, should not be changed without reason.

We *requested* that we [might] *be* permitted to examine the documents.

If we *must* [had to] obey such a rule, we *should have* no freedom left.

II. REPETITION OF INTRODUCTORY WORDS

Coördinate phrases and clauses consist of two parts: the words which introduce them and indicate their relation to the rest of the sentence, and the words which express their substantial meaning. Such introductory words are articles, auxiliary verbs, prepositions, and relative pronouns. In the case of coördinate elements it is often a question whether the introductory words should be expressed with each element, or used only with the first.

In some cases it is plain that the introductory words cannot be omitted. For example, in the sentence: "The life-line, which commences between the thumb and the first finger, is a sign when extending to the wrist of long life, but when interrupted a severe illness, and when broken off death," the initiatory word "of" *must* be repeated before "a severe illness" and "death"; the English idiom will not tolerate the long interruption between the preposition "of" and its second and third objects. At other times the introductory word may or may not be repeated according to the idea to be expressed;—"He was a gentleman entitled to make a noise and [to] give trouble in a country inn."

Introductory Words Must Be Expressed when not Identical.—Nearly always the introductory word must be expressed when it is not exactly the same for each of the coördinate elements. Thus with auxiliary verbs:

Walking the rounds, too, was often neglected, and most of the nights [were] spent in tippling.

Franklin, *Autobiography.*

This large castle is all built with my own hands, and the materials [are] extracted altogether out of my own person.

Swift, *Battle of the Books.*

Surfaces become grimy, materials are rotten, and much discomfort and ill-health [are] caused.

The repetition of the copulative verb *to be* with adjectives or nouns is not so necessary as is that of the auxiliary verb, but is usually preferable.

The street was small and dirty; the houses equally small and dirty.

Introductory Words in Comparisons.—The omission of introductory words with one member of a comparison sometimes produces inconsistency of parts.

One star did not seem so far away [as], and was more brilliant than, the rest.

This sentence would be made consistent by inserting *as* after *away;* but the expression "so far away as, and more brilliant than, the rest," lacks unity of effect, because it gives disproportionate emphasis to unimportant parts. Consistency and proper emphasis are both secured by writing, "One star did not seem so far away as the rest, and was more brilliant than they."

Repetition of Introductory Words for Clearness of Relation.—The repetition of the introductory word is sometimes necessary to make the connection of the parts of a sentence unambiguous or free from suggestions of absurdity. For example: "I think more of her than any of my other pets." This brings to the mind the absurd idea, "than any of my other pets think," a suggestion avoided by writing, "I think more of her than I do of any of my other pets." Or consider the sentence: "He was a descendant of those Van Winkles who figured so gallantly in the chivalrous days of Peter Stuyvesant, and accompanied him to the siege of Fort Christina." Does it mean *he* accompanied? or *his ancestors* accompanied? The latter evidently:—"He was a descendant of those Van Winkles who figured . . . and *who* accompanied. . . ."

Repetition of Introductory Words for Separation.—The repetition of the introductory word insists on the separateness of the elements introduced by it; and hence the repetition may be necessary when the elements are in their very nature separate. For instance: "My only companions were a foxhound, a mustang, a rifle, shotgun and revolver," should mean a compound weapon, all three at once. "A rifle, *a* shot-gun, and *a* revolver" means three distinct weapons. Similarly, "Half-way between the house and *the* barn" is better than, "Half-way between the house and barn."

It is plain that the introductory word should be repeated when for any reason it is desired to separate the elements, even though the repetition may not be necessary to indicate logical relations. Thus Burke described King Charles II as "a man without any sense of duty as a prince, without any regard to the dignity of his crown, without any love for his people—dissolute, false, venal, and destitute of any good quality whatsoever, except a pleasant temper and the manner of a gentleman." All the *withouts* after the first might be omitted with no loss of clearness, but with a weakening of the insistence on each separate count in the indictment.

The vigor of the following passage is certainly increased by the employment of the introductory words:

We have a kindness for Mr. Leigh Hunt. We form our judgment of him, indeed, from his own works, and from the works of other writers, who have generally abused him in the most rancorous manner. But unless we are greatly mistaken, he is a very clever, a very honest, and a very good-natured man. We can clearly discern, together with many merits, many faults, both in his writings and in his conduct. But we really think there is hardly a man living whose merits have been so grudgingly allowed, and whose faults have been so cruelly expiated.

Macaulay, *The Comic Dramatists of the Restoration.*

Introductory Words Omitted to Assemble the Elements.—When, on the other hand, it is the sum of the elements that is to be insisted upon, and not their separateness, the introductory word should not be repeated. Particularly, when two words in the same construction are both modified by the same word, the introductory word cannot be repeated:

My mother had given her *a new Bible and Prayer-book.*

There at length *the swarthy Moor and Spaniard* were seen to meet the blue-eyed Gaul.

Newman, *Historical Sketches.*

A very dry and difficult subject.

A simple and beautiful treatise.

Gifted with a rare energy, self-possession and imperturbability, the English people have been able to carry self-government to its limits.

III. THE INSERTION AND OMISSION OF CONJUNCTIONS

A and B and A'.—The maintenance of consistency in a group of coördinate elements sometimes depends upon the presence or absence of a conjunction connecting

them. Such expressions as the following, for example,
are inconsistent:

> She was very hospitable, gave me a dinner of ox-cheek with
> a great good will, accepting only a pot of ale in return; and I
> thought myself fixed till Tuesday should come.

Was and *gave* belong to one class,—the group of verbs
of which *she* is the subject; but *I thought* is not in that
class, and hence cannot be coördinated with the members
of it. If the word *and* were inserted before *gave,* the
group of verbs would be complete, and the whole clause,
She . . . was . . . and gave, may be coördinated with
the clause, *I thought.*

A, B, C, D; A, B, C, and D.—A series of coördinate
grammatical expressions is ordinarily without connectives except before the last member: "a, b, c, and d."
Such an arrangement produces an effect of clear-cut completeness. It causes the series to be viewed as a whole
made up of distinct parts. When no connective is used,
—"a, b, c, d,"—the series may not make up a whole,
and each member is viewed separately. For example:

> The Headmaster is obviously a figure which his creator re-
> gards with respect. He is fair-minded, human, generous [each
> by itself is a fine quality; he may have more]. . . . But he is
> a Roman father at best . . . he is acute, brisk, and sensible,
> but [yet in spite of being all this at once] he has (at least to
> me) neither grace nor wisdom.
>
> > Benson, A. C., *Upton Letters.*

Moreover, when a single connective is used at the end,
each member is added to the others, from which it is
different; but when no connective is employed, the different ideas need not be mutually exclusive.

> I have talked to a good many boys who have read the book;
> they have been amused, [yes, I may say] interested, [nay even]
> delighted.

Commonly, however, the effect of omitting connectives is to present the members of the series as casual examples, of which there might be many more.

> It is pleasurable enough within the house, but still more pleasurable to walk abroad; the little circle of dim vision passes with you just revealing the road, the field, the pasture in which you walk.

In this sentence, only one thing at a time is visible in the fog; it makes little difference what it is.

A and B and C and D.—When connectives are used throughout,—"a, and b, and c, and d,"—the effect is to dwell on each as independently important, and as added to all that goes before.

> I scorn and detest lying, and quibbling, and double-tongued practice, and slyness, and cunning, and smoothness, and cant, and pretense, quite as much as any Protestants hate them.
>
> Newman, *Apologia.*

IV.   NON-COORDINATE EXPRESSIONS

As pains should be taken to express the coördinate relation of members of the same class by parallelism of grammatical structure, so likewise pains should be taken to prevent the appearance of such coördination where it does not exist.

a) by avoiding the incorrect insertion of a coördinating conjunction, or a relative pronoun.

He worked at some time or other in all parts of the yard, *and becoming* well acquainted with all the processes in the manufacture of steel.

He worked at some time or other in all parts of the yard, *becoming* well acquainted with all the processes in the manufacture of steel.

Her impulsiveness could be laid to her youth, and *which,* if properly guided, would have preserved her youth.

Her impulsiveness could be laid to her youth, and if properly guided, would have preserved her youth.

We reached the American border with the officers only half a mile behind, and *who* at last gave up the chase.

We reached the American border with the officers only half a mile behind, and *they* at last gave up the chase.

b) by avoiding the introduction of non-coördinate parts with the same introductory phrase.

During vacation a friend invited me to visit her school. *It was* several miles up in the mountains, so *it was* a long drive.

During vacation a friend invited me to visit her school. *It was* several miles up in the mountains, so *we had* a long drive.

In the old baccalaureate address,—and *in* many places the custom is still the same,—much of the speaker's time was taken up with warning.

In the old baccalaureate address,—and *there are* many places where the custom is still the same,—much of the speaker's time was taken up with warning.

Tandem Constructions.—A common type of the fault of improperly suggesting coördination by the form occurs when a modifying element has attached to it a subordinate modifier of the same nature with itself,— when elements are harnessed tandem, as it were. The following are examples of tandem participles.

Seated on a rickety wooden chair, [which was] placed on the rough cobble-stones near the edge of the sidewalk was an old woman.

I was repenting with my eye to the key-hole, trying [*better:* in the attempt] to see the result of my plans.

Soon we were proceeding on our journey, Miss X. carrying [*better:* with] the headless rattler in her hand triumphantly leading the way.

Clauses are often awkwardly placed in the same way.

We were following a guide along one of the narrow streets of Chinatown, *when*

While we were following a guide along one of the narrow streets of Chinatown, we we drew near a doorway, *whence* issued sounds suggestive of the lower end of the Midway Plaisance.

drew near a doorway, whence issued sounds suggestive of the Midway Plaisance.

The first process in the manufacture of the best paper is the cutting of the rags, *which* is done by women standing behind a table on *which* is fastened a knife in an oblique position.

The first process in the manufacture of the best paper, the cutting of the rags, is done by women standing behind a table on which is fastened a knife in an oblique position.

The same fault is to be seen in prepositional phrases.

In shading the leaves, it is best *to* make no two alike, *to* prevent a stiff, awkward look.

In shading the leaves, it is best to make no two alike, in order to prevent a stiff, awkward look.

RECAPITULATION

Coördinate elements should be consistent alike in thought and in form. Consistency in thought requires that the elements should be parallel members of the same class of things; consistency in form that the elements should be parallel in expression. Coördinate independent clauses should keep the same point of view, an object often attained best by avoiding a change of subject or of voice. The subordinate elements of clauses are substantives, verbs, adjectives, and adverbs. Verbs may be single words or phrases; substantives, adjectives, and adverbs may be words, phrases, or clauses. The principle of coördination has a special application to each of these grammatical elements. In general all forms of concrete substantives may be coördinated. Of the four types of abstract substantives,—abstract nonverbal nouns, abstract verbal nouns, infinitives, and noun-clauses,—it is best not to coördinate one type with any other.   Adherent adjectives may be words or short phrases; both types may be coördinated. Appositive word and phrase adjectives may be freely coördinated, but it is best to avoid coördinating these types with adjective clauses. Predicate word and phrase adjectives may be coördinated with each other, and sometimes even with predicate nouns. Adverbs of all types may be freely coördinated. In general, care should be taken in coördinating verbs to maintain the same point of view as to time. The repetition of introductory words often serves to bring parallel elements into clear relation. Such repetition separates and distinguishes elements, and may therefore be required with elements essentially separate, and may be useful with elements which it is desired to emphasize individually. The use of but one introductory expression with a series of elements gathers the elements into a group. In a series, introducing the last member only by a conjunction unites the elements and make the series seem complete. Omitting all conjunctions separates the elements and gives the impression that more elements of the same kind might be added to them. Connecting each element to the preceding by a conjunction produces the effect of deliberate heaping up. Expressions not coördinate in idea should not be coördinate in form. In particular, "tandem" constructions should be avoided.

CHAPTER V

THE SENTENCE: EMPHASIS

I. WORD-GROUPS

Language when real is a spoken thing.—Written language is only a record of speech. A good writer speaks with his pen, though not quite as he would talk; a good reader listens with the ear of his mind to the printed page, though not quite as he would hear the physical sound of the words. "There is a method of trying periods on the ear or weighing them on the scales of the breath, without any articulate sound. Authors, as they write, may be said to 'hear a sound so fine, there's nothing lives 'twixt it and silence'. Even musicians generally compose in their heads. I agree that no style is good that is not fit to be spoken or read aloud with effect. This holds true not only of emphasis and cadence, but also with regard to natural idiom and colloquial freedom." The written record at its best remains imperfect; it cannot quite so easily as can the spoken language suggest the most intimately delicate shades and subtleties of feeling, or even the more mechanical transitions of thought. An ideally perfect arrangement of the words of a written sentence would *compel* the reproduction of the sentence in speech just as the author thought it. No one can write so surely as that; but in a more or less rough way it is possible to determine the movement of the related parts. The following chapter deals with the direction of the logic of the spoken sentence by the form of the written one.

Logic and Emphasis.—It is not enough for the parts of a sentence to be consistent; if the sentence is to be a unit, the parts must also be so arranged as to make manifest the relations which they bear to each other. Modifying expressions must be connected with the expressions which they modify; important words must stand out, unimportant words be placed in the background; in brief, the sentence must have distinctness of form. Imagine a sentence repeated by an idiot or by a child learning it word after word without understanding it: every word is separate from every other, is as important as every other; there is no change of pitch or inflection of the voice, but all proceeds with a steady monotone.

The—day—is—cold—and—dark—and—dreary—
It—rains—and—the—wind—is—never—weary—

Compare this imbecile utterance with a natural way of speaking the passage. The differences consist chiefly in three points. The first is that rational speech utters words in groups, separated by pauses; the second that rational speech makes a central word in each group more prominent than the rest; the third that in rational speech changes of pitch indicate this main word, and also make plain other relations of the words in each group, and of the groups as a whole. The following way of printing the sentence indicates the grouping and the important words, but it is beyond the power of type to indicate inflections of the voice.

The day is *cold,* and *dark,* and *dreary;*
It *rains,* and the *wind* is never weary.

Grouping of words, pauses, stress on particular words, changes of pitch indicating logical relations with the sentence; all these constitute the *emphasis* necessary to make the unity of the sentence obvious. The problem of emphasis includes the formation of groups, the indication of the relation of words within the groups, and the indication of the relations of the groups as wholes.

Groups Cohere about Single Words.—Let us begin by considering sentences so short that they each make but a single group. If two friends meet at a railroad station, and one says to the other, "My father will be here to-day," the emphasis will fall upon the word uppermost in the mind of the speaker, whatever that may be. "*My* father will be here to-day," means *not yours.* "My *father* will be here to-day,"—not my *mother.* "My father *will* be here to-day,"—I did not make a *mistake,* as you think. "My father will *be* here to-day," not merely *send a letter.* "My father will be *here* to-day,"—not *in England.* "My father will be here *to-day,*"—not *next week.*

The emphasized word each time is the focus or cohering-point of the sentence. It is in the light, and all the rest in the half-light. It is the most forcibly uttered word. It is at the highest point of the voice, and at the point where the voice begins to go downward. In brief, it is the center of attention. Sometimes two important points are found in one group; as, "*My* father will be here *to-day,*"—*yours* was here *last* time. But such sentences are far less common than those in which one main idea is dominant in a group. Three foci could not occur in one group. Indeed, when a second word becomes the center of attention, a new group is nearly always formed. If one declares, "My father will be

here,—to-day," he must make *to-day* a group by itself.
The thought of which each group is the expression
coheres about a single central idea, and the group contains a single central word.

The following sentence, which contains many groups,
is so printed as to indicate the division into groups and
the emphatic word within each group.

> *As,*
> When a man is given *over,*
> he may die at any *moment,*
> yet *lingers;*
> as an implement of *war*
> may at any moment *explode,*
> and *must*
> at *some* time;
> as we listen for a *clock* to strike,
> and at length it *surprises* us;
> as a crumbling *arch*
> *hangs,*
> we know not *how,*
> yet it is not safe to *pass* under;
> *so*
> creeps on this feeble weary *world,*
> and *one* day,
> before we know where we *are,*
> it will *end.*

Newman, *Sermons.*

The Emphatic Word.—In this sentence, as is commonly the case, there is but one emphatic word in each
group. The place of this word, though it may be at the
beginning, the middle, or the end of the group, tends
to be toward the end. The emphatic words are generally
nouns and verbs. The most important fact to be observed about the emphatic words, however, is that they
mainly express ideas in contrast to what has preceded.
Thus, the sentence offers instances of things sure to meet
with a sudden catastrophe, a catastrophe which may

come at any instant, or may be indefinitely delayed. Each new instance contrasted with an instance of the same class already given receives emphasis; the *implement of war* contrasted with the sick *man; explode* as against *die; must* as against *may; at some time* as against *at any moment.* Thus the words which present ideas suggested by preceding ideas but in contrast to them receive stress. Again, the emphatic word conveys not only its own meaning, but its meaning with the accompaniment of the rest of the group. *Over,* in the group *when a man is given over,* carries the weight of the whole expression, takes the color of the whole. *Moment* is the center, it is the new idea, of *he may die at any moment,* but it takes with it the significance of the whole group, in the connection in which it is used. Thus the emphasized words are symbols of the whole of which they are parts.

Place of the Emphasized Word in the Group.—The two chief principles of emphasis, accordingly, are these; the emphatic words are those which carry the ideas additional to what has preceded; and the emphatic words are charged with a meaning derived from the other words of the group. It is natural, therefore, for the place of emphasis to be toward the end of the group. As our minds proceed in continuous thinking, each successive idea has, as it were, a footing upon the ideas which have come before it, and takes a step toward the ideas which come after it. So, in each group of words, a part looks back to that which has preceded, and a part looks forward to that which is about to follow. The group, in its advance, takes a step from the old to the new, and the old will tend to come before the new, though it need not do so. Again, since the central word takes the color of the context, it must have a context before it to give it color.

Continuity of Word Groups.—The bearing of these principles will be evident from a study of the following passage in Macaulay's Essay on Lord Clive. The author has been describing the process of degeneration in some European kingdoms and empires. He proceeds:

Such, or *nearly* such, [as against *such in itself*] was the change which passed upon the *Mogul* [as against *the European*] Empire during the forty years which followed the death of *Aurungzbe* [his name fixes the time as against the rest of its history, and carries with it from the context the thought of him as dead]. A succession of nominal *sovereigns* [no antithesis; one word carries the weight of the whole new central idea], sunk in indolence and *debauchery* [debauchery stands for the whole combination *indolence and debauchery*], sauntered away life in secluded *palaces* [carries the meaning of the whole], chewing *bhang* [adds a descriptive new idea; *chewing* is taken into the idea because it is the ordinary thing to do with bhang], fondling *concubines* [analogous to *bhang*, adds the new point, and takes *fondling* into the idea], and listening to *buffoons* [like *bhang* and *concubines* in emphasis]. A succession of ferocious *invaders* [opposed to sovereigns] descended through the western *passes* [carries the whole idea], to prey on the defenseless wealth of *Hindostan* [*preying on wealth* is the natural business of invaders; *Hindostan* adds the idea defining the scope of their activity]. A *Persian* conqueror crossed the *Indus*, marched through the gates of *Delhi*, and bore away in *triumph* those *treasures* of which the magnificence had astounded *Roe* and *Bernier*, the Peacock *Throne*, on which the richest jewels of *Golconda* had been disposed by the most skilful hands of *Europe*, and the inestimable *Mountain of Light*, which, after many strange *vicissitudes*, lately shone in the bracelet of *Runjeet Sing*, and is now destined to adorn the hideous idol of *Orissa*. The *Afghan* soon followed to *complete* the work of devastation which the Persian had *begun*.

The two forms of the following paragraph from a student's theme will illustrate the effect of following and of neglecting the method of emphasis exemplified by the quotation from Macaulay. In the first form of the paragraph no consideration has been given to the connection of the groups or to the emphatic place in each. In the second, the groups begin with ideas suggested by what precedes, and leads on to the new idea.

The two most cruel and harmful ways of treating children are teasing and snubbing them, and showing tolerance and condescension for them. A child's natural development may be seriously stunted by teasing and snubbing. A child of six or seven may begin to have original ideas on various subjects. They may be false or absurd, but it is certainly preferable that children should have incorrect ideas than that they should have none. How can a child learn to think if he is purposely checked at the outset? It may be convenient to have one's small brothers and sisters quiet and untroublesome while they are passing through the awkward and formative period; yet, with these same children when their fathers and mothers wish them to outshine their neighbor's children, it is very exasperating to find that Ethel and Jack are unable to make as observant remarks or to get as good grades at school as Jerry and Molly Harris?

The two most cruel and harmful ways of treating children are teasing and snubbing them and showing tolerance and condescension for them. Teasing and snubbing a child may easily stunt its natural development. Even at the age of six or seven, children begin to have original ideas on various subjects. These ideas may be false or absurd; but that children should have incorrect ideas is certainly better than that they should have no ideas at all. How can a child learn to think, if he is purposely checked at the outset? To have one's small brothers and sisters quiet and untroublesome while they are passing through the awkward and formative period is certainly convenient for an older brother; but by and by these little children will reach the age when they are brought into comparison with the neighbor's youngsters; and then what will Father and Mother think if Ethel and Jack fail to make as observant remarks or to get as good grades at school as Jerry and Molly Harris?

Interruption.—If a group of words be interrupted, the effect is to throw emphasis on the word preceding the interruption. For instance, if a group be broken off: "True: from all men thou art emancipated: but from thyself and from the Devil—?" —"I like him; but—" An interruption is sometimes produced by an antithesis: "The prince who refuses to be the judge, instructs his people to consider him as the accomplice, of his ministers." Commonly interruptions are produced by parentheses, that is, modifying expressions loosely connected with the context as a whole and inserted into the middle of the expression which it modifies. The effect of such parentheses in throwing emphasis upon the words preceding them is easily perceived. Compare such a sentence as, "I have lost all my mirth," with, "I have, of late, lost all my mirth." The stress on *have* is obvious. Certain words of logical connection,—*however, on the other hand, to be sure, indeed; then, therefore, accordingly; moreover, further,*—are the commonest of parenthetic expressions. They are most skillfully used to increase the emphasis on important words. For example:

If ye, *then,* being evil, give good gifts unto your children, how much more shall your heavenly Father feed you, O ye of little faith.

Each day thou daff'st me with some device, Iago; and rather, *as it seems to me now,* keep'st from me all conveniency, than suppliest me with the least advantage of hope.

King Henry, *on the other hand,* had already arrived in camp.

Some of the adventurers pressed Monmouth to take a severe course. Monmouth, *however,* would not listen to this advice.

II. EMPHASIS UPON GROUPS AS MEMBERS OF THE SENTENCE

Transitions between Sentences.—The principles which govern the place of the words in separate groups govern also the place of the groups in the sentence. Just as in the groups, the beginnings tend to be in close connection with what precedes, while the ends add new elements, so in the sentence as a whole, the introductory group tends to be connective, while the last group tends to contain the most important substantially new idea toward which the whole sentence has been moving. Thus the last group—not the last word—of the sentence is commonly the most important, and the introductory group the next in importance. The following passage illustrates this close connection of sentences, already exemplified in the order of the new words within the groups.

In the midst of the night, an uproar rose within the walls of Zahara, more fearful than the raging of the storm. A fearful alarm cry—"The Moor! The Moor!" rang through the streets, mingled with the clash of arms, the shriek of anguish, and the shout of victory. Muley Abul Hassan, at the head of a powerful force, had hurried from Granada, and passed through the mountains in the obscurity of the tempest. While the storm pelted the sentinel from his post, and howled round tower and battlement, the Moors had planted their scaling ladders, and mounted securely into both town and castle. The garrison was unsuspicious of danger, until battle and massacre burst forth within its very walls. It seemed to the affrighted inhabitants, as if the fiends of the air had come upon the wings of the wind, and possessed themselves of tower and turret. The war-cry resounded on every side, shout answering shout above, below, on the battlements of the castle, in the streets of the town; the foe was in all parts, wrapped in obscurity, but acting in concert by the aid of preconcerted signals. Starting from sleep, the soldiers were intercepted and cut down as they rushed from their quarters; or if they escaped, they knew not where to assemble, or where to strike. Wherever lights appeared, the flashing scimeter was at its deadly work, and all who attempted resistance fell beneath its edge.

Irving, Conquest of Granada.

Explicit Connectives.—When the emphasis does not of itself sufficiently indicate the connection of successive sentences, explicit connectives are required. (See p. 27.) *But* and *and* are very often used as connectives between sentences. There is no objection to them except that they may be too weak to bear the burden of connection between sentences in which it is of importance to emphasize the logical relations of one sentence to another, and that if too frequently used they produce an effect of vagueness and indecision.

The following extract from Mr. Ford Madox Hueffer's *Ancient Lights* would lose much both in continuity and strength if the explicit connective words were omitted.

The principal . . . set it down to my dismay that my second study must be the piano. *Now* I could not play the piano; I dislike the piano, which seems to me to be the most soulless of instruments, and, in any case, to acquire the mastery of the piano, or indeed of any other instrument, requires many hours of practising a day which would interfere, as it seemed to me, rather seriously with the deep study that I hoped to make of the theory of music. I *accordingly* asked to be allowed to interview the principal—an awful being who kept himself splendidly remote. Having succeeded with a great deal of difficulty in penetrating into his room, I discovered a silent gentleman who listened to my remarks without any appearance of paying attention to them. *But* when I had finished and was waiting in nervous silence, he suddenly overwhelmed me with a torrent of excited language. *What it amounted to* was that, during his lifetime my father had domineered over that institution; and that, if I thought I was going to keep up the tradition I was exceedingly mistaken. *On the contrary*, the professors were determined to give me a hot time of it, or—as Sir C—— D—— put it—to treat me with the utmost rigour of the rules.

Monotonous Connections.—In the passage just cited, the connectives are managed with much ease and variety. Care should be taken not to depend too much upon a single method of transition. Do not use too many *this's, these's* and *those's* as in the following example.

The old inhabitants of Norway were called Northmen or Norsemen. *These* people were bold and hardy sailors, and in the ninth and tenth centuries were famous sea-robbers. In order to find new fields for plunder and adventure they sought strange coasts. On one of *these* expeditions they reached Iceland and on another Greenland. In each of *these* islands they made settlements. The brave deeds of *these* old warriors are preserved in the old Sagas, which were written in Icelandic prose. For a long time *these* Sagas were transmitted orally, but finally they were committed to writing.

Vigorous Ending of Sentences.—As sentences should begin distinctly, so they should end vigorously. Compare the following sentences, as originally written, with a minor group at the end, and as rewritten, with an important group in the last place.

Care should be taken in watering not to splash water on the leaves, for the pores of the leaves will be stopped up and the growth of the plant retarded if this is done.

Care should be taken in watering not to splash water on the leaves, for if this is done the pores of the leaves will be stopped up and the growth of the plant be retarded.

Furthermore, a college education is supposed to give a student training along moral and social lines, and if a student finishes his course without having been improved along those lines his college course is incomplete, for a person is not prepared to be a useful leader among men as he should be after taking a course in college.

Furthermore, since a college course should equip those who have received it to be useful leaders of men, no such education is complete which does not conduce to moral and social development.

[An introductory sentence.] The course in physical education covers two years at most institutions. [The curriculum follows.]

The top of the hill is covered with tangled blackberry thickets, and glows with golden-rod and sumach in the fall.

The so-called fusser is the happy-go-lucky, well-dressed fellow who gives most of his time and attention to the fair sex. Before and after classes, and sometimes during recitations, he smiles and talks to the ladies. Every dance, every party, every football game is attended by him in company with a charmer. Once or twice a week he must take a girl to the Fuller or the Orpheum, for college life is short and girls must be shown a good time, regardless of accumulated back work. In the Library you will find the fusser talking first to one girl and then to another. In the intervals he glances from table to table and compares the pretty face of a blonde with that of a brunette. In general, a fusser is fussing wherever he may be.

The course in physical education usually covers two years. [The time covered is important in determining the curriculum.]

The top of the hill is covered with tangled blackberry thickets and in the fall glows with golden-rod and sumach.

The so-called fusser is the well-dressed, happy-go-lucky fellow who gives most of his time and attention to the fair sex. He is smiling and talking to the ladies before and after classes, and sometimes during recitations. You see him with a charmer at every dance, every party, every football game. Once or twice a week,—for college life is short, and girls must be shown a good time, regardless of accumulated back work,— he must take a girl to the Fuller or to the Orpheum. But it is in the Library that you will find the fusser busiest. There he is talking first to one girl and then to another, and in the intervals glancing from table to table and comparing the pretty face of a blonde with that of a brunette. In general, the fusser, wherever he may be, is always fussing.

The Last Word not Necessarily Emphatic.—It is the important group that should conclude the sentence,— not necessarily the important word. The concluding group, like any other group, may perfectly well end in an insignificant word, a preposition for example, when there is no special reason to the contrary. Thus, in such expressions as, "What is the moon made of?" the preposition *of* is almost one word with *made;* and to change the sentence to, "Of what is the moon made?" would produce an effect of extreme formality. English literature of the highest order abounds in sentences which end with prepositions;—*Faith is the substance of things hoped for. Do as you would be done by* is less noble than, *Do unto others as ye would that they should do unto you;* but it is more pungent and rememberable. Even in a style of considerable formality the prepositional ending of a sentence is not infrequent.

We must have the real thing [history] before we can have the science of a thing [the philosophy of history]. . . . But until this real thing is given, philosophical history is but an idle plaything to entertain children with.

Froude, *Life of Carlyle.*

III. LOGICAL RELATIONS OF GROUPS AS AFFECTED BY EMPHASIS

The principles of emphasis thus far discussed apply to all groups in sequence, whatever their grammatical relation. Next come the principles governing the order of grammatically subordinate expressions in the sentence.

Introductory Adjectives.—The tendency of the language is to connect adjective expressions beginning the sentence with the subject; and any other connection will, in most cases, shock or disturb the reader. This principle, of course, applies to participles and prepositional phrases as well as to ordinary descriptive adjectives. (*Viewing, looking at,* and similar words are exceptions.)

Now *apart* from all others, *alone,* and *in secrecy, sinking* in the extremity of her sorrow before the shrine of her patroness, *she* besought the protection of kindred purity for the defence of her freedom and her honor, and invoked vengeance on the wild and treacherous chieftain who had slain her father.

Scott, *The Betrothed.*

You could not be angry with [Coleridge] for using this privilege [of talking all the time without listening], for it was a privilege conferred by others and a privilege which he was ready to resign as soon as any man demurred to it. But *though reconciled* to it by these considerations, and by the ability with which he used it, *you* could not but feel that it worked ill for all parties. Himself it tempted into a pure garrulity of egotism, and the listeners it reduced to a state of debilitated sympathy or of absolute torpor. *Prevented* by custom from putting questions, from proposing doubts, from asking for explanations, *reacting* by no mode of mental activity, and *condemned* also to the mental distress of hearing doctrines stream past them by flights which they must not arrest for a moment so as even to make a note of them, and which yet they could not often understand, or seeming to understand could not always approve, *the audience* sank at times into a listless condition of inanimate vacuity.

De Quincey, *Second Essay on Conservation.*

Ardent and intrepid on the field of battle, *Monmouth* was everywhere else effeminate and irresolute.

Macaulay, *History of England.*

Introductory Elliptical Clauses.—Very similar to introductory adjective expressions are groups of words introduced by such subordinating conjunctions as *while, though,* and *if,* and implying though not expressing predication. These groups of words are in effect clauses, with an ellipsis of the verb, and are known as *elliptical clauses.* Such expressions are almost always naturally referred to the subject of the sentence.

Although the victor, we submit to Caesar.

If rich, they go to enjoy; if poor, to retrench; if sick, to recover; if studious, to learn; if learned, to relax from their studies.

Rogers, Italy.

This principle is often violated by careless writers, as in the following sentences.

Maggie went to school at Mrs. Firmin's. *While there* [i. e., While she was there] *her father* lost a case in court.

I suppose some people laugh at the idea of treeing a fox; but the grey fox trees readily. *Though not so good* at climbing as cats and coons [i. e., *Though the creatures are not so good*, etc.; the sentence suggests that it was the writer who could not climb very well], *I* have often shot them thirty feet from the ground.

Introductory Gerunds.—Likewise, initial gerund phrases which imply predication almost always are felt to refer to the subject.

Instead of reforming others, let *each* man reform himself.

Without plunging into any very deep mysteries, *without committing ourselves* to any very dangerous theories in the darker regions of ethnological inquiries, *we* may perhaps be allowed to doubt whether there is any real primeval kindred between the Ottoman and the Finnish Magyar.

Freeman, Race and Language.

In other cases, the gerund does not imply predication of a specific action by a particular subject. In such cases, the principle stated above does not apply.

In dealing with differences of temperature arising between different kinds of surfaces, it *is essential to observe* that these arise in consequence of different rates of cooling. *By assuming* that these conditions are actually realized, the barometer *may be used* to obtain approximate measurements of the heights of mountains.

Loosely Attached Adjectives.—Not only at the beginning of the sentence, but anywhere within it, predicative and adjective expressions are easily connected with the subject when they are not closely attached to some nearer word. This is particularly the case with the participle and gerund; less so with the attributive adjective. The following sentence illustrates the difference.

Eveline, restored to her own fair castle and domains, failed not to provide for her confessor, as well as for her old soldiers, servants and retainers, *forgetting* their errors and *remembering* their fidelity. The confessor was restored to the flesh-pots of Egypt, *more congenial* to his habits than the meagre fare of his convent.

> Scott, *The Betrothed.*

In the following sentence, the ease with which the adjective may be associated with the subject as readily as with a nearer substantive, is very plain, while the participle, in spite of its meaning, gravitates toward the subject.

We went up the hill, silent, calm, grass-grown, and with no path to show where others had gone before us.

Adverbs.—Within the body of the sentence, it is more often adverbial expressions which cause difficulty. In particular, the connection of adverbial expressions is sometimes ambiguous, inasmuch as it is, or for an instant *feels*, uncertain whether they modify a portion of a group, a whole group, or a larger total of which the group is a part. Thus in the following sentence, it is indifferent whether *with a vicious grin* modifies the whole expression *to look down on the wreck he had made,* or only the part *look down;* but for an instant it is felt only with the word *made,*—an absurd connection. "The villainous driver flicked his horses with his whip and dashed away, but not before he had time to look down on the wreck he had made with a vicious grin."

In correcting such sentences, care should be taken to avoid stiffness and dislocation. In this case, *with a vicious grin* easily follows *look down,* and should be placed immediately after it.

In the sentence, "The knight brought her the roses he found growing by the wall, in his mantle," the correction, "brought her in his mantle," though accurate, is stiff. Probably expansion is needed,—"picked the roses, and brought them to her in his mantle."

Modifiers which Look Two Ways.—Another type of faulty order, due to the fact that the printed sentence will not always clearly indicate the emphasis of the spoken sentence, arises from placing a modifier between the two groups, with either of which it might be associated. This construction, which is said to squint, that is, to be cross-eyed, so as to look in two directions, is practically confined to adverbial phrases.

Arriving at the foot of the mountain with little difficulty they soon reached the top.

(Is this: *Having arrived with little difficulty at the foot of the mountain?* or: *After arriving at the foot of the mountain, they reached the top soon and with little difficulty?*)

We all took fence-rails, and using them as levers after half an hour's hard work succeeded in overturning the rock [*i. e., succeeded after half an hour's hard work*].

I had discovered if you sat on the foot the legs turned up [*i. e., I had discovered that if,* etc.].

Only, Merely, Simply, Etc.—Certain words throw their emphasis in strict formal use upon the expressions immediately following them; but the idiom of the language permits some freedom in employing them. The commonest of these words is *only;* others are *merely, simply, as well . . . as, not only . . . but also.*

The following illustration brings out the principle in the case of *only*. If a man has been staying in a town six days, he would say in strict logic, "I have been here only six days," but he would actually say in idiomatic English, "I have only been here six days." Whether to follow logic or idiom depends on circumstances. Whenever the looser way of writing produces real ambiguity or awkwardness, the exact way is to be preferred, and the exact way is never wrong. Most writers would prefer, "The stillness was broken only by the noise of a rushing stream," to, "The stillness was only broken by the noise of a rushing stream." Probably most writers of this day would not write as Dryden did two hundred years ago; "We do not only build upon their foundations but by their models," but; "We build not only upon their foundations but by their models." But it is certain that while some would write: "The car struck him with force sufficient only to knock him to the ground," nobody would write: "with force enough only to knock him to the ground." With the colloquial word *enough* the colloquial order, "The car only struck him with force enough to knock him to the ground," or: "with only force enough," would be employed.

Groups Ending with Modified Word.—Especially in complicated sentences, it is frequently desirable to bring the modified word to the end of a group, and thus to emphasize it and to connect it closely with a following modifier. Thus it is natural to write: "Each tribe had a chief at its head," but: "Each tribe had at its head a chief, who fought for his place."

Other examples are:

| The spiral screw-driver has lately been invented, which, it | A late invention is the spiral screw-driver, which, it |

is thought, will save much labor.

There is a certain privacy that one feels in a small house, which is entirely wanting in a dormitory, where everything is in common.

By the system of land tenure, lords held land from the king called feudal demesnes.

is thought, will save much labor.

In a small house there is a certain privacy which is entirely wanting in a dormitory, where everything is in common.

By the system of land tenure, lords held from the king land called feudal demesnes.

IV.   SUSPENSE

Word-groups may follow each other either with or without suspending the sense.   For example, the following sentence has no effect of suspense; the clause *as I remember* is added after a clause already complete in meaning: "The youngsters were always breaking their legs, as I remember."   On the other hand, if the sentence is arranged as follows, the sense is suspended after *remember:* "As I remember, the youngsters were always breaking their legs."   The following sentences illustrate this difference on a larger scale.   The first is suspended in form, the second is not.

Everything about him [Johnson], his coat, his wig, his figure, his face, his scrofula, his St. Vitus's dance, his rolling walk, the outward signs which too clearly marked his approbation of his dinner, his insatiable appetite for fish-sauce and veal-pie with plums, his inextinguishable thirst for tea, his trick of touching the posts as he walked, his mysterious habit of treasuring up scraps of orange-peel, his morning slumbers, his midnight disputations, his contortions, his mutterings, his grumblings, his puffings, his vigorous, acute and ready eloquence, his sarcastic wit, his vehemence, his insolence, his fits of tempestuous rage, his queer inmates, old Mr. Levett, and blind Mrs. Williams, the cat Hodge, and the negro Frank, all are as familiar to us as the objects by which we have been surrounded from childhood.

Macaulay, *Essay on Boswell's Life of Johnson.*

The Mitre Tavern still stands in Fleet Street; but where is now its scot-and-lot paying, beef-and-ale loving, cocked-hatted, pot-bellied landlord; its rosy-faced assiduous landlady, with all her shining brass pans, waxed tables, well-filled larder shelves; her cooks, and bootjacks, and errand-boys, and watery-mouthed hangers-on? Gone! Gone!

Carlyle, *Boswell's Life of Johnson.*

Means of Suspense.—The chief means of suspense are four. The first is presenting a series of subjects, or of modifiers of the subject, before introducing the predicate,—as in Macaulay's sentence already quoted.

The second is placing a number of modifiers before the expression modified,—as in the following sentence:

If a man were a profligate or a drunkard; if he lied or swore; if he did not come to communion, or held unlawful opinions; if he was idle or unthrifty; if he was unkind to his wife or his servants; if a child was disobedient to his father, or a father cruel to his child; if a tradesman sold adulterated wares, or used false measures or dishonest weights,—the eye of the parish priest was everywhere, and the Church court stood always open to examine and to punish.

Froude, *Short Studies.*

The third is the introduction of parentheses,—as:

In that same village, and in one of those very houses (which, to tell the precise truth, was sadly time-worn and weather-beaten) there lived a simple good-natured fellow of the name of Rip Van Winkle.

The fourth is the employment of expressions requiring something to complete them. Such words are: words of comparison,—*as . . . as, more . . . than, so . . . as;* demonstratives expecting a definition,—*the . . . who, those . . ., etc.; not only . . . but; not . . . but.*

As Lord Shaftesbury would desire, it [civilized self-respect] prefers playful wit and satire in putting down what is objectionable, as a *more* refined and good-natured, as well as a more

effectual method, *than the* expedient *which* is natural to the
uneducated minds.

Newman, *Idea of a University.*

Loose and Periodic Sentences.—Sentences in which
there is an effect of suspense carried so far as to render it
impossible to get a complete sense from a statement until
the end is reached, are *periodic;* those in which the sense
is grammatically complete before the end are termed
loose. The periodic sentence can bind together into a
firm and clear unity a number of parts which might
scatter if not so bound. It manifests and elicits intellectual energy. On the other hand, by requiring close
attention and intellectual power of combination, it
wearies the attention. It tends to become formal and
artificial. The loose sentence of more than a few members almost inevitably fails to bring out the relations
among them. It is, at its worst, intellectually scattering
and indistinct. Finally, in the loose sentence, the necessity of picking up the attention frequently may become
even more exhausting than the severe task of attention
required to apprehend the periodic sentence as a whole.

The effects of the loose and periodic sentences are illustrated by the following passages. The first is a simple
narrative entirely composed of loose sentences.

He [the Emperor of Lilliput] first calls for my scimitar,
which I took out, scabbard and all. In the meantime he ordered three thousand of his choicest troops (who attended
him) to surround me at a distance, with their bows and arrows
just ready to discharge; but I did not observe it, for mine
eyes were wholly fixed upon his majesty. He then desired
me to draw my scimitar, which, though it had got some rust
by the sea-water, was in most parts exceeding bright. I did
so, and immediately all the troops gave a shout between terror
and surprise; for the sun shone clear, and the reflection daz-
zled their eyes, as I waved the scimitar to and fro in my hand.

His majesty, who is a most magnanimous prince, was less daunted than I could expect: he ordered me to return it into the scabbard, and cast it on the ground as gently as I could, about six feet from the end of my chain.

Swift, *Gulliver's Travels.*

The second, which is expository, contains some completely periodic sentences, and many in which there is a considerable element of suspense. A composition in which all the sentences are wholly periodic could not be endured.

Among sayings that have a currency in spite of being wholly false on the face of them for the sake of a half-truth upon another subject which is accidentally combined with the error, one of the grossest and broadest conveys the monstrous proposition that it is easy to tell the truth and hard to tell a lie. I wish heartily it were. But the truth is one; it has first to be discovered, then justly and exactly uttered. Even with instruments specially contrived for such a purpose—with a foot-rule, a level, or a theodolite—it is not easy to be exact; it is easier, alas! to be inexact. From those who mark the divisions on a scale to those who measure the boundaries of empires or the distance of the heavenly stars, it is by careful method and minute, unwearying attention that men rise even to material exactness or to sure knowledge even of external and constant things. But it is easier to draw the outlines of a mountain than the changing appearance of a human face; and truth in human relations is of this more intangible and dubious order: hard to seize, harder to communicate. Veracity to facts in a loose, colloquial sense—not to say that I have been in Malabar when as a matter of fact I have never been out of England, not to say that I have read Cervantes in the original when as a matter of fact I know not one syllable of Spanish—this, indeed, is easy and to the same degree unimportant in itself. Lies of this sort, according to circumstances, may or may not be important, in a sense they may not even be false. The habitual liar may be a very honest fellow, and live truly with his wife and friends; while another man who never told a formal falsehood in his life may yet be himself one lie—heart and face, from top to bottom. This is the kind of lie which poisons intimacy. And *vice versa* veracity to sentiment, truth in a relation, truth to your heart and to your friends, never to feign or to falsify emotion—that is the truth which makes love possible and life happy.

> Stevenson, *Virginibus Puerisque;* by permission of C. Scribner's Sons.

Sentences Periodic in Effect, though not in Form.— Often sentences which are not periodic in their grammatical form are yet periodic in effect because of the relation of their parts. The second of the following sentences is such a one. Grammatically, it may end at *identical,* but practically a conclusion at that point would sound intolerably abrupt and unsatisfactory.

> Consider . . . how different has been the political history, and yet how similar is the social condition, of Great Britain, France, Germany, Holland, and Belgium. Though these five nations do not for the most part speak the same language, nor profess the same religion, nor claim the same ancestry; though the events by which they have been moulded, and the institutions by which they have been governed, are apparently widely dissimilar; yet their culture is at this moment practically identical; their ideas form a common stock; the social questions they have to face are the same; and such differences as exist in the material condition and well-being of their populations are unquestionably due more to economic differences in their position, climate, and natural advantages, than to the decisions at which they may have from time to time arrived on the various political controversies by which their peoples have been so bitterly divided.   Balfour, *Essays and Addresses.*

V.   COORDINATE WORD-GROUPS

The discussion of emphasis thus far has dealt chiefly with the order of word-groups in relation to the sentence as a whole, and to some extent with the order of words in the group. Next to be considered is the form of the group in relation to other groups.

Balanced Groups.—Word-groups may be balanced— may be alike in syntax and in form and cadence. For example:

Studies serve for delight, for ornament, and for ability. Their chief use for delight, is in privateness and retiring; for ornament, is in discourse; and for ability, is in the judgment and disposition of business. . . . To spend too much time in studies, is sloth; to use them too much for ornament, is affectation; to make judgment wholly by their rules, is the humour of a scholar.

Bacon, Essays.

Or again:

It may be observed that the oldest poets of many nations preserve their reputations, and that the following generations of wit, after a short celebrity, sink into oblivion. The first, whoever they be, must take their sentiments and descriptions immediately from knowledge; the resemblance is therefore just, their descriptions are verified by every eye, and their sentiments acknowledged by every breast. Those whom their fame invites to the same studies copy partly them, and partly nature, till the books of one age gain such authority as to stand in the place of nature to another, and imitation, always deviating a little, becomes at last capricious and casual. Shakespeare, whether life or nature be his subject, shows plainly that he has seen with his own eyes; he gives the image which he receives, not weakened or distorted by the intervention of any other mind; the ignorant feel his representations to be just, and the learned see that they are complete.

Johnson, S., Shakespeare.

Antitheses.—One form of balanced sentence is called an antithesis. An antithesis is formed by the balancing of word-groups in which the central words are opposed in idea, as in the following sentences.

Some in their discourse rather commendation of wit, in being able to hold all arguments, than of judgment, in discerning what is true; as if it were a praise to know what might be said, and not what should be thought.

Bacon, Essays.

The Turkish empire would be more formidable were it less extensive,—were it not for those countries which it can neither

command, nor give entirely away: which it is obliged to protect, but from which it has no power to exact obedience.

Goldsmith, *Citizen of the World.*

If the lower ranks are actuated by envy and uncharitable-
ness towards the upper, the latter have scarcely any feelings
but of pride, contempt, and aversion to the lower. If the
poor would pull down the rich to get at their good things, the
rich would tread down the poor as in a wine-press, and squeeze
the last shilling out of their pockets and the last drop of blood
out of their veins. If the headstrong self-will and unruly
turbulence of a common ale-house are shocking, what shall we
say to the studied insincerity, the inspired want of common-
sense, the callous insensibility of the drawing-room and bou-
doir? I would rather see the feelings of our common nature
(for they are the same at bottom) expressed in the most naked
and unqualified way, than see every feeling of our nature suppressed, stifled, hermetically sealed under the smooth, cold,
glittering varnish of pretended refinement and conventional
politeness. The one may be corrected by being better informed; the other is incorrigible, wilful, heartless depravity.

Hazlitt, *Table Talk.*

An antithetic element is to be perceived in many of
the most impressive sentences, because it is by the perception of contrasts that the mind often advances to the
discovery of truth. Conversely, the failure to perceive
the real point of a contrast is a frequent sign of weakness of thought, and the failure to shape a sentence so
as to bring out a contrast is a frequent cause of weakness of expression. The following sentences from
students' exercises, as originally written and as recon-
structed illustrate the value of the antithetic form in
bringing out a real contrast of thought.

There were only three peo-ple in sight, two girls and a boy, but the principal object in view was a large, well-humped Arabian camel.	The principal object in view was not one of the three human beings to be seen—two girls and a boy—but a large, well-humped Arabian camel.

After all it is not so much the quality in these grades as it is the power that the child gains that is worth the most.	After all, in these grades what is worth the most is not so much the quality of the work done as the power gained by doing it.

The dangers of the antithesis are the ordinary dangers of vigorous forms of expression: insincerity, sensationalism, and monotony. First, the danger of insincerity. A writer striving for antithetic effect is easily led to say more than he really believes in order to obtain the liveliness of the exaggerated contrast. Secondly, the danger of sensationalism. In course of time, the habit of exaggeration, harmless when it is understood as exaggeration, perhaps playful, may grow upon a writer to such an extent that he seasons his writings with extravagance or even absurdity, in order to excite the reader's attention. And finally, the danger of monotony. The exaggerating habit once having taken possession of a writer, he falls into a mannerism of superficial cleverness, as tiresome as any other mannerism.

Climax.—A second method of emphasis by means of structure is an increase of the intensity of the ideas expressed in a series of groups of the same general form. This is called a climax.

Every change of season, every change of weather, indeed, every hour of the day produces some change in the magical hues and shapes of the mountains.

W. Irving, *Rip Van Winkle.*

There is one coffee-house in town, and I see one old gentleman goes to it.   Thackeray, *Roundabout Papers.*

What need have the inhabitants for walls and ramparts, except to build summer-houses, to trail vines, and hang clothes to dry on them?   *Ibid.*

A series in which the less follows the greater is called
an anti-climax, and is peculiarly weak and flat. Inexperienced writers are specially liable to produce anti-
climaxes by placing the more general and less interesting
expressions after the more specific and vivid ones. For
example:

I went to bed with visions of porter-house steak, of toast
browned to the queen's taste, of milk sweet as nectar, and of
other necessaries.

The vines are being cut down, the trees trimmed, and the
place put in order generally.

Oh! how I longed to see my home, the trees, the walks, and
the large roses that grew along the front fence! A whole
year, oh! how long it seemed! I was truly homesick.

The effect of an anti-climax is sometimes due to defects of form in the sentence and to no real falling off in
thought. Compare the two forms of the following sentence.

These people will not only
enter upon a struggle for life,
but their failure will cause
Europe to lose certain advantages.

These people will enter
upon a struggle not only for
their national life but for the
future of their country and
of all Europe.

By using words which seem to form an anti-climax
but which in reality do not, writers sometimes add a spice
of surprise.

The laws are cemented with blood, praised, and disregarded.
                    Goldsmith, *Citizen of the World.*

The lion roars with terror over his captive; the tiger sends
forth its hideous roar to intimidate its prey; no creature shows
any fondness for its short-lived prisoner, except a man and
a cat.
                                        Ibid.

Increase in Volume.—Generally speaking, the length of groups tends to increase towards the end of the sen' tence; and especially in a series it is usually unsatis- factory for the shorter to follow the longer group.

> The Council was met; a new Treasurer appointed; the troops were devoted to the king's cause; and fifty loyal gentlemen of the greatest names were assembled to accompany the Prince of Wales, who might have been the acknowledged heir to the throne, or the possessor of it by this time, had your Majesty not chosen to take the air.
>
> Thackeray, *Henry Esmond.*

> It is said that history is not of individuals; that the proper concern of it is with broad masses of facts, with tendencies which can be analyzed into laws, with the evolution of human- ity in general.
>
> Froude, *Life of Carlyle.*

Variety.—Students should be on their guard against using any means of effect so often that it becomes monotonous. Some writers balance their sentences con- stantly, others make constant antitheses, with others the length and cadence of their phrases are constantly the same. As for all the means by which sentences may be made clear and emphatic, the advice which Bacon quotes from Queen Isabella about manners is applicable,—"To attain them it almost sufficeth not to despise them; for so shall a man observe them in others, and let him trust himself with the rest: for if he labor too much to ex- press them, he shall lose their grace, which is to be na- tural and unaffected."

VI. REPETITION OF WORDS

Are there principles determining when words ought to be repeated? The question has already been discussed with regard to such words of relation as prepositions and articles, and introductory words in general; we now come to the problem of repeating words of substantial meaning such as nouns, verbs, and significant modifiers, whether introductory or not.

It is to be observed that a repeated word may either give emphasis to other words or receive emphasis itself. Thus in the following sentence *believes, perfection,* and *new,* when repeated, emphasize either the words which precede or those which follow them, but *culture* is itself emphatic. "Now, then, is the moment for culture to be of service, culture which believes in making reason and the will of God prevail, believes in perfection, in the study and pursuit of perfection, and is no longer debarred by a rigid invincible exclusion of whatever is new, from getting acceptance for its ideas, simply because they are new."

Unemphatic Words Repeated.—It is clear, moreover, that the unemphatic words have two functions: the introductory word *believes* makes plain the parallelism of the word-groups which it introduces and brings them into connection with the idea *culture;* the words *perfection* and *new,* when they appear the second time, throw stress on *study* and *pursuit,* and on the unrepeated elements of the parallel expressions. In general terms, then, words may be repeated without emphasis in order to bring out logical relations of parallelism, and to increase the sharpness of antitheses.

Repetition for Clearness of Relation.—Of the former use of repetition, that of indicating the direction and relation of ideas, and gathering them together, so that they can be easily grasped and held, the following sentences contain examples. They exemplify no new principles, being like the sentences already discussed, in which the initiatory words are repeated.

He who works for sweetness and light, *works* to make reason and the will of God prevail. *He who works* for hatred, works only for confusion. *Culture* looks beyond machinery, *culture* hates hatred; *culture* has one great passion, *the passion for* sweetness and light. It has one even greater!—the passion for making them prevail.

. . . There is poetry enough in East London; poetry in the great river that washes it on the south, in the fretted tangle of cordage and mast that peeps over the roofs of Shadwell or in the great hulls moored along the wharves of Wapping; poetry in the "Forest" that fringes it to the east, in the few glades that remain of Epping and Hainault,—glades ringing with the shouts of schoolchildren out for their holiday and half mad with delight at the sight of a flower or a butterfly; poetry of the present in the work and toil of these acres of dull bricks and mortar where everybody, man, woman and child, is a worker, this England without a "leisure class"; poetry in the thud of the steam-engine, and the white trail of steam from the tall sugar refinery, in the blear eyes of the Spitalfields weaver, or the hungering faces of the group of labourers clustered from morning till night round the gates of the docks and watching for the wind that brings the ships up the river; poetry in its past, in strange old-fashioned squares, in quaint gabled houses, in grey village churches, that have been caught up and overlapped and lost, as it were, in the great human advance that has carried London forward past Whitechapel, its limit in the age of the Georges, to Stratford, its bound in that of Victoria.

> Green, J. R., *Stray Studies;* by permission of Harper and Brothers.

Repetition to Strengthen Antithesis.—The following passage illustrates the use of repetition of some words to enhance the contrast between others. *Ancient* stresses *institutions* and *principles*. *Free from, preventive, honor,* all have a similar function.

But power, of some kind or other, will survive the shock in which manners and opinions perish. The usurpation, which, in order to subvert ancient institutions, has destroyed ancient principles, will hold power by arts similar to those by which it has acquired it. When the old feudal and chivalrous spirit of fealty, which by freeing kings from fear, freed both kings and subjects from the precautions of tyranny, shall be extinct in the minds of men, plots and assassinations will be anticipated by preventive murder and preventive confiscation, and that long roll of grim and bloody maxims which form the political code of all power not standing on its own honour and the honour of those who are to obey it. Kings will be tyrants from policy when subjects are rebels from principle.

Emphatic Words.—The second class of repeated words includes those which are themselves emphatic. Such words are repeated commonly because the ideas which they express fill the writer's mind and occupy it wholly. Hence such repetitions as, ''Nonsense! Nonsense!''—''I will! I will!''—''And many, many more were there.'' ''Fallen, fallen is Babylon, that great city.''

Clumsy Repetitions.—Repetitions are faulty when they correspond with no reality of thought or feeling,—when they do not serve to bring ideas into relation, or to emphasize other words, or to carry an emphasis of their own. Casual repetitions of the same word, especially in different senses, produce the effect of poverty of resource and slipshod habits not only of speech but of thought.

For example:

One form of house is *one* that stands up about four feet from the surface of the water.

The trees should be *planted* in ditches deep enough to cover the roots. The *plants* should be *planted* about two inches apart in the rows.

No war vessels may be built on the Great Lakes. That is the reason why the imitation warship for *exhibition* was built at the World's Columbian *Exhibition*.

Repetitions which Violate Emphasis.—The bad effects of faulty repetitions are aggravated when, as in the sentence just quoted, the word repeated closes groups of words or sentences, especially when the groups are successive. Not only does such a way of concluding the word-group or sentence make the word repeated unduly conspicuous, but it violates the principle already considered, that each sentence as a whole and each word-group within the sentence shall progress from what has been said towards what is to be said. By stopping forward motion, it destroys the effect of intellectual energy and purpose.

He soon had his chores done and was in the house getting ready to go; and at a quarter past nine he came down stairs ready to go.

Muskrat houses have two stories inside: one high and dry and the other under water. The outlet being under water, it is important to find out where it is before setting a trap.

His chief inheritance was from his mother. He inherited the ability to draw from his father. But this talent was never cultivated. He also inherited a hot temper and tenacity of purpose from his father.

It is a delicate feeling for the necessity of advance that causes the writer of the following sentences to place the repeated word at the beginning of the group of words in which it occurs.

He who cannot look forward with comfort must find what comfort he can in looking backward.

Cowper, *Letters.*

The purport of the letter is a direct accusation of me, and of her an accusation implied, that we have both deviated into forbidden paths.   *Ibid.*

RECAPITULATION

Within a sentence, the actual units of thought are not single words, but groups of words, each of which is uttered at one impulse, and in each of which a single word is generally central and dominant. This central word tends to come toward the end of the group. Groups in general naturally take their beginning in something suggested by what has passed, and lead on to what follows. The result is a continuous linkage of group with group. The final group tends to be the most emphatic in the sentence, the introductory group the next so. The introductory group generally relates to what has preceded, the final group to what is to follow; in this way by the emphasis of the groups connection of sentence with sentence is secured. In addition explicit connectives are sometimes required. There is a danger of excessive closeness of connection in this method, and there is a danger of depending too much on a single type of transition. Weakness in the ending of a sentence is to be avoided; the last group, not necessarily the last word, should be relatively important.

In general, introductory groups implying predication, for example, adjectives, participles, gerunds, and elliptical clauses, tend to be connected in idea with the grammatical subject. Loosely attached adjective expressions in other parts of the sentence may refer to the subject, or to the nearest important substantive; loosely attached participles in particular, in all parts of the sentence, tend to refer to the subject. As to adverbial expressions, it is sometimes uncertain whether they are connected with what precedes or with what follows.

Among the most important means of heightening emphasis is suspense, which is attained: (1) by expanding the subject before presenting the predicate; (2) by placing modifiers before the words modified; (3) by the use of parentheses; (4) by the use of correlatives. Sentences in which the meaning is not grammatically complete until the end of the sentence are called periodic, in the strict sense; other sentences are loose. There may be an element of suspense in loose sentences, and the effect of suspense sometimes results from the general movement of the sentence, not strictly from its syntax. Emphasis is heightened by giving to coördinate groups (1) balance, (2) antithesis, (3) climax, and (4) an increase in volume. Such forms of structure should correspond to the true logic of the sentence, and not be mere artifices of effect. The repetition of words is sometimes a means of emphasis; that of unemphatic words by contributing to clearness of relation or to vigor of antithesis, of emphatic words by expressing emotional intensity. Untrained writers repeat words clumsily, and often in violation of the real connection of their ideas.

CHAPTER VI

THE SENTENCE: THE BROAD RELATIONS OF SOUND AND SENSE

I. PLEASANTNESS OF SOUND

Good Prose Agreeable.—Many writers feel that it is insincere to give conscious attention to the sound of their sentences. There is, for example, a saying of Cato the Censor, which has been Englished, "Take care of the sense and the sounds will take care of themselves." This is not true. It is not enough to take care of the sense, that is, of the exact meaning and the logic of a sentence. To take care of the sense will write a sentence to an intelligent tune; but a well written sentence should have other excellences which are manifested through the sound;—dignity, charm, movement, beauty. Language is a social affair—a matter between writer and reader. A well written sentence is in "English sweet upon the tongue."

Elements of Attractiveness in Prose.—Agreeable prose has at least these two qualities: it is easy of utterance, and it has a certain patterning or recurrence of sound. In other words, it is free from obstruction, and it has a pattern, not too exact.

II. EASE OF UTTERANCE

As for ease of utterance, it depends mainly on the actual sequence of the separate sounds which make up

the words.   The most fluent language is made up of a
single vowel at a time followed by a single consonant
at a time, and so on.   Vowels without consonants between them must be mouthed:—

> Tho' oft the ear the open vowels tire.

Masses of consonants close the mouth and make enunciation difficult.

> Amidst the mists
> With stoutest boasts
> He thrusts his fists
> Against the posts
> And still insists
> He sees the ghosts.

Excess of Consonants.—The English language is consonantal, and in it care is most needed to avoid accumu-
lations of harsh and close sounds.   The sounds of *t*, in
a less degree of *k*, and above all of *s* give the greatest
amount of trouble.   The following sentences illustrate
some of the commoner forms of obstruction.

How can anyone expect that the subje*ct sh*ould be of any
advantage to the student if he ju*st st*udies it to make a passing
grade?

The highe*st p*anegyric tha*t p*riva*t*e *v*irtue can receive is the
praise of servants.

During hi*s st*ewardship he ha*s st*eadily resi*st*ed the wor*st*
distractions and the subtle*st* seductions which were mo*st s*uited
to hi*s* sanguine disposition.

Sibilance.—The English language has a bad reputation for its sibilant or hissing character.   Tennyson
used always to revise his verses "to kick the geese out
of boat," that is, to put out the s's; and in the work
of the Irish poet, Mr. W. B. Yeats, "S must never mee*t*

S: 'for his sake' was inadmissible. [It was] a terrifying cacophony."

If Mr. Yeats was too fastidious, the writers of the following sentences may justly be charged with the opposite fault.

The Gauls had for some centuries ceased their wanderings.

Steele's style has been severely criticized.

Examples.—The following passages illustrate the nature of the fluency and ease attainable in the English language without artificiality and effort by writers who are sensitive to the effects of sound.

[The writer dramatically represents the ancient writers as contending with the moderns. One of the Ancients compares the Moderns to spiders, and themselves to bees.] As for us, the Ancients, we are content with the bee, to pretend to nothing of our own beyond our wings and our voice: that is to say, our flights and our language. For the rest, whatever we have got has been by infinite labour and search, and ranging through every corner of nature; the difference is that instead of dirt and poison, we have rather chosen to fill our hives with honey and wax; thus furnishing mankind with the two noblest of things, which are sweetness and light.

Swift, *The Battle of the Books.*

A loving Heart is the beginning of all Knowledge. This it is that opens the whole mind, quickens every faculty of the intellect to do its work, that of *knowing;* and therefrom, by sure consequence, of *vividly uttering forth.* Other secret for being *graphic* is there none, worth having; but this is an all-sufficient one. See, for example, what a small Boswell can do! Hereby, indeed, is the whole man made a living mirror, wherein the wonders of this ever-wonderful Universe are, in their true light (which is ever a magical, miraculous one) represented, and reflected back on us. It has been said, "the heart sees farther than the head"; but, indeed, without the seeing heart there is no seeing for the head so much as possible; all is mere *oversight,* hallucination and vain superficial phantasmagoria, which can permanently profit no one.

Carlyle. *First Essay on Boswell.*

III.   RECURRENCE OF SOUNDS

Alliteration.—The second grace of sound is *pattern;* —symmetry, some sort of recurrence. The most mechanical recurrence is that of a consonantal sound. Repeating the consonant at the beginning of stressed syllables, but not the following vowel, is a frequent means of decoration or emphasis. This jingle of initial sounds, which is called alliteration, has helped to keep alive many current phrases: "safe and sound"; "sick and sorry"; "widows' weeds"; "tip-top"; "fat, fair, and forty"; "a pig in a poke." Alliteration sometimes heightens an emotional passage, or sharpens an antithesis; though an excessive or conscious pursuit of the letter easily makes writing gaudy, or smart, or mechanical, yet there can be no doubt that when appropriate a certain amount of alliteration, especially if it is not too obvious, lends to style sometimes charm, sometimes vivacity.

The following passages illustrate the use of alliteration as an emotional heightening.

The flame of liberty, the light of intellect, was to be extinguished with the sword—or with slander, whose edge is sharper than the sword.

> Hazlitt, *Coleridge and Godwin.*

In one of those beautiful valleys through which the Thames, not yet polluted with the tide, the scouring of cities, or even the minor defilement of the sandy streams of Surrey, rolls a clear flood through flowery meadows and under the shade of old beech woods, and the smooth glossy greensward of the chalk hills. . . .

> Peacock, *Crotchet Castle.*

The wreath was to be of wild olive, mark you:—the tree that grows carelessly; tufting the rocks with no vivid bloom, no verdure of branch; only with soft snow of blossom, and scarcely fulfilled fruit, mixed with grey leaf and thorn-set

stem; no fastening of diadem for you but with such sharp em-
broidery.   Ruskin, *Crown of Wild Olive.*

The per*f*ume of the *l*ittle *f*lowers of the *l*ime-tree *f*ell through
the air upon them like rain; while time seemed to *m*ove ever
*m*ore slowly to the *m*urmur of the bees in it, till it *st*ood almost
*st*ill on June afternoons.   Pater, *The Child in the House.*

The following examples illustrate the use of alliteration
tion to give spice to an antithesis by insisting on the
balance of opposed words.

Spare the rod and spoil the child.

Take care of the pence and the pounds will take care of
themselves.

The Puritans hated bear-baiting not because it gave pain to
the bear, but because it gave pleasure to the spectators.

Excessive alliteration, either for emotional, or for
opigrammatic effects, produces the impression of insincerity, or of sentimental weakness, and may stop forward
motion.   The following sentences illustrate one or the
other of these faults.

No clearer or diviner waters ever sang with constant lips of
the hand which "giveth rain from heaven"; no pastures ever
lightened in spring with more passionate blossoming; no
sweeter homes ever hallowed the heart of the passer-by with
their pride of peaceful gladness—fain-hidden—yet full-con-
fessed.   Ruskin, *The Crown of Wild Olive.*

O divine nature, O heavenly nobility, what thing can there
more be required in a prince than in greatest power to show
greatest patience, in chiefest glory to bring forth chiefest
grace, in abundance of all earthly glory to manifest abundance
of all heavenly piety! O fortunate England that hath such
a Queen, ungrateful, if thou pray not for her, wicked if thou
do not love her, miserable, if thou lose her.

                              Lyly, *Euphues.*

Rhyme, Actual or Approximate.—The recurrence of
a whole syllable, or even of a consonant followed by a

vowel, is commonly unpleasant, especially at the ends of words.   For example:

This is due both to the fact that the land is rolling, and that this part of the state is comparative*ly* dense*ly* populated.

How is this enlightenm*ent* to be brought to the stud*ent*?

. . . seated immovable by the dead fire and *dy*ing lights in the *di*ning-room; *rating* her in harsh tones, *reiterating* old *re*-proaches.

The student *fi*nally *fi*nds the truth.

Actual rhyme in prose,—the identity of that part of two words beginning with the stressed vowel sound,—is effective only when the words stand near together, and the balanced in a group.   Such groups are: *high and dry; near and dear; rough, and tough, and hard to bluff; John Doe and Richard Roe.*

The crudity of recurring syllables is of course the greater when supplemented by alliterations.

A *g*ood *g*ra*d*e of *grain* must be produced, if he is to *rea*lize a *rea*sonable profit.

By this means we gain an *in*sight *into* an *in*teresting phase of life.

A *seem*ingly *sim*ple substance may prove to be compound.

Finally, there was a law, carefully framed, *De repetundis,* to exact retribution from pro-consuls or pro-praetors of the type of Verres, who had plundered the provinces.   All governors were *re*quired, on *re*linquishing office, to make a double *re*turn of their accounts, one to *re*main for inspection among the archives of the province, and one to be sent to Rome; and where peculation or injustice could be proved, the offender's estate was made answerable to the last sesterce.

Rhythm.—A less mechanical and more attractive kind of pattern than the recurrence of sounds is the arrangement of stressed and unstressed syllables in order; that is to say, rhythm. An entire absence of rhythmic quality, or the abrupt inadequacy of rhythm at the end of a sentence or important word-group is unpleasant.

I believe that Chemistry is a subject that every student who desires a thorough education should take; and from my study of this branch of science, I have found that I have derived many benefits.

The loose plot of the Heart of Mid-Lothian may be explained by Scott's having for his chief character a real woman, for in real life it is very seldom if ever that two people's lives run parallel from birth to death, and have the same circumstances affecting both.

At Athens the word music comprehended from the beginning everything appertaining to the province of the Nine Muses, not merely the use of the lyre, or how to bear part in a chorus, but also the hearing, learning, and repeating of poetical compositions, as well as the practice of exact and elegant pronunciation—which latter accomplishment, in a language like the Greek, with long words, measured syllables, and great diversity of accentuation between one word and another, must have been far more difficult to acquire than it is in any modern European language.

On the other hand, exact rhythm, or a close approach to exact rhythm, sounds very affected and sentimental. In the following passage, a number of lines of blank verse follow each other, and a number of others are enclosed by brief phrases of connection. The verse is not sufficiently finished to be good poetry, but it is definite enough to become bad prose.

> Thus the child came to be an old man, and
> his once smooth face was wrinkled and his step
> was slow and feeble and his back was bent.
> And one night as he lay upon his bed,
> his children standing round, he cried, as he
> had cried so long ago:—"I see the star!"
> They whispered one another, "He is dying!"

And he said: "I am;
my age is falling from me like a garment,
and I move toward the star as a child.
    "And, O My Father, now I thank thee that
it has so often opened to receive
those dear ones who await me!" And the star
was shining; and it shines upon his grave.

Dickens, A Child's Dream of a Star.

The best prose, however, has a broad rhythm, a rhythm not to be measured by syllables, but of groups of words somewhat alike as a whole in emphasis and sound, having a certain balance but not standing still or returning later to any point already passed over, either in throught or sound.

I have of late, but wherefore I know not, lost all my mirth, foregone all custom of exercises; and indeed it goes so heavily with my disposition that this goodly frame, the earth, seems to me a sterile promontory; this most excellent canopy, the air, look you,—this brave o'erhanging firmament, this majestical roof, fretted with golden fire,—why, it appears no other thing to me than a foul and pestilent congregation of vapors. What a piece of work is a man! how noble in reason, how infinite in faculty; in form and moving how express and admirable; in action, how like an angel, in apprehension, how like a god! the beauty of the world, the paragon of animals! And yet to me, what is this quintessence of dust?

Shakespeare, Hamlet.

To begin them with Shakespeare. He was the man who of all modern, and perhaps ancient poets, had the largest and most comprehensive soul. All the images of nature were still present to him, and he drew them not laboriously, but luckily: when he describes anything, you more than see it, you feel it too. Those who accuse him to have wanted learning, give him the greater commendation: he was naturally learned; he needed not the spectacles of books to read nature; he looked inwards, and found her there. I cannot say he is everywhere alike; were he so, I should do him injury to compare him with the greatest of mankind. He is many times flat, insipid; his comic wit degenerating into clenches, his serious swelling into bombast. But he is always great, when some great occasion is presented to him: no man can say he ever had a fit subject for his wit, and did not then raise himself as high above the rest of poets,

Quantum lenta solent inter viburna cupressi. [As do the cypresses among the laggard shrubs.]

Dryden, *Essay of Dramatic Poesy.*

When we could endure no more upon the water, we to a little ale-house on the Bankside, over against the Three-Cranes, and there stayed till it was dark almost, and saw the fire grow; and as it grew darker, appeared more and more; and in corners and upon steeples, and between churches and houses, as far as we could see up the hill of the city, in a most horrid, malicious, bloody flame, not like the fine flame of an ordinary fire. Barbary and her husband away before us. We stayed till, it being darkish, we saw the fire as only one entire arch of fire from this to the other side the bridge, and in a bow up the hill for an arch of above a mile long: it made me weep to see it. The churches, houses, and all on fire, and flaming at once; and a horrid noise the flames made, and the cracking of houses at their ruin. So home with a sad heart.

Pepys, *Diary,* 2d September, 1666.

Night is a dead monotonous period under a roof; but in the open world it passes lightly, with its stars and dews and perfumes, and the hours are marked by changes in the face of Nature. What seems a kind of temporal death to people choked between walls and curtains, is only a light and living slumber to the man who sleeps afield. All night long he can hear Nature breathing deeply and freely; even as she takes her rest, she turns and smiles; and there is one stirring hour unknown to those who dwell in houses, when a wakeful influence goes abroad over the sleeping hemisphere, and all the outdoor world are on their feet. It is then that the cock first crows, not this time to announce the dawn but like a cheerful watchman speeding the course of night. Cattle awake on the meadows; sheep break their fast on dewy hillsides, and change to a new lair among the ferns; and houseless men, who have lain down with the fowls, open their dim eyes and behold the beauty of the night.

Stevenson, *Travels with a Donkey;* by permission of C. Scribner's Sons.

RECAPITULATION

Prose should, except for special reasons, be agreeable in sound. It should be easily spoken, not clogged by consonants, and it should have a certain symmetry or recurrent pattern. Alliteration is a form of recurrence, ugly if casual and inappropriate, disagreeable if excessive, but effective in moderation, either for intellectual or emotional heightening of style. Actual or approximate rhyme is usually unpleasant. A total absence of rhythm is repellent, an excess of rhythm is intolerable, but a large rhythm, not of syllables but of groups, may be pleasant and natural. The conscious cultivation of any of these elements of style is fraught with danger to sincere directness; variety is essential.

CHAPTER VII

WORDS

I. LEVELS OF DICTION

The Mastery of Words.—To put the parts of a composition together effectively is a fine achievement. It manifests admirable mental qualities;—sound judgment, steady attention, insight, energy, logic, tact. Yet after all the most important question about a piece of writing is not whether B comes before A or A before B, but whether either A or B is worth saying. When the bee blundered into the spider's web and tore it to pieces, he was willing to praise the engineering, but could not compliment the materials. The materials—the substance —the things thought out and put into words, these are what give real value to a piece of writing. Vision and force, liveliness and charm, the genuine qualities of the writer's mind, are expressed in the individual ideas in his work, and these are manifested most of all by his words. The structure is a storehouse; the riches to which the structure gives display shine out in the words. Skill in arrangement depends upon a few principles, which may be learned by any sensible person who will submit to a brief discipline; effectiveness of vocabulary results from a special energy of the mind;—keenness of the senses, vivacious interests, the imaginative power to see likeness in unlikeness, together with a sensitiveness to the effects of words, both natural and developed. Words must be learned by thousands, one at a time, and cannot be reduced to principles; they must be learned not only with the intellect but with the imagination and the feelings. The mastery of words, then, is the most difficult and the most interesting part of the skill of language.

Special Languages.—Imagine yourself listening to the grateful acknowledgments of someone who hears of an unexpected favor. In what words will they be uttered? In different words to different people, and certainly in very different words by different people. A girl of the period will not say to her aunt, "Fine! fine!" or an enterprising young business man to a fellow member of the Rotary Club, "You are very kind," or a lively boy to a companion in mischief, "Oh, how dear of you!" or an elderly lady of formal manners to her clergyman, "Bully for you!" To each kind of speaker and for each kind of situation a special language, differing in many points, but differing above all in vocabulary. Within the great circle of English there are many languages, limited and peculiar to certain sets of people and to certain relations. Everybody's language is more or less individual, and every group of people has in a sense its own group-language. Craftsmen must name their processes and their tools and the things they make. Towns have their ways of speech. The game of marbles has a set of technicalities and a body of technical terms in one place which are never heard of in another place: *taws* and *knuckles* and *fend-dibs* are unknown here and sacred formulas there; *vant* is a common word of incantation in most towns but not in all; and the game itself is *mibbles* in one slang but not in another. Families have their own little languages, and the more vigorous their life, the more their speech will abound in peculiar expressions and allusions unintelligible to an outsider. Sometimes two brothers will have their own secret words; who has not seen boys go into fits of laughter at the comic suggestion of *dibbits* or *pyrums*—words of their own in which no one else has any rights and of which no one else has any knowledge?

Dialects.—The people of a little neighborhood group speak very much in the same way; those of a bigger group speak roughly alike; those of a still bigger group have a language easily intelligible, though the most remote members speak in a way that seems odd to the others. Southeh-nehs, and Westerr-nerrs, and East-anas, all Americans; Scotsmen, Irishmen, and London-ers,—all speak good English, and all speak the same language. But how different it sounds!

Varieties of English.—The English language, then, is the name for a great many various ways of speaking, all more or less unlike, some very unlike the others, but all centering about a body of usages having much in common. The written language, of course, is much more at one than the spoken. An English humorist rhymes:

> They said, "Caccabee, caccabaw,"
> And they said nothing more.

An American could not make the two words sound enough alike to make a joke of such a rhyme. An American rhymes *clerk* and *work;* an Englishman *clerk* and *dark*. But all English-speaking people spell the words *more* and *clerk*.

The Lower Levels of Diction.—The mass of the English language, accordingly, has a central body of common words, belonging to everybody's vocabulary, and in place as part of every type of speech, formal and informal, technical, professional, east, west, north, and south,—words recognizably alike in sound in everybody's pronunciation, and practically identical in everybody's spelling. Such are all short words indicating connection, logic, and the relations of thought: *the, to, and; shall, can; me, who.* Such are the names of the common things and actions which are part of daily life: *sleep, hat, dislike, brown, telephone, know.* These words everybody not only is familiar with, but must use if he uses the English language at all. Now in a certain sense below this central group of words, and almost but not quite so universally well known, there are words which nearly everybody employs in familiar talk, but does not freely use on formal occasions, or in writing and print. Such are the common contractions—it *is n't,* he *has n't,* they *would n't,*—which are acceptable to every English-speaking person in free-and-easy conversation, but which would be ventured upon by few in perfectly serious printed prose on any important matter. A *crack* tennis player, to *back down,* a *regular* (*i. e.* thorough) villain, a *stand-by,* a *cad,* a *chap,* a *chum,* a *chunk, galore,* a *slump* in prices, the play was *a success,* are examples of expressions, known to all the world, not out of place in the speech of ordinary familiar intercourse, but carrying with them a certain tone of informality, which makes them noticeable in serious writing. And it is possible to carry this tendency to informality further and further from the center. He *does n't* is familiar; he *don't* is a mistake, but not a vulgar mistake; he *ain't* is uneducated but not impossible for half-educated people; he *hain't* is an illiterate and

socially disqualifying error. *I have drank* is disagree-
ably incorrect; it is incorrect as people are incorrect
who try to be correct without knowing how; *I clumb out
of the window* is incorrect as people are incorrect who
accept an obsolete tradition without knowing the difference. It is not so unpleasant as *I have drank,* but it
makes most people wonder where the speaker was
brought up. *Goin'* is free-and-easy; *go'n'* (I 'm *go'n'*
away) is slovenly and unpleasant. *Gwine* is over the
line of what is recognized as quite tolerable. Thus there
are grades of departure from the center;—recognized
colloquialisms, disapproved improprieties, and unac-
cepted vulgarisms, marks of imperfect education or of
ignorance.

Bookish Words.—Similarly, on the other side of the
mass of common words, are words appropriate especially in more formal speech and in written language.
The transition from class to class is gradual. Of a
given word it may not be easy to say that it is distinctly
a book-word or a talk-word; but of the body of words
in a composition it is not difficult to perceive whether
they are bookish or familiar. We recognize the language
of a formal man as a trifle stiff for daily intercourse.
Omit and *proceed* and *postpone* are not unfamiliar
words or at all out of place in ordinary conversation; but
a man who habitually *omits* and *proceeds* and *postpones*
and never *leaves out* or *goes on* or *puts off* is an intolerable prig. *Detach* and *desist* and *scintillate* and *com-
modious* are somewhat more formal still. (Compare
unloose and *release, stop* and *cease, sparkle* and *flash,
roomy and spacious.*) *Irretrievable, cismontane, sibyl-
line, saturnine, oxygenate,* are decidedly book-words, and
would each be conspicuous in common talk.

Elevated Diction.—Again, some words belong to language not so much bookish as exalted, and adapted to occasions of a certain warmth and sacredness—to oratory if not to poetry. Such are *clad* and *forth* (for *out* or *away*), *whatsoever, billows, fraught.* To say of a group of nurses, "We sent them forth clad in the white garb of mercy," is neither book-language, nor common language, but the language of decorative solemnity. "The cismontane countries had met with irretrievable disaster," is book-language of learned uncommonness. "We measured the detached scintillations emitted by the substance in a state of radio-activity," is book-language meant to be very accurate. "We shall omit the next chapter" has just a tinge of formality, and sounds like a teacher, not like a pupil.

Dialect Words.—Now, all these classes of words, whether appropriate or inappropriate in any given case, belong within the central body of the English language. They are not the language of a region, or a sect, or an occupation. They are words special not to persons, but to circumstances,—smoking-jacket words, business-coat words, or dress-coat words. They are familiar, scholastic, low or lofty, everywhere and to all English-speaking persons. But there are more divergent and special vocabularies still. For example, my language is English: well, what do I fetch up coal in? a hod, a bucket, a scuttle, or perhaps even a pail? If I live in Nebraska, I mean by a *gopher* a little animal like a chipmunk, in mid-California a creature as big as a good-sized rat, in some parts of the South a burrowing tortoise, and in other parts of the South a snake. Thus to some extent my language is colored or at least tinged by the place where I live. If I am not at all book-learned, and

live in an isolated region, where the population has not
mixed much with the rest of the world, my speech may
diverge so much from that of common English as to be
quite unintelligible except to those who are within my
particular circle. I am likely to say, "Draw the sneck
(latch) and come ben (in)"; or, "Those thunder-bugs
(midges) did kiddle (tickle) me so that I couldn't keep
still no hows." Thus, there is a divergence from central
English in what we call dialect, affecting everybody's
language, but extreme only for the uneducated.

Foreign Words.—Again, take such a word as *piano;*
that is certainly an English word. So is *violin.* Is
'cello? is *violoncello?* Is *legato?* Certainly not, yet it
ought to be in an English dictionary. *Cantabile* is an
Italian word borrowed, not naturalized, but not wholly
strange. *Lo stesso tempo* is really and completely foreign. So one may follow an unbroken sequence of Latin
words from resident aliens like *ex tempore* and *sine die*
to Latin that has no idea of migrating into English, like
monumentum aere perennius, or of French words from
rendezvous to *peu de chose.* There is, then, a body of
foreign words, once foreign, now quite naturalized; there
are others less completely a part of the language; and
so gradually away from the center of English to a
clearly and completely non-English vocabulary. In the
main these foreign words are related to the language
of books and learning, not in the same way, but in a
way somewhat such as that in which dialect is to the
colloquial language.

Technical Words.—Moreover, there is a language for
every occupation. Every English-speaking person uses
the words *plow* and *hammer, jacket* and *anvil;* he understands *plowshare, face of a hammer, gore,* and *auger-*

bit; but *clevis, peen, felled seam,* and *terret* are words
of the farmer, the mechanic, the seamstress, and the
harness-maker. These words, to those who have occasion to use them, are words of common talk; they have
no color of learning or trace of bookishness. On the
other hand, scientists have their special terms, capable
of being classified in a series gradually more and more
remote from the central vocabulary. A *degree* on a
thermometer, a *volt,* the *force of gravity* are now fairly
established in the language of most people. *Isotherm,
static electricity, ultra-violet rays* are more remote from
common knowledge and from common speech. *Endo-
tropic, geosyncline, sextile, spinthariscope* are far within
the central territory of the branches of learning to
which each belongs. It is plain that the language of
learning and of familiar life has each its groups of
divergences from the common language, current for
special occupations, technical and scientific words being
in a way correlative to each other.

Slang.—There remains a special part of the colloquial
vocabulary by which the ocean is known as the *Pond,*
or the *Fish-pond,* the high-way as the *grit,* the human
face as the *picture,* and in which *Nit!* and *Nix!* and
Not so, but far otherwise are familiar negatives. This
is slang. It is not easy to define slang, for the name
and the thing shade off from a central meaning to cover
colloquial, vulgar, and dialectic usages. As the word
is employed here, it does not mean the special language
of the disreputable or the vulgar—the *cant* of thieves
or the *low language* of the debased, nor is it simply an
intentional novelty or irreverent freedom with the language. The first man who called the head a *cocoa-nut*
was not using slang, but giving a free-and-easy turn to

his speech. When he kept on using the term and when others took it up—when it "caught on"—it became slang. "You bet your boots," was slang once; it is now "old." "Believe *me*," was the later slang for the same idea; "*I 'll* say it is," is current at the present minute (10 A. M. January 3, 1919). Slang has three characteristics: it is colloquial, it is irreverent in spirit, and it is a fashion.

Poetic Diction.—On the other side there is a vocabulary specially assigned to exalted occasions or to verse, and so far remote from standard usage that it is not part of the central vocabulary. Milton's *auxiliar* for *auxiliary,* Tennyson's *rathe* for *early,* Keats's *lush* for *luxuriant, enfetter, compare* as a noun, *lucent, yestereve* belong to the language of verse.

The following diagram, slightly modified from that given in the preface of Murray's great dictionary,

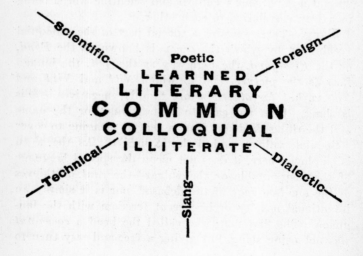

roughly illustrates the relation of these groups of words in the English vocabulary.

Cultivate the Upper Part of the Central Vocabulary.—Now what of this immeasurable English vocabulary, with its clear center and its indefinite margin, ought a writer to use, or let us say to cultivate? Why, plainly, that depends upon his object and his public. A thief, speaking to thieves, and quite at home among them, ought to use thieves' cant. A geologist, talking to geologists about geology, uses his scientific language without thinking about it. There are a place and a function for every type of speech—for dialectic remoteness, and poetic strangeness, and slangy freedom, and mercantile curtness, and industrial technicality. But in general, for most purposes and as a matter of practice, one who uses English should make an effort to command the central part of the language. Most people, most of the time, wish to be understood; and they can count most safely on being understood if they use the vocabulary most widely current. That is to say, they had better keep to the center, avoiding the technical, the scientific, the dialectic, the foreign,—avoiding also the uncommon words of learned curiosity, and avoiding slang, an expert knowledge of which at any time is confined to the initiated. Yet it is not enough to be understood; a writer would wish his language to be acceptable—to be such that the mere look or sound of his words should at least not be unpleasant to the people whom he addresses and make them disinclined to pay attention to him. Now, it is the "common" vocabulary—the familiar but not distinctly colloquial—that is most acceptable; and next to that the familiar part of what may be called educated language. To be free-and-easy always, to use colloquial speech on serious matters, is felt to savor of frivolity and discourtesy, and hence tends to close the ears of the public to one's message. A stump speaker will not help his party by calling his opponent a "chump"; the writer of a letter of apology will not smooth over a difficulty by hoping that he will not "get in bad." "Cheeky," and "spliff," and "limelight," and "pep" in serious writing will prejudice at least some people against the writer, while *pert,* and *fine,* and *foreground,* and *fire* will not offend anyone. Likewise, to go too far the other way, to suggest condescension or pedantry of speech, is as fatal to the acceptability of one's language. An author who says, "It is my intention,"—"It is my expectation,"—"Permit me to register an objection," for "I mean,"—"I expect,"—"I object," who is very free with such words as *pragmatic* (fussy), *lugubrious* (mournful), *irrefutable* (unanswerable), *meticulous* (finical), raises a strong prejudice against himself. The most generally acceptable part of our language is the language of educated people not scholastic, not artificially elevated, not strange, not foreign or scientific, not in any way special,—and at the same time not taking liberties, not low, not flatly commonplace. That is to say, one should strive to write, not as one talks, but as, if given a trifle of time to think, one would like to talk to a company of people whom one respects and would be glad to influence.

From this standard it is comparatively easy on occasion to depart; but it is not so easy to obey it if your language is habitually centered elsewhere. It is not hard to be colloquial; it is not hard to be impertinent and slangy; it is not hard to be formal. It is easy to be technical or scientific. But it is not at all easy with-

out the support of habit to reach the center: to be at
ease without becoming slipshod or flippant, to be self-
respecting and respectful of others without becoming
academic or pompous, to be exact without being pedantic,
and serious without being solemn, and gay without being facetious. Yet to aim at any standard lower than
this is likely to make one's writing cheap, tedious, vulgar,
or provincial.

II. ON ACQUIRING A VOCABULARY

Good Reading the Basis.—How acquire the mastery
of words? We acquire a language as members of a
company. We imitate our parents and the older persons
in our family; we imitate our school-fellows; we pick
up the language of our trade and of our social set from
our fellow-craftsmen and our acquaintances. In all
these parts of our language we learn by direct conscious
or unconscious imitation of the ways of individual people. It is the same with the language of print and
writing. The language that befits writing is learned
from good writing, and most easily and naturally by
great familiarity with it. There is a tradition of the
best in English, namely, the usage of those who most
truly,—that is, with the most delicate exactness, most
movingly,—that is, with the greatest power to awaken
sympathy, and most tactfully,—that is, most acceptably
to all the world, have expressed their ideas in English
books. The fundamental step, therefore, for those who
are learning to write is to get into the tradition of Good
English by reading standard books. English-speaking
people who do not do this, who do not know the great
English books, are not full sharers in the civilization
which controls their lives. Having rejected the wealth

of ideas which belongs to every member of the English-speaking community who will open his hand to it, they have earned a penalty which comes of itself—the penalty of being unintelligent, common, raw, and poor in word as well as in thought. Frequent, accurate, and careful reading of books worth the pains is the foundation of simply decent writing, of the writing, that is, of decently educated people.

Thorough Reading.—Much reading may well be done with great rapidity, but some reading should be done with minute and exact thoroughness,—with a scrupulous weighing of each word, utilizing a large dictionary and every necessary help, until the exact meaning of the words literally used, and the full emotional weight of allusions and of figures of speech are mastered and taken home to the reader. Not every kind of writing will endure or reward such scrutiny, but the best writing will abundantly repay the labor spent upon it, in the enrichment of the ideas as well as in the enrichment and improvement of the vocabulary of the student. Consider, for instance, the following passages.

A man that can succeed in working is to me always a man. How one loves to see the burly figure of him, this thick-skinned, seemingly opaque, perhaps sulky, almost stupid Man of Practice, pitted against some light adroit Man of Theory, all equipt with clear logic, and able anywhere to give you Why for Wherefore! The adroit Man of Theory, so light of movement, clear of utterance, with his bow full-bent and quiver full of arrow-arguments,—surely he will strike down the game, transfix everywhere the heart of the matter; triumph everywhere, as he proves that he shall and must do? To your astonishment it proves oftenest No. The cloudy-browed, thick-soled, opaque Practicality, with no logic utterance, in silence mainly, with here and there a low grunt or growl, has in him what transcends all logic-utterance: a Congruity with the Unuttered. The Speakable, which lies atop, as a superficial film,

or outer skin, is his or is not his: but the Doable, which reaches
down to the World's centre, you find him there!

Carlyle, Past and Present.

(Define: burly, opaque, pitted, adroit, equip, utterance, transcend, congruity, superficial. Is the man
opaque because the light within cannot shine out, or because the light without cannot shine in? Why should
an effective worker in the world be sulky? Pitted,—
for a contest, as game-cocks used to fight in a pit.
Light,—nimble; adroit,—full of resource in delicate
rather than massive ways of attack. The figure from
archery makes tangible and real the common phrase,
"the heart of the matter." Proves,—how? Cloudy-
browed,—grim of countenance, as the conflict with the
facts of the world has made him. Thick-soled,—clumsy
of step and not delicate of sensibility, so as to tread down
negligible obstacles. Congruity with the Unuttered.
The Speakable, which lies atop, as a superficial film, or
outer skin, is his or is not his.—The most fundamental
laws of the world are incapable of being fully expressed
in speech, but men of insight can detect them, and act
in accordance with them, often without being able to explain why. Skin, or film, like the crust of the earth;
the World's centre, the essential depths of fact.)

. . . Look at the manner in which the people of New England have of late carried on the whale-fishery. Whilst we follow them among the tumbling mountains of ice, and behold
them penetrating into the deepest frozen recesses of Hudson's
Bay and Davis's Straits, whilst we are looking for them beneath the arctic circle, we hear that they have pierced into
the opposite region of polar cold, that they are at the antipodes, and engaged under the frozen serpent of the South.
Falkland Island, which seemed too remote and romantic an
object for the grasp of national ambition, is but a stage and
resting-place in the progress of their victorious industry. Nor

is the equinoctial heat more discouraging to them than the accumulated winter of both the poles. We know, that, whilst some of them draw the line and strike the harpoon on the coast of Africa, others run the longitude, and pursue their gigantic game along the coast of Brazil. No sea but what is vexed with their fisheries. No climate that is not witness to their toils. Neither the perseverance of Holland, nor the activity of France, nor the dexterous and firm sagacity of English enterprise, ever carried this most perilous mode of hardy industry to the extent to which it has been pushed by this recent people,—a people who are still, as it it were, but in the gristle, and not yet hardened into the bone of manhood. When I contemplate these things, when I know that the colonies in general owe little or nothing to any care of ours, and that they are not squeezed into this happy form by the constraints of watchful and suspicious government, but that through a wise and salutary neglect, a generous nature has been suffered to take her own way to perfection,—when I reflect upon the effects, when I see how profitable they have been to us, I feel all the pride of power sink, and all presumption in the wisdom of human contrivances melt and die away within me,—my rigor relents,—I pardon something to the spirit of liberty.

Burke, *On Conciliation with America.*

(What is the general meaning of the passage? How do the *mountains of ice tumble?* What are *recesses* in the Straits? What is *the frozen serpent of the South?* What is the point of bringing in the Falkland Islands? Why a *romantic* object of ambition? Why *accumulated* winter? What exactly does *draw the line* mean? *strike the harpoon? run the longitude?* Why is the sea *vexed?* What is the point of attributing to Holland *perseverance,* to France *activity,* to England *enterprise* conducted with *dexterous and firm sagacity?* Why should these nations be mentioned in connection with fisheries? How can *constraint* be said to *squeeze?* How can *neglect* be wise and *salutary?* To take her *own* way-to-perfection? or, to take her own *way* to perfection? *Pride of power,* natural in a people having subject colonies.

Presumption: just what does it mean, especially with *in* instead of *upon? Melt,* a gradual but complete change to a wholly new and less rigid state of mind.)

The Active and the Passive Vocabulary.—Words are most usefully studied in a context, either of one's own writing, or of the writings of others; but there are exercises upon words considered independently which are not without value. For instance, we have all of us two vocabularies—our active and our passive vocabulary; the words we use and the words we only understand without using. We understand *danger, peril,* and *risk,* but it may be we do not use any but the very general word *danger.* Why not say *peril* in cold blood some day, and see if there is any echo? If we become aware that a word is perfectly familiar as a member of our passive vocabulary, we may do well to make a conscious effort to add it to our active vocabulary. Do we say: *abridge, uproar, plausible, innate, feeble, extricate, benevolent, endure, abide, babble, tolerate?* Avoid uncommon words, avoid the appearance of effort and ingenuity, but make a frank effort to widen the active vocabulary to the full extent of the familiar passive vocabulary.

Accuracy.—To do justice to the ideas which they are intended to express, words must be accurate—that is, they must fit the ideas closely, not loosely. A student in an autobiography tells his readers about his schooling. He says, ''The next year I went to work for the first time.'' Does this mean that he then began really to study, or that he then first found paid employment, or that he then for the first time did some physical labor? All these things are *work;* but for any one of them the word work is a very indistinct name.

A soldier-student writes of the difficulty of studying in barracks.

There *are* [better: *The room contains*] no study-tables, and no places to *put* [*lay* is better] books but the window-sill. Another *thing* [*fault of the system, defect of the system, obstacle to studiousness*] is that *there is* no time for study [*no time is assigned, no time is left, the time is so completely occupied as to leave no opportunity for study*].

The effort should be made to use words the extent of whose meaning goes as little beyond the idea intended as is possible. *There is, there are,* and *thing* are the most inclusive words possible; every object or idea *is,* and is a *thing*. *Work* and *are* and *put* and *thing* are loose fits for their ideas; the meaning shakes about in them.

A writer goes over the obstacles which confront a man of small capital who desires to establish a business of his own. "At this rate," he proceeds, "it is impossible for most men without millions to be anything but the hirelings of a corporation." Now a *rate* is a measure of progress, and the author has said nothing about change or movement, but has only enumerated determining facts. He meant, "Under these conditions," or, "Under these circumstances." A speaker on the problems of industrial reconstruction after the late war declared that they were difficult, but that he was optimistic as to the *chance* of a happy solution. A *chance* is a matter of hazard, over which human judgment has no control; but the *solution of a problem* is a matter of intelligence. The speaker would not have been optimistic if he really believed that the solution of this great problem, involving the happiness of millions, were a thing about which mere chance would decide. He meant that he was hopeful about the *prospect* of a happy solution. The words *rate* and *chance* are not mere loose fits for the ideas they are intended to express; they do not actually fit those ideas at all.

Loosely fitting words are too *general;* they should be made as *specific* as possible consistently with the ideas they are to express. The use of a word which does not really fit its idea at all is technically known as an *impropriety*.

The Study of Synonyms.—One means of increasing the accuracy of the vocabulary, by avoiding both generality and impropriety in the use of words, is the study of synonyms. Synonyms are usually best studied along with the definition in a dictionary of large size. Under the careful scrutiny which should be given to one's composition, a question arises with reference to some one word. For example, I have written about persons who are *generally* joking; and something raises a doubt about the use of the word *generally*. I look up [in Webster's Collegiate Dictionary, which I happen to be using] both the adverb *generally* and the adjective *general,* and find the adverb defined as *commonly,* the adjective as *common to many,* with synonyms *common* and *universal.* I turn to *common* and *commonly,* to see if I can get a hint, and find *commonly* defined as *usually, ordinarily; common* is *frequent, customary, usual, familiar. Usual* has the synonyms *customary, habitual.* "Usual applies to whatever happens in the ordinary course of events; that is customary which is according to the usual practices, conventions, usages, etc., whether of an individual, or (especially) of a community; habitual implies settled practice or regularity of repetition, especially of a person or individual." It would seem that I shall speak with most precision of those who are *habitually,* rather of those who are *generally* or *usually,* joking.

It is from one's own writing that words for study are most profitably chosen, because such words are best understood and most accurately remembered. But the study of disconnected words is also valuable; and the study of the following words, often loosely used, with their synonyms, is suggested as the basis for further exercises.

> yell: shout, cry, scream, call, halloa, shriek, vociferate, exclaim.
> start: begin, originate, initiate, inaugurate, invent; set about, undertake; set out, set off, depart; aim at, plan, propose; *start for:* attack, come at.
> ideal: fine, excellent, admirable, transcendent, superior, faultless, perfect; fit, suitable; *an ideal* place etc. *for;* the very place, etc. for, just the place for.
> handle [men, situations, affairs,]: cope with, deal with, meet, manage, conduct.
> do: finish, attain, fulfill, accomplish, execute, perform, achieve.
> business [adjective]: mercantile, commercial.
> care-free: unconcerned, careless, merry, cheerful, sunny.
> grab: snatch, seize, twitch, catch, pluck.
> feature: characteristic, quality, trait, property; point, item, particular, detail; factor, element, ingredient, component.
> tease: wheedle, importune; twit, nag, irritate, annoy.

The following synonyms will also repay study:

> appropriate, apt, suitable, pat, fitting.
> danger, peril, jeopardy, hazard, risk.
> deceit, imposture, fraud, trickery, deception, deceitfulness, sham, humbug.
> defend, protect, look out for, guard.
> find, find out, discover, perceive, detect, hit on, light on.
> hold, contain, comprehend, comprise, include, take in, cover.
> home, dwelling-place, residence, house, house and grounds.

statement, narrative, report, account.
trouble, pains, effort, application, toil, struggle.

The following synonyms contain examples of words which though homely in sound are in perfectly good use.

beat, whack, thump, drub.
bungle, fumble, muddle, botch.
clatter, clang, bang.
climb, scramble, clamber.
clinch, clench, clutch, grip, gripe, grapple.
clink, clank, tinkle, clang, jingle.
clout, patch, cobble.
clutter, rubbish, mess, hodgepodge.
chew, munch, crunch.
crack, crevice, slit, chink.
crooked, awry, askew, aslant.
nonsense, twaddle, trash, claptrap.
poke, nudge, jog, jostle.
roll, trundle.
rub, chafe, fret.
squeak, squawk, cackle; mumble, grumble, mutter; gabble, jabber, chatter.
throw, chuck, toss, flip, heave, fling.
wrestle, tussle, scuffle.
writhe, wriggle, squirm.

The following synonyms have to do with physical impressions.

big, large, great, bulky, ample, vast, huge, voluminous, immense.
heavy, weighty, massive, dense.
yellow, golden, saffron, tan, tawny, sallow, buff, blonde, amber, sandy.
iridescent, prismatic, opalescent, pearly, rainbow-tinted, changeable, watered, shot.
boom, roll, rumble, hum, drone, buzz, murmur, gurgle, purl.
crash, dash, splash, lap.
bland, insipid, tasteless, vapid, mawkish, flat, wishy-washy.
neat, tidy, trim, prim, spruce, smart.

fusty, musty, frowzy.
stir, budge.
halt, limp.
rend, tear.
shake, tremble, quaver, quiver, shiver.
leap, vault, spring.
nestle, squat, perch.
tranquilize, lull, hush.

Translation.—Next after careful writing and reading in one's own language, the most effective discipline in the use of words is to be obtained by translation from foreign languages; but it must be done in the right way, for translation wrongly done will result in more harm than good. A translator should first of all master his original to the last point—catch the author's logic in each little matter of syntax, receive his finest shade of distinction in the choice of synonyms, follow his thought as it develops in the sequence of his words, and if possible feel the suggestions of the intangible elements of his style. A good translation must rest upon better knowledge than is sufficient for a merely literal rendering. Having mastered the original, the good translator must then strive to express all that he can in his own idiom, by the equivalent devices of his own language. Caesar says: *Gallia est omnis divisa in partes tres.* What does Caesar mean by *omnis?* There is no sense in his saying *all* Gaul—*all Gaul* is nothing more than *Gaul.* There were in Caesar's day several territories known to the Romans as Gaul—at least these three: Gaul south of the Alps, a province in what is now southern France, and a vaguely defined part of Europe somewhat larger than modern France. Caesar means this last —"Gaul in the larger sense"—"Gaul as a whole"— "Greater Gaul." *Est divisa* is a perfect tense: does

Caesar mean *has been divided,* as by geographers, or *is divided?* The latter evidently; he deals with a condition attained, not going on. *Partes:* the Latin vocabulary is smaller than the English, and usually less exact in the definition of its thought by its words. *Parts* has too extensive a meaning to suit the English tendency. A *geographical part* is a *region.* "Gaul regarded as a whole is divided into three regions."

His rebus cognitis exploratores centurionesque praemittit qui locum castris idoneum deligant. His rebus cognitis; the Latin language expresses many relations as circumstances of an action, without defining just what relation to the action the circumstances bear; the English vocabulary usually defines the relation: "As soon as." *His rebus:* the Latin language does not define the type of "thing" dealt with as closely as the English usually does: these *facts. Cognitis:* again the English language defines the kind of knowledge—*were ascertained;* or if the relative sequence of time is important, *had been ascertained. Exploratores centurionesque praemittit.* Our idiom places the verb in general before the object; and does not freely use a present tense in narrative: "he sent forward." *Exploratores*— "persons to make an investigation, 'to spy out the land.'" We have no convenient single word; *scouts* will not quite do: "a reconnaissance party." *Centurionesque:* "and several centurions." *Qui . . . deligant:* Caesar states the purpose they were to carry out. We have many ways of indicating a purpose, the least formal being probably an infinitive—"to select," *locum castris idoneum*—"a place—ground—suited for a camp" (*i. e.,* a *fortified* camp). "As soon as this information was received, he sent ahead a reconnaissance party with some centurions to select a place suitable for an encampment.''

Other languages afford the same sort of practice in beating over the ground for the most appropriate synonym, the most effective and natural syntax, and the most expressive order, French having a special vocabulary rich in many fields, especially in color, German affording practice in abstract words and syntax, but on the whole none yielding such valuable results in so many ways as carefully translated Latin and Greek.

III. WASTE WORDS

Closely allied with the habit of using words vaguely and loosely is the habit of using too many words; and the practice of scrutinizing the meaning of words will tend to correct this fault also.

From a theme on the subject: *Is Movie Acting True to Life?*

If we may take for example the average photo-drama, [only an individual instance can be an example; the idea of *average* repeats the idea of *example*.], we find [students are always *finding*] usually [the average must be usual] that the cast consists of a well known hero or heroine, supported by a fairly well known cast [the cast is made both to exclude and to include the hero and heroine], in which we find [*find* again] a villain and not infrequently a comedian. I believe that I can safely say that in the above statement I have diagnosed

Rewritten: In at least four fifths of the motion pictures made, the cast consists of a star hero or heroine, supported by a company of tolerably well known actors, including always a "villain," and not infrequently a comedian.

[*diagnose* involves the idea of detecting an imperfection] eighty per cent of the casts that make motion pictures.

Two students who are rooming together may be of entirely different characters. One of them may pursue his studies vigorously, while the other may loaf at his work. The latter, by his association with his room-mate, will be influenced to devote more attention and time to his studies. This is naturally always true, because the first student has naturally the stronger personality and through his studies has developed it, and will therefore influence the second student. A good example of this kind of influence of student upon student is in the fraternities. The fraternities are anxious that their own shall be rated among the best, and therefore all must attend to their studies. If one student lags behind, the example of the rest of the students is an incentive for the lagging student to spend more time on his work.

Rewritten: Sometimes, of two students who are rooming together, one is diligent, the other a loafer. The latter is likely to be controlled by the inevitably stronger personality of the former. A similar influence of student upon student for good is to be found in the fraternities. Each fraternity is anxious to be rated among the best, and therefore insists that its members shall attend to their studies. Thus the example of the rest of the men pushes on the occasional laggard.

Otiose Words.—One form of wordiness is the use of otiose expressions, such as the following:

We may safely say,—
As we see it today,—
In this day and age,—
Another thing that we may note,—
We find,—

Tends to indicate (for the direct verb *indicates*),
To a large extent,—
There are many who are desirous of obtaining a college
    education [many desire].
He has a witty way about him [a witty way].

Tautology.—A second is tautology, or the useless repetition of an idea in other words, as:

The *contemporary* life of the *time,*—
He is *generally* popular *all over* the *entire* country.
I had not many *fellow classmates.*
Throughout the *entire* story, nature reflects the feelings of
    the characters.
Enough so that, . . .
The *reason* is because, . . .
The makers of the constitution seemed *more* bent on se-
    curing the freedom of the individual *rather* than on
    framing a strong and vital government.

IV. ADAPTATION

The Central Standard.—The main suggestions about vocabulary thus far made amount to this: do not waste words, use exact words, and use familiar words. In practice it will generally be the case that these directions do not conflict, but sometimes the last two will be found to be inconsistent with each other. A writer who strives to be very exact will sometimes be compelled to go a long distance from the familiar body of common words. It is often not practicable to deal with the minutiae of technical subjects except by the use of technical terms, and even about common things, about hearing and seeing, right and wrong, thoughts and actions, very exact ideas and very exact words are not really familiar. A problem for the writer thus arises sometimes—a problem which must be solved in accordance with the circumstances of the case. In truth, there is nothing in writing which is always right, and nothing of which it can be said with certainty that it is always wrong. An old saying runs:

> When of another you would speak,
> Five things observe with care:
> Of whom you speak, to whom you speak,
> And how, and when, and where.

The adage holds good more widely than it was intended. A writer must aim at that degree of exactness and at the same time of familiarity which is demanded by his subject, by his public, and by his particular purpose. When definitely writing as one member of a profession to another member of the same profession, he would waste time by avoiding or explaining the technicalities of the subject:—*off-side plays, or butterises, or interference, or opsonic index, or sigma distance.* These are short-cuts or open roads for the professional mind. With other less instructed publics, such technicalities would be impossible, or would have to be explained. What is needed is a basis,—a way of writing which shall be the most natural and the most adaptable daily habit, a standard to which all one's writing may be referred. To this end, it is best to think of one's public as made up of intelligent, mature people, educated in a general way, but not technically trained, and to think of oneself as addressing this public seriously in print. This is the sound basis, the reliable standard, by accepting which the art of writing is most safely learned. From this standard, as has been suggested, it is possible to depart on occasion, but it is not easy to take it up on a sudden necessity.

Adaptation to Circumstances.—Even with such a public clearly in mind, the degree of accuracy about any particular thing must vary with the particular object of one's writing. There are times when it would be a sheer waste of energy to strive for great exactitude, and other times when no effort is too great for the occasion. If one were thinking what the weather was likely to be, it would commonly be absurd to define the color of a sunset cloud or sky by any but the vaguest adjectives —*red,* or *bright;* but if one desired to share the pleasure excited by the color, it might be quite reasonable to speak of a *saffron cloud,* or *an apple-yellow streak of sky near the horizon.* An eye might be casually spoken of as *black;* the same eye might under other circumstances be described as having the *hue of obsidian,* for instance, if a writer desired to insist on marks of Indian descent, and to suggest the peculiar dense, impenetrable, shining, dark, unchanging Indian eye. In advising persons little experienced in business about the effect of contracts which they might make for buying or selling land, it might be important to draw a sharp distinction between a *broker,* who arranges purchases or sales for another, and an *agent,* who acts in any business as the representative of another. Under most circumstances it might make little difference whether you called a man a real estate *agent* or a real estate *broker.* In one story of Arizona, it would be important to distinguish between a *side-winder* and a *diamond-back;* in another it would be enough to speak of a *rattlesnake,* of a *snake,* or even of a *reptile.* Speaking broadly, writing is good in proportion as it is exact in ideas, especially in the line of the special purpose for which it is intended, and at the same time as it is free from technicality in expression.

V. INDIVIDUALITY OF DICTION

Flatness of Diction.—On the other hand, language which makes no energetic effort at all to communicate any definite impression about anything at all, which is simply and dully common, is intolerable.

The Club had long planned to go on a picnic. At last the expected day arrived. We started out carrying our provisions to Thompson's Grove, a beautiful resort on a lake near by. Here we spent the afternoon playing games; and after building a fire and cooking our supper, we walked back the four miles by moonlight, a weary but happy crowd.

The music was good, and all passed an enjoyable evening.

One of the things that interested me most at the State Fair was the livestock show. Seeing a crowd going into the Pavilion, I joined them, and found that many of the seats had been filled. Many fine animals were shown, and I came away feeling well repaid for my time.

The view which I am about to describe was one which I shall never forget. Cattle were grazing happily in the valley, which seemed like a garden of Eden, with the dew-covered grass, shining like so many diamonds in the morning sun. The smoke rising from the chimneys was in harmony with the peace and quietness of the surroundings.

Sincerity of Diction.—Such writing suggests a torpid mind. This may be the fact—the writer may never have waked up, or he may be naturally dull. Or perhaps he has never made his language genuinely the servant of his ideas; he may have been satisfied to keep his ideas to himself. Effective language is always sincere language —not merely negatively sincere, in that it pretends to no more than the writer has seen and felt, but positively and energetically sincere, in that it strives not to fall further short of his feelings and thoughts than is inevitable. The result of such effort is always a certain freshness of expression, a certain impress of originality. Words so used are not simply exact, but are *different;* they are not anybody's words, but somebody's words.

The first day I went to school, I was teased about my little lunch-pail and my long curls.	The first day I went to school, the boys pretended that they meant to steal my lunch out of my little tin pail, and the girls, one after another, begged for one of my long curls.
The old slave quarters, which are kept very neat and clean, seem very quiet and reposeful as one stands among them, thinking of the past.	The old slave quarters, clean whitewashed, bask in a century's doze.

What a man needs in gardening is a cast-iron back with a hinge in it. The hoe is an ingenious instrument, calculated to call out a great deal of strength at a great disadvantage.

Warner, C. D., My Summer in a Garden.

Gray twilight poured
On dewy pastures, dewy trees.

Tennyson, Palace of Art.

A lightning-flash literally bores a hole through the atmosphere, just as a bullet would force its way through a mass of jelly.

Wurts, A. J., "The Protection of
Electrical Apparatus Against
Lightning," Century Magazine.

Second-hand Diction.—Writers sometimes take away from the life of their style by using second-hand expressions,—expressions, that is, which without becoming absolutely colorless have yet lost their freshness. The insincerity of such writing becomes particularly obvious when the expression used is very striking in itself, but is plainly not really thought anew by the writer.

Strange fascination
Vernal freshness
A financial giant
A mantle of glistening snow
Badly hit; as, "The commerce of the country has been
    badly hit by the failure of the crops."
Out of commission
Dropped in his tracks
Loomed up [often incorrectly used; *to loom* is to appear
    through a mist, often in such a way as to look larger
    or nearer than reality.]
With an eye to the practical rather than the useful
Reached the scene
The situation was becoming serious
Rendered a selection
Suddenly a gun spoke
The blizzard raged in full blast
The wind howled through the gaunt branches

Solemnity.—One of the most offensive forms of insincerity is solemnity,—the ordinary use of words only
suited for occasions of a formal nature, or the use of
words of exact and serious thought without any real
seriousness and exactness to justify them. Some people
always say *pursuant to,* never *in accordance with,* or *following.* They *take the matter under advisement* (like
a supreme court); they never *consider the business,* or
reflect upon the subject; they would shrink in horror
from *thinking the affair over.* When they *reach a decision* (not *make up their minds*), they will *advise* you,
(never *inform* or *notify* you, still less *let you know*).
They *request;* they do not *ask.* Things *superinduce*
(never even *induce*) a belief. For such people something
eliminates a possibility; with them a committee *limits
its activities* to the *consideration* of routine matters.
They are fond of abstract nouns and roundabout ways of
expressing action;—"His popularity has no wise diminished since that time, as is evinced by the fact that his

nominating papers received a number of signatures far in excess of the legal number required." ["He is as popular now as he was then; for there were many more signatures on his nominating papers than the law required." It is characteristic of these formal writers to fall into inaccuracy of expression; for *legal number required,* read *number required by law.*]

Formulas.—Such language is formal,—not human but mechanical. A writer in the *American Magazine* for March, 1919, brings out the ineffectiveness of mechanical formulas in business letters.

The danger I have constantly to guard against is that familiarity with mail in the mass should breed in our people a certain contempt. In other words, that they should come to look at mail as merely mail, and fail to see and feel behind every individual letter a human hand and heart. It is a danger that applies to every man in business, whether his day's mail consists of a thousand letters or of ten.

One afternoon last week I had, in the office of a doctor friend of mine, an excellent illustration of that fact. He was just then getting around to his morning's letters. They dealt with purely professional matters; and being in the same room with him, I could not fail to overhear his dictation. It was very interesting. In each instance he began by reading off the full name and address of his correspondent, although both were written or printed on the letter which went into his stenographer's hands a moment later. His answers ran something like this:

> New York, July 15th, 1918.
>
> *Mr. John H. Robinson,*
>
>   25 Maple St., Chicago, Illinois.
>
>   Dear Sir: In answer to your letter of July 11th, in which you inquire about the condition of your brother Samuel Robinson, who is under treatment at the Roosevelt Hospital, I beg to state that there has been no special change in his condition.
>
>   I will state further that should any

> change of serious character occur in the
> next few days I shall be glad to advise
> you by wire, as per your request.
>
> Assuring you that you will be advised
> immediately of any important develop-
> ments, I am, etc.

Each letter made a simple inquiry, which the doctor in conversation or over the telephone would have answered in a half
dozen words. Yet because his answer was to be written instead of spoken he invariably used the same wordy, stilted
form. Apparently it had never occurred to him that good
letter-writing is simply good conversation, and that the more
fully a letter embodies the individuality of the writer the better
it becomes. To him, the dictation of his mail was a thing
entirely apart from the other functions of his personality and
must follow forms worked out long ago.

I have tried to picture Mr. John H. Robinson, of Maple
Street, Chicago, as he would receive the doctor's letter. There
are forty-three words in the first paragraph, and thirty-four
of these Mr. Robinson would have to read before gaining any
information whatever.

"In answer to your letter of July 11th."

It was the only letter Mr. Robinson had ever written the
doctor. The doctor's printed letterhead would cry out to him
that this *must* be an answer to that epistle.

"In which you inquire about the condition of your brother,"
etc. All poppycock and camouflage! There was only one
subject on which Mr. Robinson would write to the doctor, and
he does not have to be reminded, four days later, what that
subject is.

If the doctor should have forgotten for a moment that he
was dictating a letter and have imagined himself answering
Mr. Robinson's question in person, he would have said something like this:

> *Mr. John H. Robinson,*
> 25 Maple Street, Chicago, Ill.
>
> DEAR MR. ROBINSON: Your brother
> is receiving the best possible care at
> Roosevelt Hospital. You may count on
> me to wire you the minute there is any
> change in his condition. Meanwhile
> don't worry. Until you hear from me to

the contrary you may rest assured he is
all right.

In those few lines there is something of the doctor's own
radiant and confidence-inspiring personality. The other was
an ill-fitting cloak, hiding the qualities that have made him so
successful.

As he plowed on conscientiously through the other letters,
never varying the formula of his reply, I wondered how many
thousand times that scene is repeated in business every day;
how many hours are wasted by patient stenographers in making pothooks to represent "In answer to your letter of," and
"Yours received and contents noted."

Copyright by the *American Magazine;* by permission.

Undue familiarity is as bad as undue formality. This
truth is illustrated by the abuse of slang.

Vivacious Slang.—There are two kinds of slang, the
vivacious and the lazy. Vivacious slang is part of the
joyousness of life. It expresses the cheer and superficial irreverence of youth, and is a way of having fun
with things in general. A writer in the London *Daily
Mail* says:

The picturesque imagery with which he [the American
soldier] adorns his speech may be an old story in "God's
country"—to me it is a thing of wonder and a joy forever.

He came over "the big drink" some months ago. He had
a pleasant voyage, saw no "tin fish," and had plenty to eat—
"six meals a day, three up and three down." On arrival at
the port they got into "the dinkiest train ever." Before the
train started, the captain asked for a key to wind it up with.
Sammy [what would an American soldier say to the Englishman who called him Sammy?] says that he personally intends
to take one home as a charm to hang on his watchchain.

They went into camp, where they spent their time "hiking"
about the countryside. The "eats" here were not overgood.
They were given tea "which tasted like the last water Noah
kept afloat in" and fish "that was never caught but must have
given itself up." However, they made their motto, "Work

like Helen B. Happy," and stuck it out bravely. The one thing that really "got their goat" was having to sleep on *terra firma*. That, Sammy says, is Latin for "terribly hard."

Ultimately he and his companions crossed to the front. The country pleased Sammy, but he found the language difficult and the French people slow of comprehension. On one occasion he wanted a pair of duck shoes, so he went into a bootmaker's and quacked—but he couldn't get the old dame "wise" to it.

For the fight that put him out of action Sammy says his lieutenant was responsible. "He was sure tired of his position and crazy on becoming a captain or an angel." Sammy was ready enough to help, but a *Boche* shell intervened and insisted on sending his name with an application "for immediate transfer to the Flying Corps."

Hence his presence in hospital.

Some of these expressions which charmed the English writer are colloquial figures of speech; some are examples of vivacious slang, good-naturedly impertinent to all the world thinks or can do.

Lazy Slang.—Lazy slang is the bandying of second-hand catch-words and phrases out of which the vitality they once had is gone: such are, as generally used (a man of originality can bring even dead slang to life), *swell,* and *grand* as words of praise (''We had a swell rest down to Atlantic City'';—''This is grand weather, isn't it?'') ; *guy* for person (''That 's the guy that gave me the shoes,''—applied to an elegant lady) ; *boob, bonehead, fish,* as words of blame; *four-flusher, the big idea, I would n't put it past him.*

The Danger of Slang.—Slang is appropriate where free-and-easy speech is appropriate, inappropriate where that is inappropriate. At best, it has the flavor of irreverent ingenuity. Now, to be always irreverent, always free-and-easy, takes away the point of being ever irreverent. Moreover, it is dangerous. There are serious things. It is an intellectual loss to be impertinent or flippant about them. This saying applies to good slang, to the best slang, and even to that original wit which is better than the best slang. But most people's slang is not so good as this. It is simply a way of writing blank checks on the bank of ideas, to be filled up by the bearer at will. I mean that the poorer sort of slang, by providing a writer with a conventional term having an apparent though not a real vivacity affords a cheap and easy way of avoiding original thought. Even such a way of using language achieves ends that may sometimes be desirable, but they belong to the familiar companionship of those who wish to avoid the appearance of assuming to feel warmly or to think seriously. To use the word *peach* as a term of general commendation saves the labor of defining one's ideas, and so protects one from seeming to put on airs in a company of persons self-consciously afraid of pretending to intellectual strenuousness. Sometimes, too, it avoids committing oneself emotionally. "He handed me out a *peach* of a swat!" (Perhaps it was professionally admirable because delivered with a maximum of power, perhaps because the minimum of effort was expended, perhaps for all these reasons.) "Say! That was a *peach* of a quiz!" (Easy? fair? comprehensive? well balanced?) "Prexy gave a *peach* of a lecture." (Perhaps it was simply well made, perhaps original, perhaps it was more impressive than one likes to acknowledge.) "I got a date with a *peach* of a dame." (I am not committing myself emotionally at all, as I might be by defining the nature of her charm.) But this kind of slang, convenient and safe as it may sometimes be in some circles, tends, if habitually employed, to deprave the mind. To tell the truth, the plain truth, about plain things, is not easy; even that requires observation, thought, care, pains, and training; but to tell the truth about difficult things as exactly as at times one needs to tell it in order to get on well with life is almost beyond what language can do at its best. No one can afford to prejudice his intellectual accuracy and his command of language by systematically practising vagueness and unreality of speech; yet this is what the users of lazy slang do.

Second-class Diction.—The same lazy habits of mind are encouraged by accepting those current usages which without being illiterate are essentially incorrect. *Due* is an adjective; to write, "*Due* to the epidemic of influenza, the schools will be closed to-morrow," where an adverbial expression, such as, "*Because of* the epidemic," is required by the syntax, marks a writer as belonging to the careless group who do not think with precision. Arrived *home, most all,* equally common *as* this, the *enormity* of the amount, have the same half-educated sound. "There is much danger of unemployment. The *situation* [evil, danger] is likely to be aggravated by the return of our soldiers." *Series* means a number of things in a regular order, a number of things arranged on some principle; the word is carelessly used to mean a number of things, without any reference to their being in a sequence. An article on the American system of courts-martial speaks of "revelations of a *series* of shocking injustices," where all that is meant is that there were a great many. The same article in the next sentence calls the same narratives "accounts of a *series* of alleged brutalities," and then speaks of "the latter *series* of accounts." The effect of what may be called second-class English is exemplified in the following sentence. "A few weeks ago army

officers from the General Staff in Washington were holding a *series* (number) of *consultative meetings* (con-
ferences; round-about-*ative* adjectives are favorites of
people who do not know the meaning of English words)
preparatory to (in preparation for; they *were holding*
the meetings, a verb, to make preparations, and hence
the modifier should be an adverbial expression, not an
adjectival one) the army that is to be." Such expressions mark those who use them as "outsiders" in language. They are the blunders of the unobservant and
the insensitive. To use second-class English is more injurious than to have the habit of slang, because it is
more insidious, and hence more difficult to resist. A
slangy speaker may be tongue-tied and unready if he
wishes to speak with propriety, but at least he knows
what he wishes to avoid; but the user of second-class
English cannot be sure whether he is right or wrong.

VI. VIVIDNESS OF DICTION

Concrete Diction.—Thus far stress has been laid upon
thinking and writing definitely and sensibly; but writing may be definite and sensible and at the same time
faint and dry. A good writer grasps his ideas with
energy and therefore uses his words with vividness. One
manifestation of this energy is to be found in the concrete definiteness with which he apprehends and expresses general ideas. A man of vigorous mind does not
know a general truth simply as a convenient formula,
like an algebraic statement, but seizes it also as a thing
vividly true in individual cases. If it is a truth of
economics he knows not only that two and two are four,
but knows it with conviction as a man knows it who is
trying to pay his debts; if it is a truth of morals, he

knows that the Samaritan was neighbor to him that fell
among thieves. An idea firmly grasped is known as a
blacksmith knows bar-iron, or as an aviator knows five
thousand feet up, as a tangible reality. Compare the
two following passages, in which the same idea is expressed, first abstractly, then concretely.

Though the other papers which are published for the use
of the good people of England have certainly very wholesome
effects and are laudable in their particular kinds, they do not
seem to come up to the main design of such narrations, which,
I humbly presume, should be principally intended for the use
of politic persons, who are so public-spirited as to neglect
their own affairs to look into transactions of state. Now these
gentlemen, for the most part, being persons of strong zeal and
weak intellects, it is both a charitable and necessary work to
offer something whereby such worthy and well-affected members of the commonwealth may be instructed, after their reading, what to think; which shall be the end and purpose of this
my paper, wherein I shall from time to time report and consider all matters of what kind soever that shall occur to me,
and publish such my advices and reflections every Tuesday,
Thursday and Saturday in the week, for the convenience of the
post.

Steele, The Tatler.

There is another set of men that I must likewise lay a
claim to, whom I have lately called the blanks of society, as
being altogether unfurnish'd with ideas, till the business and
conversation of the day has supplied them. I have often
consider'd these poor souls with an eye of great commisera-
tion, when I have heard them asking the first man they have
met whether there was any news stirring? and by that means
gathering together materials for thinking. These needy persons do not know what to talk of, 'till about twelve o'clock
in the morning; for by that time they are pretty good judges
of the weather, know which way the wind sits, and whether
the Dutch mail be come in. As they lie at the mercy of the
first man they meet, and are grave or impertinent all the day
long, according to the notions they have imbibed in the morning, I would earnestly entreat them not to stir out of their
chambers till they have read this paper, and do promise them,
that I will daily instil into them such sound and wholesome

sentiments, as shall have a good effect on their conversation for the ensuing twelve hours.　　Addison, *The Spectator*.

Consider also the following examples.

The Turkish empire would be more formidable, were it less extensive; were it not for those countries which it can neither command, nor give entirely away; which it is obliged to protect, but from which it has no power to exact obedience.
　　　　　　　　　　Goldsmith, *Citizen of the World*.

The last cause of this disobedient spirit in the colonies is hardly less powerful than the rest, as it is not merely moral, but laid deep in the natural constitution of things. Three thousand miles of ocean lie between you and them. No contrivance can prevent the effect of this distance in weakening government. Seas roll, and months pass, between the order and the execution; and the want of a speedy explanation of a single point is enough to defeat an whole system. You have, indeed, winged messengers of vengeance, who carry your bolts in their pounces to the remotest verge of the sea; but there a power steps in, that limits the arrogance of raging passions and furious elements, and says, "So far shalt thou go, and no farther." Who are you, that should fret and rage, and bite the chains of Nature? Nothing worse happens to you than does to all nations who have extensive empire; and it happens in all the forms into which empire can be thrown. In large bodies, the circulation of power must be less vigorous at the extremities. Nature has said it. The Turk cannot govern Egypt, and Arabia, and Kurdistan, as he governs Thrace; nor has he the same dominion in Crimea and Algiers which he has at Brusa and Smyrna. Despotism itself is obliged to truck and huskster. The Sultan gets such obedience as he can. He governs with a loose rein, that he may govern at all; and the whole of the force and vigor of his authority in his centre is derived from a prudent relaxation in all his borders. Spain, in her provinces, is perhaps not so well obeyed as you are in yours. She complies, too; she submits; she watches times. This is the immutable condition, the eternal law, of extensive and detached empire.
　　　　　　　　Burke, *On Conciliation with America*.

The second of the following passages is on the whole the more concrete.

The cultivation of these lands appears to have been the worst, the most wasteful, and the most exhausting in England. The pasture land was usually of a wretched description, and often enormously over stocked. Nothing was done for it in the way of draining or manure, and the greater part of common land appears to have been perfectly uncultivated and almost wholly unproductive. It has been estimated, probably without any exaggeration, that the enclosure and separate cultivation of the common lands must have increased their produce at least five-fold. It is not true that these lands were public property. The rights that have been described belonged to the surrounding freeholders in defined and recognised proportions, or were conveyed to tenants in the leases of their farms. There were claims, however, of an uncertain and vague character, resting on long prescription; there were numerous squatters who had settled on these great wastes without any legal rights, and who obtained from them a scanty and precarious livelihood, and a large vagrant population of gypsies, tramps, poachers, smugglers, and nomadic mendicants found them an important element in their existence.

Lecky, *England in the Eighteenth Century.*

In one respect it must be admitted that the progress of civilization has diminished the physical comforts of a portion of the poorest class. It has already been mentioned that, before the Revolution, many thousands of square miles, now inclosed and cultivated, were marsh, forest, and heath. Of this wild land much was, by law, common, and much of what was not common by law was worth so little that the proprietors suffered it to be common in fact. In such a tract, squatters and trespassers were tolerated to an extent now unknown. The peasant who dwelt there could, at little or no charge, procure occasionally some palatable addition to his hard fare, and provide himself with fuel for the winter. He kept a flock of geese on what is now an orchard rich with apple blossoms. He snared wild fowl on the fen which has long since been drained and divided into corn fields and turnip fields. He cut turf among the furze bushes on the moor which is now a meadow bright with clover and renowned for butter and cheese.

Macaulay, *History of England.*

How is Concrete Diction Acquired?—Of these passages, the more concrete, the more physically definite, are the more vivid and energetic. They are actual to the imagination, because what is said is plunged in real life, not academic, not a matter to be reflected upon, but an experience directly felt. What can be done to increase the physical definiteness of one's words? In no small degree, the habit of searching for exact synonyms will be of use as to words of sensation as well as of abstract thought. The lists already given contain examples, especially of concrete and exact verbs, which will repay study. But it is not from words alone, perhaps not from words mainly, that the command of words can be obtained—least of all as to the words appealing to the senses and dealing with physical life. One must see colors rightly to name them rightly. It is not from the dictionary or from tradition but from life that one learns such things. A healthy keenness of sense is at the basis of vigorously picturesque writing. Without an alert interest in the world about one, in which everything is unlike everything else and perpetually changing, without a delight in the characteristic bearing of men, in the perpetual drama of tones of voice and movements of the eyes, as people greet each other, in the vast tower of cloud, white on its rolling bosses, blue and black in its shadowy recesses, in the crackle of wind-brushed rushes, in the circle on the lake where a fish has broken the quiet surface—without a rich, exact, ample, and delighted experience of the world about him, no writer can learn the secret of the vivid word.

VII.   TROPES

Synecdoche.—A writer who has a strong and vivid sense of physical reality is likely to go further in his language than the bare facts warrant. Such a writer will not only perceive the physical facts, but will snatch from the facts that part or that aspect which is typical or significant for the whole, and will make it true for the whole. A man who does not care for what others think about him or his ways lets his hair go untrimmed, and gets shaggy on the back of his neck—he is a *rough-neck*. Scripture speaks of a haughty man as a man of a *high stomach*. A certain group of politicians used to be spoken of as *silk-stockings;* another was called the *plug-hats*. A vessel moving in the waters is called a *keel*—"thirty-thousand keels plowed the waters." In old days, as seen on the horizon, a vessel was a *sail*—"a fleet of fifty sail." As a thing to float cargo upon it was a *bottom;* the marine insurance companies undertake the risks of all kinds of *bottoms*. A man with spectacles is *four-eyes;* a stiff elderly lady is a *false front*. This use of the part for the whole is called synecdoche.

Metonymy.—Just as one makes of the significant or characteristic part a symbol for the whole, so one may make a symbol out of something connected with the idea. Newspapers are the *Press,* or *Printer's Ink;* a regiment equipped with rifles are the *Rifles;* those on horses are the *Horse*. I give my *voice* for a resolution—my approval that is, expressed by my voice. A carpenter is *Chips;* an iceman is *Tongs;* a big gun is *Big Bertha,* because associated with Bertha Krupp, one of the owners of the Krupp cannon factory. A bullet is *zip-zip-zip,* because of the noise it makes. This use of an associated thing for the thing with which it is associated is called *metonymy*.

Metaphor.—Each of these diversions of words from their literal sense is due to a natural impulse, an impulse to insist upon the vivid physical aspect which makes the greatest impression, or perhaps upon that one which excites and amuses. The same impulse may go even further. A lively mind, intent upon the one significant aspect of the thing before it, finds a resemblance as to this point with something very remote, and uses the second thing as a symbol of the first. I scorn a mean rascally fellow, who has got a tricky advantage of me, and I will not give in to him. I might yield to a lordly oppressor. There are animals, one great, powerful, handsome, bold, and at the same time ferocious; another also ferocious, but small, ugly, tricky, greedy, and loathsome. They are the same in relation as these two oppressors. "It is no disgrace to yield to a lion, but who with the figure of a man will submit to be devoured alive by a rat?" A big cannon-shell sent up a mass of dark smoke, and delivered a terrible blow; the fighter Jack Johnson was black and heavy and a champion hitter. The shell is a *Jack Johnson*. The relation between honesty and dishonesty is like that between straightness and crookedness—a dishonest man is *crooked;* a manner is *warm* or *cool* or *distant*. Prospects are *blue* (cold-looking and promising chill), or *rosy* (dawn-colored and promising fair weather); men are *yellow* or *green* or *white* (white is clean of stain; a green thing is immature; many yellow things are disgusting). This identification of things in different regions of thought because their relations are alike is called *metaphor*.

Fossil Tropes.—Such expressions,—metonymy, synecdoche, and metaphor,—in which a symbol is used for the literal statement of an idea, and in which words are turned aside from their natural meaning, are called *tropes*. Historically studied, language is nothing but a vast collection of tropes, and especially of metaphors,

once used in order to express ideas for which there were
no words, but now used without any feeling that their
present meaning was ever anything but literal. *Literal*
means according to the letter, *metaphorical* turned aside,
sense means feeling, *language* the action of the tongue,
express squeeze out, *idea* form or shape.

Dying Metaphors.—These words, once metaphorical,
are now no longer so, but have become literal in their
secondary meaning. There are also words on their way
to new meanings, but not yet without a feeling of their
original signification. It is these dying metaphors which
give most trouble to inexperienced writers, who often be-
tray a lack of vivid sense of what their words mean by
combining such metaphors with each other or with literal
expressions in absurd or awkward ways. For example:

Upon this economic basis [the effectiveness of the cotton-gin]
the institution of slavery which it had been confidently supposed by all statesmen, South as well as North, was in process
of extinction, reared a more significant growth, and became a
social and political factor of the most formidable magnitude.
[Upon a *basis* stands an object which the basis supports; a
growth does not stand upon a basis, but is rooted in a soil. A
fire, not a growth, suffers *extinction,* and a *factor* is a constitu-
ent of a total, not a separable object, like a growth.]

On the heels of this laudable desire [to have the army under-
stood] has come a *crusade* against the court-martial system as
it exists in our army.

Some adherents of the Scheidemann cabinet insist that the
Anglo-American combination is a *myth*. It will be *foiled* anyhow by the socialization of the whole German metal industry.

As Pater says: "A lover of words for their own sakes,
to whom nothing about them is unimportant, a minute
and constant observer of their physiognomy, he [the
artist in writing] will be on the alert not only for the
obviously mixed metaphors of course, but for the meta-

phor which is mixed in all our speech, though a rapid
use may involve no cognition of it. . . . Still opposing
the constant degradation of language by those who use
it carelessly, he will not treat colored glass as if it were
clear; and while half the world is using figure unconsciously, will be fully aware . . . of all that latent
figurative texture in speech.''

Mixed Metaphors.—Sometimes writers so far forget
the obvious metaphorical significance of their words as
to combine distinctly incongruous metaphors, producing
what are called *mixed metaphors*.

How absorbed we became in the incident-crowded *skein* of
an inconsequential and *half-baked* scenario!

A *streak* of economy *struck* us the other day.

Now from the *smoke* of the world's mightiest conflict of
arms, the goddess of democracy *arises full grown* as an *impulse*
to all mankind in the great work of reconstruction before it.

The eye *drinks in* the wonderful *shades* which the setting sun
is *throwing* over the landscape, until darkness *covers* all.

All such forms of confusion manifest a certain insincerity; they show that one is writing without having
one's mind on what one is really saying.

The Source of Metaphor.—The gift of figurative
speech is a sign of a vigorous and energetic mind. The
power of metaphor, in particular, arises from a special
mental force, and accordingly excites the reader's attention and stimulates his mind. It is the effective metaphor which more than any other element of style has
power over the emotions, arousing scorn or pity, or touching the sense of the ludicrous, the beautiful or the
sublime. It is the felicitous metaphors which catch the
imagination, and extend and raise the thought of

thousands,—*the open door, race-suicide, tender-minded* and *tough-minded thinkers.*

Some books are to be tasted, others to be swallowed, some few to be chewed and digested.

Mr. Godwin's faculties have kept at home, and plied their tasks in the workshop of the brain, diligently and effectually: Mr. Coleridge's have gossiped away their time, and gadded about from house, as if life's business were to melt the hours in listless talk.

Villon, who had not the courage to be poor with honesty, now whiningly implores our sympathy, now shows his teeth upon the dungheap with an ugly snarl.

Your Bonaparte represents his *Sorrows of Napoleon* Opera, in all-too stupendous style; with music of cannon-volleys, and murder-shrieks of a world; his stage-lights are the fire of Conflagration; his rhyme and recitative are the tramp of embattled hosts and the sound of falling cities.

A good book is the precious life-blood of a master-spirit, embalmed and treasured up to a life beyond life.

The power to create effective metaphors is a gift and a grace. They come, if they come at all, unsought. The deliberately invented metaphor can hardly avoid betraying itself, and appearing insincere and cold. Yet there is equal insincerity in adopting a dry, hard, barren literalness, in which a figure of speech would shine like a flower in the desert. The young writer is as much in danger of excessive timidity and repression as of showiness and fine language.

Simile.—In connection with the metaphor should be mentioned the simile—an expressed comparison between things belonging to wholly different classes. Examples follow:

Hardly a speculation has been left on record from the earliest time, but it is loosely folded up in Mr. Coleridge's memory, *like a rich, but somewhat tattered piece of tapestry.*

His mind goes round and round, *like a dog chasing his own tail.*

There is no literal resemblance in these cases, but a resemblance of relations.   On the other hand, in the following expressions, a real comparison between things in the same class is made.

He was unmercifully thrashed by one *Noe le Joly*—beaten, as he says himself, like dirty line on the washingboard.

[The beating of a man is like the beating of linen in the river, to clean it, after the method still used in France.]

No past event has any intrinsic importance.   The knowledge of it is valuable only as it leads us to form just calculations with respect to the future.   A history which does not serve the purpose is as useless as the series of turnpike tickets collected by Sir Mathew Mite.   [Both are simply useless things.]

A Metaphor is not Merely a Condensed Simile.—Any metaphor may be changed into a simile by the insertion of words of comparison, and a simile into a metaphor by the omission of such words.   But as regards the effect of the two figures and the impulses to which they owe their origin, the metaphor and the simile are not at all alike.   The intensity of imagination and of feeling which produces the sense of likeness does not stop with saying *like;* it identifies.   It is too little self-conscious to know that it is figuring out resemblances.   A simile is not so entirely a spontaneous form of expression as a metaphor, but is almost always consciously conceived.   It is intellectual and cool, while the metaphor is emotional and imaginative.   The simile is sometimes effective, is satire and attack, as in the following similes of Franklin.

The destroying of our ships by the English is only like shaving our beards, that will soon grow again.   The loss of provinces is like the loss of a limb, which can never again be united to the body.

A great empire, like a great cake, is most easily diminished at the edges.

Similes also are often useful in explanation.

All his [Thucydides'] general observations in these subjects [of government and policy] are very superficial. His most judicious remarks differ from the remarks of a really philosophical historian, as a sum correctly cast up by a book-keeper from a general expression discovered by an algebraist. The former is useful only in a single transaction, the latter may be applied to an infinite number of cases.

VIII. THE TONE OF WORDS

A review of the objects to be sought after by the student who wishes to master the use of words, shows that they fall into three main classes. Two of these classes have already been sufficiently considered: propriety of usage, and intellectual accuracy. The third is truth of association, the use of words with the greatest power to convey by intimation the mood, spirit, sentiment, temper of the writer. Words have not only a definable meaning of the dictionary, but an equally important, though less distinct, meaning of spirit or suggestion. *Dad, Father, Papa* (it makes a difference whether it is *Póppa,* or *Papá*), the *Old Man,* the *Governor* all mean the same person, but they mean it differently or under different circumstances. ''A lad is not the same as a boy; a lad is a boy with a man's hand on his head.'' The *Ancient Mariner,* the *Venerable Seaman*, the *Old Sailor,* and the *Old Salt* may mean the same individual, but they do not mean the same thing. Words, then, have a quality, a flavor, a fringe, an *aura,* as well as a definition, and it is this which most carries the feeling from author to reader. The power of emotional suggestion, indeed, is a quality of the style as a whole, not of the single word alone, but is especially subserved by those ways of using words which are called forth by the excited imagination, —by the concrete word, and by all the tropes considered, especially by the metaphor. The concrete word is a more effective symbol of emotion than the abstract, and sincere tropes in general have power of communicating the truth of feeling—a more difficult result to achieve than the communication of the truth of fact, and yet in some degree essential to any truth of speech. "In the highest as in the lowliest literature, then, the one indispensable beauty is, after all, truth:—truth to bare fact in the matter, as to some personal sense of fact, diverted from men's ordinary sense of it in the former; truth there as accuracy, truth here as expression, that finest and most intimate form of truth, the *vraie vérité* [true truth]."

In the highest forms of this truth of the spirit, adequacy in the expression of feeling, only specially gifted writers can reach great results, but everybody can avoid falsity, even the falsity of writing which is *out of tone,* that is, jarringly inconsistent with its context and its evident spirit.

RECAPITULATION

The English language includes a great many special languages of varying extent and of various words. Standard English is that English which belongs to the upper level of common speech. This English is best acquired by the careful reading of books which are recognized as in the great tradition of the language. Special exercises of many kinds are valuable but subsidiary. From such exercises exactness and economy in the use of words will naturally follow. Exactness, however, should not be sought for at the expense of intelligibility to the public addressed—appropriateness is an essential quality of good writing. In practice and as a basis, it is best to conceive of one's writing as seriously addressed to an intelligent, fairly educated, non-technical public. Diction, if sincere, is not likely to be flat but personal and characteristic of the writer. Insincere writing is conventional, second-hand, pompous, or mechanical. Slang, like every other language not central, may under some circumstances be effective and appropriate; at its best it possesses an irreverent vivacity. It is more often a mere dull convention; and the habit of slang at its best is dangerous to truth and effectiveness of diction. Second-class or half-educated diction is in some ways even more injurious than slang to the command of language. Vivid diction tends to be concrete; and the quality of concrete definiteness results primarily from trained and vigorous physical senses. Alert and energetic minds tend to find expression in figurative diction, especially in synecdoches, metonymies, and metaphors. Synecdoche is the use of a part for the whole, or the whole for a part; metonymy of an associated thing for the thing with which it is associated; metaphor symbolizes a thing by something not of the same class with the thing itself, but like it in the relation which the symbol has to the class to which it belongs. Language is full of wholly faded and of fading metaphors. Insensitive and careless writers often use fading metaphors incongruously, or they awkwardly combine literal with metaphorical expressions, or mix their metaphors. The repression of a natural tendency to metaphor and a conscious striving for metaphor are alike insincere. The simile, an expressed comparison of things in unlike classes, is essentially different in nature from the metaphor, though the two are mechanically interchangeable. The simile is most effective in explanation and satire. Appropriateness of tone is as essential to sincerity of expression as is exactness of idea.

CHAPTER VIII

THE FORMS OF DISCOURSE

Writing that means anything, writing which is of any use to the reader and which gives any satisfaction to the writer, is done with a purpose. Books on the art of composition classify the kinds of purpose with which one writes, not that a writer needs to be thinking of the classes when he actually has his own purpose in mind, but because it is possible thus to be sure of a more definite and complete kind of training than is gained by writing without being limited to each class in turn. The kinds of purpose are four: to tell a story, to describe the physical aspect of objects, to express the reflections of the mind, and to lead the reader to a conclusion;—to narrate, to describe, to expound, and to argue. From these four purposes there result four kinds of composition, or, as they are technically termed, *forms of discourse:* narration, description, exposition, and argument. Two are alike in that they deal mainly with concrete physical facts,—narration and description. In them the writer and reader are concerned not with the workings of the mind, but with things external to it. The other two, exposition and argument, deal with what goes on in the writer's mind, as he reflects on the things about him—not with things but thoughts. Again, two are alike in that they deal with processes, with a line or course of movement proceeding from a start to a finish; namely, narration and argument. Two are concerned with more fixed conditions, not with the course through which the subject of the writing goes, but with the state in which it is; namely, description and exposition. It is true that a piece of writing may serve two purposes at once; a writer may tell his story, as Aesop tells the fable of the lion and the mouse, or of the fox and the grapes, not only to record a transaction, but at the same time to set forth ideas, and to bring the reader to act in a certain way. The narrative itself expounds and argues. A writer may also expound and persuade by description, as Dickens described Squeers' school, in order to let people know what kind of schools existed in some places, and to make them determined to have no more of them. There is also a "twilight zone" about each of the forms of discourse; it is not easy to classify every piece of writing distinctly as narrative, descriptive, expository, or argumentative. Conrad tells how the *Nan-Shan* in *Typhoon* came into port after the storm, and how it looked. Is he describing, or narrating? A teacher of manual training shows a boy what will happen if he tries to saw a board in an incorrect way. Is he expounding, or arguing? At the same time, it is quite easy to see that typical examples are well within the clear daylight of each class; and for discipline and study it is well worth while to make the distinction and to practice each form separately.

Each of the forms of discourse, moreover, may be more or less touched with the emotions of the writer. One may narrate or describe or expound merely to communicate information, with a strictly practical purpose, and may argue only to produce a cold logical conviction; or one may narrate or describe or expound with a sense of delight or interest, to communicate a mood as well as merely to state a fact. So one may argue to fire the blood, or to stir the compassion, or to move the whole being of the reader, as well as merely to convince his mind. Each form of discourse, then, may be strictly utilitarian, or may be artistic. These purposes, also, need not exclude each other, though they may do so. There are romantic story-tellers, and poetic describers, and lyric expositors, and purely emotional orators; there are matter-of-fact historians, and scientific describers, and purely rational debaters. Speaking broadly, it is true, those who add some touch of the imagination to solid practical sense are able to achieve both the ends of writing better than those who can only write sensibly. Yet for most of us in most circumstances, good sense and clear processes of mind are the fundamental things, the objects to be most sought after, and those which we can be most sure of acquiring by effort.

CHAPTER IX

NARRATION

I.   THE CENTRAL THEME

Narrative the Most Natural Form of Discourse.—A narrative is the account of something done.   In general, an effective narrative is the account of some *one* thing done—not of a string of happenings with no definite result, but of a succession of events which make up a transaction, a single completed affair.   Language itself is an action, consisting of successive acts which take up time.   That is to say, uttering a sound or writing a letter of the alphabet is an act, and many of these acts in succession make up the action of expressing ideas in language.   Narration, then, which records actions, is the most natural form of discourse, and the easiest for most people to begin with, though an artistic narrative of a high order is exceedingly difficult.

Scientific Narratives.—The simplest form of narrative consists of the recital of bare facts in order, making up as a whole one transaction,—such a thing, for example, as the "write-up" of a laboratory experiment in which a process is carried out.   I tell how I have roasted so much potassium permanganate to make so much oxygen; in doing so I am writing a narrative. Even the bare outline of facts which makes up my report illustrates some of the fundamentals of good narration.   It divides naturally into three parts: (1)

a beginning,—an account of things which would stay
as they are indefinitely unless something happened to
them (namely, the application of heat); (2) a middle,
—an account of the things that result from the initia-
tion of action (namely, the formation of bubbles and the
catching of the gas); and (3) an end,—an account of a
new set of things (namely, a lot of gas in bottles, and
a black cake of new material in the flask), which will
stay as they are until a new force acts upon them.
Moreover, this narrative proceeds throughout by successive steps, as has been long since explained. The
salts are measured; they are placed in the flask; the
flask is set in the stand; the tubing is connected; the
heat is applied; the bubbles come one after the other.
In general, well made narratives deal with single, complete transactions, which advance by orderly successive
steps from a beginning, through a middle, to an end.

Practical Narratives.—The object of a scientific narrative is to record observed facts. Similarly, a physician's "history" of a case, a court reporter's outline of
the "facts" in a law-suit, or an engineer's record of
the steps taken toward the carrying out of a project are
narratives intended to give information about practical
matters. Sometimes these reports are dry, sometimes
they are full of human interest, but always, if they are
well done, they deal with a single piece of business,
indicate clearly the beginning of action, follow the
sequence of events systematically, and come to a distinct
end.

The Point of View.—Typical narratives, however, do
not deal with a course of events prepared and guided
in advance, like the events of a laboratory, or with
events selected in advance, by special conditions, like

the events recorded in a physician's office. Even for a
brief newspaper report of facts a writer has to solve a
new problem,—a problem which does not arise in a
technical report. He must decide which of many points
of view, all true, all perhaps alike important, shall be
chosen as the central point of view for the telling of the
story. He must decide whose story he is telling, and
why he is telling it. For example.—An automobile was
left standing on a slight incline near the end of a street.
The brake-lining was worn, and the car gradually began
to move downward, gathered momentum, plunged across
the sidewalk, and rushed twenty-five or thirty feet down
a very steep slope into the shallow waters along the
shore of a lake. An elderly lady who was sitting in
the rear seat had presence of mind to crouch down and
brace herself against the back of the front seat, and
escaped with some severe bruises and a slight nervous
shock. Workmen from a garage drew the car up by
means of a winch and cables over an improvised wooden
platform and across the rocks, to level ground, found
only two wheels broken and the frame bent a little, put
on new wheels and the old tires, and took the car away
under its own power. Now with what purpose should
one tell the story of such an incident? Is the point
to be dwelt upon the carelessness of people who do not
keep their brake-linings in repair? or the negligence of
the city engineer, in laying out streets with unprotected
steep ends? or the extraordinary escape of the lady in
the car? or the excellence of the Nonesuch car, which
passed so well through such a test? or the ingenuity of
the workmen who hauled out the car with so little
trouble? The order, the proportions, the whole tone
and method of the story will differ as the main purpose

of the story differs. If the writer has before his mind
chiefly the lady's story, he will give space and prominence to the fearful swiftness of the plunge, to her
terrors, to her quick and resolute action in protecting
herself, to the reaction when the car stopped, in brief
to everything she suffered and did. If he wishes to
praise the make of the car, he will touch lightly on the
things that might have happened, and will afterwards
bring out how little harm was done. If he is thinking
of the skill of the workmen, he will say not much of
the details of the accident, but will expand upon the
hopeless look of the car tipped up in the water; if
he is amused by the contrast between the alarm and
the trifling damage, he will expand upon the details of
the noise of the rush and the breaking sounds that followed and the excitement of the neighbors, but will have
little occasion to describe the car standing in the lake.
Thus each point of view makes a new combination of the
facts necessary, makes it necessary, indeed, to write a
new story.

Narratives about Propositions.—The idea directing a
narrative may be a general proposition; perhaps an
age-old truth, such as is perpetually being proved anew
in human experience. The doctrine of the following
anecdote is the French saying, *"Il n'y a pas d'homme
nécessaire,"*—"Do not flatter yourself; there is no man
who is indispensable."

I reflected upon the story of a minister, who, in the reign
of Charles II, upon a certain occasion, resigned all his posts,
and retired to the country in a fit of resentment. But as he
had not given the world entirely up with his ambition, he sent
a messenger to town, to see how the courtiers would bear his
resignation. Upon the messenger's return he was asked,
whether there appeared any commotion at court? To which
he replied, there were very great ones.

"Ay," said the minister, "I knew my friends would make a bustle; all petitioning the king for my restoration, I presume."

"No, sir," replied the messenger, "they are only petitioning his majesty to be put in your place."

Goldsmith, *The Bee*.

The Presentation of Character.—Another purpose or idea which may direct a narrative and contribute to give it unity is the presentation of character. In a narrative which embodies such an idea, the character need not be consciously analyzed, but is expressed in the actions of which the narrative makes record.

There was a boy in my class at school, who stood always at the top, nor could I with all my efforts supplant him. Day came after day, and still he kept his place, do what I would; till at length I observed that, when a question was asked him, he always fumbled with his fingers at a particuar button in the lower part of his waistcoat. To remove it, therefore, became expedient in my eyes; and in an evil moment it was removed with a knife. Great was my anxiety to know the success of my measure; and it succeeded too well. When the boy was again questioned, his fingers again sought the button, but it was not to be found. In his distress he looked down for it; it was to be seen no more than to be felt. He stood confounded, and I took possession of his place; nor did he ever recover it, or ever, I believe, suspect who was the author of his wrong.

Scott, in *Lockhart*.

I dressed myself as neat as I could, and went to Andrew Bradford, the printer's. I found in the shop the old man, his father, whom I had seen at New York, and who, traveling on horseback, had got to Philadelphia before me. He introduced me to his son, who received me civilly, gave me a breakfast, but told me he did not at present want a hand, being lately supplied with one; but that there was another printer in town, lately set up, one Keimer, who perhaps might employ me; if not, I should be welcome to lodge at his house, and he would give me a little work now and then, till fuller business should offer.

The old gentleman said he would go with me to the new printer; and when we found him, "Neighbor," said Bradford, "I have brought to see you a young man of your business; perhaps you may want such a one." He asked me a few questions, put a composing stick in my hand to see how I worked, and then said he would employ me soon, though he had just then nothing for me to do. And taking old Bradford, whom he had never seen before, to be one of the town's people that had a good will for him, entered into a conversation on his present undertaking and prospects; while Bradford, not discovering that he was the other printer's father, on Keimer's saying he expected soon to get the greatest part of the business into his own hands, drew him on by artful questions, and starting little doubts, to explain all his views, what influence he relied on, and in what manner he intended to proceed. I, who stood by and heard all, saw immediately that one was a crafty old sophister, and the other a true novice. Bradford left me with Keimer, who was greatly surprised when I told him who the old man was.

Franklin, *Autobiography*.

Interest in the Events.—The reason for telling a story may be the sheer interest of the thing done. The writer may wish to bring out something marvelous or comic or odd or exciting in the events themselves. In such a story, it is usually best, as in other kinds, not to give the reason for telling it, but to leave that for the reader to infer.

Since our conflagration here, we have sent two women and a boy to the justice for depredation; Sue Riviss, for stealing a piece of beef, which, in her excuse, she said she intended to take care of. This lady, whom you well remember, escaped, for the want of evidence; not that evidence was indeed wanting, but our men of Gotham judged it unnecessary to send it. With her went the woman I mentioned before, who, it seems, has made some sort of profession, [of evangelical christianity], but upon this occasion allowed herself a latitude of conduct rather inconsistent with it, having filled her apron with wearing apparel, which she likewise intended to take care of. She would have gone to the county gaol had Billy Raban, the baker's son, who prosecuted, insisted upon it; but he good-naturedly, though I think weakly, interposed in her favor, and begged her off. The young gentleman who accompanied these fair ones, is the junior son of Molly Boswell. He had stolen some iron-work, the property of Griggs, the butcher. Being convicted, he was ordered to be whipt, which operation he underwent at the cart's tail, from the stone-house to the high arch, and back again. He seemed to show great fortitude, but it was all an imposition upon the public. The beadle, who performed it, had filled his left hand with red ochre, through which, after every stroke, he drew the lash of his whip, leaving the appearance of a wound upon the skin, but in reality not hurting him at all. This being perceived by Mr. Constable Hanscomb, who followed the beadle, he applied his cane, without any such management or precaution, to the shoulders of the too merciful executioner. The scene immediately became more interesting. The beadle could by no means be prevailed upon to strike hard, which provoked the constable to strike harder; and this double flogging continued, till a lass of Silver End, pitying the pitiful beadle thus suffering under the hands of the pitiless constable, joined the procession, and placing herself immediately behind the latter, seized him by his capillary club, and pulling him backwards by the same, slapt his face with a most Amazonian fury. This concatenation of events has taken up more of my paper than I intended it should, but I could not forbear to inform you how the beadle thrashed the thief, the constable the beadle, and the lady the constable, and how the thief was the only person concerned who suffered nothing.   Cowper, W., *Correspondence.*

II. INTENSIFICATION

By subserving these or other definite purposes, a narrative is given point and unity. But it may be dull in the telling, it may lack movement and life. It may need to be *intensified,*—that is, to be freed from weakening elements, and to have its significant elements accentuated.

Beginning with the Action under Way.—First of all, a narrative should be freed from the tedious beginning which explains too much; it should march from the very outset.

One is going to tell how a very respectable (a most uncommonly respectable and sensitive) professor of

zoölogy, while making an excursion in a remote region
for the purpose of collecting specimens, was arrested
by the town constable, who took him for an escaped
forger, how the professor was kept in jail over night,
and how he was released only upon the arrival of a
friend who traveled all night for the purpose, and who
brought the county sheriff to identify the prisoner. It
is not necessary to explain who the professor was; it
is more fun for the reader to find out. It is not necessary to tell how sensitive, in fact how fastidious, he
was; that will appear from his actions. It is not necessary to explain why he was in the woods; he can explain
that himself. It is not necessary to explain that the
forger was at large; the constable can explain that.
What is the essential, the striking and vital, part of
the story? Perhaps it is the situation created as this
refined gentleman realizes with agony that he must suffer the humiliation of being confined in a common jail
on suspicion of being a despicable criminal. Then it
is well, especially since we are planning a short narrative, to begin as near the point of this crisis as possible.
Thus: "The constable shook his head. 'Look at that
notice,' said he, 'and then look at yourself'"; or thus:
"The prisoner, who had sunk in a sort of collapse into
a chair, suddenly sat up. 'Here is my collecting box;
here are some engraved cards; here is a letter of introduction to ——' " In brief, begin after action is
started, and work the necessary explanation of preliminary conditions, and as much else as can be made clear
and interesting, into the story.

He was out on the down one summer day in charge of his
father's flock, when two boys of the village on a ramble in
the hills came and sat down on the turf by his side. One of

them had a titlark, or meadow pipit, which he had just caught, in his hand, and there was a hot argument as to which of the two was the lawful owner of the poor little captive. The facts were as follows. One of the boys having found the nest became possessed with the desire to get the bird. His companion at once offered to catch it for him, and together they withdrew to a distance and sat down and waited until the bird returned to sit on the eggs. Then the young birdcatcher returned to the spot, and creeping quietly up to within five or six feet of the nest threw his hat so that it fell over the sitting titlark; but after having thus secured it he refused to give it up. The dispute waxed hotter as they sat there, and at last when it got to the point of threats of cuffs on the ear and slaps on the face they agreed to fight it out, the victor to have the titlark. The bird was then put under a hat for safety on the smooth turf a few feet away, and the boys proceeded to take off their jackets and roll up their shirt-sleeves, after which they faced one another, and were just about to begin when Caleb, thrusting out his crook, turned the hat over and away flew the titlark.

The boys, deprived of their bird and of an excuse for a fight, would gladly have discharged their fury on Caleb, but they durst not, seeing that his dog was lying at his side; they could only threaten and abuse him, call him bad names, and finally put on their coats and walk off,

Hudson, W. H., A Shepherd's Tale.

Then it was that I determined to carry out my plan.

I went to the stable and harnessed the horse to the little carriage. Jonas was not there, and I had fallen out of the habit of calling him. I drove slowly through the yard and out of the gate. No one called to me or asked where I was going. How different this was from the old times! Then, someone would not have failed to know where I was going, and, in all probability, she would have gone with me. But now I drove away, quietly and undisturbed.

About three miles from our house was a settlement known as New Dublin. It was a cluster of poor and doleful houses, inhabited entirely by Irish people, whose dirt and poverty seemed to make them very contented and happy. The men were generally away, at their work, during the day, but there was never any difficulty in finding someone at home, no matter at what house one called. I was acquainted with one of the matrons of this locality, a Mrs. Duffy, who had occasionally undertaken some odd jobs at our house, and to her I made a visit.

She was glad to see me, and wiped off a chair for me.

"Mrs. Duffy," said I, "I want to hire a baby."

Stockton, Frank R., *Rudder Grange.*

Accentuating Resistance.—Secondly, a story is intensified by accentuating the resistance overcome in carrying the transaction through. In every story there are two sides, one side including the forces that help along the hero's cause, the other side those forces which oppose him. Now if we let the hero's side have it all its own way, if we make the achievement too easy, the story will be tame. For example, if I say that I had some trouble in getting the cat down cellar, but that she went at last, there is nothing to arouse attention in my report. But if I make it plain that the cat had a mind of her own, and that she made an exhaustive experimental investigation of all the means of escape in the kitchen, I may make an entertaining narrative of our conflict. I could tell how when I went one way, the cat dodged the other, and how when I went the other way, the cat dodged back; how, when I stooped, she ran up my back to the top of the dresser, and how when I stood up and reached after her, she leaped down and hid under the refrigerator; how she scurried from one piece of furniture to another; how she sulked in the darkest and obscurest corner of the kitchen; and how, at last, when she was poked out she fled straight through the open cellar door as if to her last refuge.

As Eames paused on the road, he fancied that he recognized the earl's voice, and it was the voice of one in distress. Then the bull's roar sounded very plain in his ear, and almost close; upon hearing which he rushed on to the gate, and, without much thinking what he was doing, vaulted over it, and advanced a few steps into the field.

"Hallo!" shouted the earl. "There's a man. Come on." And then his continued shoutings hardly formed themselves into intelligible words; but Eames plainly understood that he was invoking assistance under great pressure and stress of circumstances. The bull was making short runs at his owner as though determined in each run to have a toss at his lordship; and at each run the earl would retreat quickly for a few paces, but he retreated always facing his enemy, and as the animal got near to him, would make digs at his face with the long spud which he carried in his hand. But in thus making good his retreat he had been unable to keep in a direct line to the gate, and there seemed to be a great danger lest the bull should succeed in pressing him up against the hedge. "Come on!" shouted the earl, who was fighting his battle manfully, but was by no means anxious to carry off all the laurels of the victory himself. "Come on, I say!" Then he stopped in his path, shouted into the bull's face, brandished his spud, and threw about his arms, thinking that he might best dismay the beast by the display of these warlike gestures.

Johnny Eames ran on gallantly to the peer's assistance, as he would have run to that of any peasant in the land. He was one to whom I should be perhaps wrong to attribute at this period of his life the gift of very high courage. He feared many things which no man should fear; but he did not fear personal mishap or injury to his own skin and bones. When Cradell escaped out of the house in Burton Crescent, making his way through the passage into the outer air, he did so because he feared that Lupex would beat him or kick him, or otherwise ill-use him. John Eames would also have desired to escape under similar circumstances; but he would have so desired because he could not endure to be looked upon in his difficulties by the people of the house, and because his imagination would have painted the horrors of a policeman dragging him off with a black eye and a torn coat. There was no one to see him now, and no policeman to take offence. Therefore he rushed to the earl's assistance, brandishing his stick, and roaring in emulation of the bull.

When the animal saw with what unfairness he was treated, and that the number of his foes was doubled, while no assistance had lent itself on his side, he stood for a while, disgusted by the injustice of humanity. He stopped, and throwing his head up to the heavens, bellowed out his complaint. "Don't come close!" said the earl, who was almost out of breath. "Keep a little apart. Ugh! ugh! Whoop, whoop!" And he threw up his arms manfully, jabbing about with his spud, ever and anon rubbing the perspiration from his eyebrows with the back of his hand.

As the bull stood pausing, meditating whether under such circumstances flight would not be preferable to gratified passion, Eames made a rush in at him, attempting to hit him on the head. The earl, seeing this, advanced a step also, and got his spud almost up to the animal's eye. But these indignities the beast could not stand. He made a charge, bending his head first towards John Eames, and then, with that weak vacillation which is as disgraceful in a bull as in a general, he changed his purpose, and turned his horns upon his other enemy. The consequence was that his steps carried him in between the two, and that the earl and Eames found themselves for a while behind his tail.

"Now for the gate," said the earl.

"Slowly does it; slowly does it; don't run!" said Johnny, assuming in the heat of the moment a tone of counsel which would have been very foreign to him under other circumstances.

The earl was not a whit offended. "All right," said he, taking with a backward motion the direction of the gate. Then as the bull again faced towards him, he jumped from the ground, labouring painfully with arms and legs, and ever keeping his spud well advanced against the foe. Eames, holding his position a little apart from his friend, stooped low and beat the ground with his stick, and as though defying the creature. The bull felt himself defied, stood still and roared, and then made another vacillating attack.

"Hold on till we reach the gate," said Eames.

"Ugh! ugh! Whoop! whoop!" shouted the earl. And so gradually they made good their ground.

"Now get over," said Eames, when they had both reached the corner of the field in which the gate stood.

"And what'll you do?" said the earl.

"I'll go at the hedge to the right." And Johnny as he spoke dashed his stick about, so as to monopolize, for a moment, the attention of the brute. The earl made a spring at the gate, and got well on to the upper rung. The bull seeing that his prey was going, made a final rush upon the earl and struck the timber furiously with his head, knocking his lordship down on the other side. Lord De Guest was already over, but not off the rail; and thus, though he fell, he fell in safety on the sward beyond the gate. He fell in safety, but utterly exhausted.

Eames, as he had purposed, made a leap almost sideways at the thick hedge which divided the field from one of the Guestwick copses. There was a fairly broad ditch, and on the other side a quickset hedge, which had, however, been weakened and injured by trespassers at this corner, close to the gate. Eames was young and active and jumped well. He jumped so well that he carried his body full into the middle of the quickset, and then scrambled through to the other side, not without much injury to his clothes, and some damage also to his hands and face.

> Trollope, A., *The Small House at Allington.*

Concrete Detail.—A story told in this way, and, indeed, lively narratives in general, make much use of concrete detail. It is the details which make a story seem real, and which give it the power to stir the imagination and to awaken interest. The following passage from Dickens's *The Old Curiosity Shop* only tells how six very ordinary people made their way into a theatre; but to them the adventure was a memorable experience, and to us it is made so by the enthusiastic abundance of the details.

However, it was high time now to be thinking of the play; for which, great preparation was required, in the way of shawls and bonnets, not to mention one handkerchief full of oranges and another of apples, which took some time tying up, in consequence of the fruit having a tendency to roll out at the corners. At length, everything was ready, and they went off very fast; Kit's mother carrying the baby, who was dreadfully wide awake, and Kit holding little Jacob in one hand, and escorting Barbara with the other—a state of things which occasioned the two mothers, who walked behind, to declare that they looked quite like family folks, and caused Barbara to blush and say, "Now don't, mother!" But Kit said she had no call to mind what they said; and indeed she need not have had, if she had known how very far from Kit's thoughts any love-making was. Poor Barbara!

At last they got to the theatre, which was Astley's; and in some two minutes after they had reached the yet unopened door, little Jacob was squeezed flat, and the baby had received divers concussions, and Barbara's mother's umbrella had been carried several yards off and passed back to her over the shoulders of the people, and Kit had hit a man on the head with the handkerchief of apples for "scrowdging" his parent with unnecessary violence, and there was a great uproar. But, when they were once past the pay-place and tearing away for very life with their cheeks in their hands, and, above all, when they were fairly in the theatre, and seated in such places that they couldn't have had better if they had picked them out, and taken them beforehand, all this was looked upon as quite a capital joke, and an essential part of the entertainment.

Dickens, *The Old Curiosity Shop*.

Physical Definiteness.—One way of adding to the vividness of a story by the employment of detail is telling it as a succession of physical events, of appeals to the senses, things heard, seen, felt. Thus it is less vivid to say that a man answered indignantly than that he threw his head back, opened his eyes wide, and barked out his words. "Mr. Codlin drew his sleeve across his lips, and said in a murmuring voice, 'What is it?' " is more vivid than, "Mr. Codlin asked with hungry expectancy what it was." Again, it is less vivid to say that a bird sang than that a robin shouted, or that all the universe was hushed than that,

> "The fir-trees, gathering closer in the shadows,
> Listened in every spray."

In brief, a story is intensified by the direct description of physical action which expresses emotion, not by the account of the emotion expressed; and by the recording of specific facts, not by the indication of generalities.

Conversation.—One of the ways by which detail gives reality to a story is the use of conversation. The skilful use of conversation is not easy. Conversation takes up more space than direct narrative and tends to make the story move slowly. But be the movement slow or rapid, conversations at least ought not to stand still; they should move the narrative on. Forward movement is gained by the interaction of the speakers; if by their speeches each responds to the other, and moves the other to an answering response, if their speeches are really in themselves actions toward an end, so that the conversation as a whole works out some effect, then the conversation has told its story. Conversations may thus contribute to the life of a narrative, by accenting the action and reaction of opposing forces which increase tension and expectancy, while at the same time they make the characters more vivid, and the story as a whole more natural. The things said and the language used should of course be appropriate to the character and to the circumstances. But the ordinary conversations of actual life are mostly tame and dull and fragmentary, and hence in narrative there is the same need of "intensification" in the conversations as in the other details. Significant things must be said, and the vividness of the speeches must be heightened without the loss of naturalness. In general the mixture of direct narration with conversation is most effective, the speeches making clear the working of the minds of the characters, and being in a way small climaxes.

Observe in the following passage how in spite of the ease and naturalness of the language the dialogue works out a transaction and maintains suspense. One girl is trying to find out what the other does not wish to reveal. The scene grows in intensity, and important consequences in their lives result from the relation between them which begins here.

Miss Barfoot arrived at half-past eleven, after many delays on her journey. She was pierced with cold, and choked with the poisonous air [of the London fog], and had derived very little satisfaction from her visit to Faversham.

"What happened?" was her first question, as Rhoda came into the hall with sympathy and solicitude. "Did the fog keep our guest away?"

"No; he dined here."

"It was just as well. You have n't been lonely."

They spoke no more on the subject until Miss Barfoot recovered from her discomfort, and was enjoying a much needed supper.

"Did he offer to go away?"

"It was really impossible. It took him more than half an hour to get here from Sloane Square."

"Foolish fellow! Why did n't he take a train back at once?"

There was a peculiar brightness in Rhoda's countenance, and Miss Barfoot had observed it from the first.

"Did you quarrel much?"

"Not more than was to be expected."

"He did n't think of staying for my return?"

"He left about ten o'clock."

"Of course. Quite late enough, under the circumstances.— It was very unfortunate, but I don't suppose Everard cared much. He would enjoy the opportunity of teasing you."

A glance told her that Everard was not alone in his enjoyment of the evening. Rhoda led the talk into other channels, but Miss Barfoot continued to reflect on what she had perceived.

Gissing, The Odd Women.

Selection.—We seem to have two inconsistent demands;—to tell a story without expansion, and to tell it with detail. How can the two be reconciled? A summary is cold, while extreme detail is tedious beyond expression; an energetically told story will not seem to be spun out, and will at the same time be vividly definite. How can a writer achieve both these merits? It must be by selection, by the suppression of everything insignificant, of everything which can be easily imagined or inferred, and by the consequent emphasis upon the salient and typical elements which most effectively embody the central idea of the narrative. Such selection is the most important aspect of what we have called intensification.

Major Oldyne, commanding the horse battery, was coming back from a dinner in the civil lines; was driving after his usual custom—that is to say, as fast as the horse could go.

"A orf'cer! A blooming spangled orf'cer!" shrieked Simmons; "I'll make a scarecrow of that orf'cer!" The trap stopped.

"What's this?" demanded the major of gunners. "You there, drop your rifle."

"Why, it's Jerry Blazes! I ain't got no quarrel with you, Jerry Blazes. Pass friend, an' all's well!"

But Jerry Blazes had not the faintest intention of passing a dangerous murderer. He was, as his adoring battery swore long and fervently, without knowledge of fear, and they were surely the best judges, for Jerry Blazes, it was notorious, had done his possible to kill a man each time his battery went out.

He walked toward Simmons, with the intention of rushing him, and knocking him down.

"Don't make me do it, sir," said Simmons. "I ain't got nothing ag'in' you. Ah! you would?"—the major broke into a run—"Take that then!"

The major dropped with a bullet through his shoulder, and Simmons stood over him.

Kipling, *Soldiers Three.*

I decided to become a carpenter, justifying myself by reference to my apprenticeship to my grandfather. One fine April morning I started out towards the suburbs, and at every house in process of construction approached the boss and asked for a job. Almost at once I found encouragement. "Yes, but where are your tools?"

In order to buy the tools I must work, work at anything. Therefore, at the next place I asked whether there was any rough labor required around the house. The foreman replied: "Yes, there is some grading to be done." Accordingly I set to work with a wheelbarrow, grading the bank around the almost completed building. This was hard work, the crudest form of manual labor, but I grappled with it desperately, knowing that the pay (a dollar and a half a day) would soon buy a kit of tools.

Oh, that terrible first day! The heavy shovel blistered my hands and lamed my wrists. The lifting of the heavily laden wheelbarrow strained my back and shoulders. Half-starved and weak, quite unfit for sustained work of this kind, I struggled on, and at the end of an interminable afternoon staggered home to my cot. The next morning came soon,—too soon. I was not merely lame, I was lacerated. My muscles seemed to have been torn asunder, but I toiled (or made a show of toiling) all the second day. On the warrant of my wages I borrowed twenty-five cents of a friend and with this bought a meat dinner which helped me through another afternoon.

The third day was less painful and by the end of the week, I was able to do anything required of me. Upon receiving my pay I went immediately to the hardware store and bought a set of tools and a carpenter's apron, and early on Monday morning sallied forth in the *opposite direction* as a carpenter seeking a job. I soon came to a big frame house in course of construction. "Do you need another hand?" I asked. "Yes," replied the boss. "Take hold, right here, with this man."

Garland, H., *A Son of the Middle Border;* copyright, The Macmillan Co.; by permission.

Summary of Intensification.—Intensification of effect, in fine, requires the fixing of the mind on the essential idea of the narrative, selecting that part of the possible narrative which most adequately expresses this idea,—narrating this incident not from before its beginning, but with an immediate start, suggesting or bringing in incidentally necessary information and introductory facts, and perpetually alternating between the opposing forces the conflict of which makes up the transaction accomplished. Precise detail is essential to vividness, but it should be selected, significant, typical detail, concentrating and not spreading out the action.

III. INVENTION IN NARRATIVES

Do not Invent a Setting.—All stories, of course, contain three elements:—the thing done, the actors, and the circumstances; or plot, characters, and setting. It is a mistake to try to invent a setting, because a writer's own mind cannot provide the abundant and various detail of reality, cannot make an unreal world as rich, vivid, and *dense* as his own world of experience. Hence the writer, especially at the beginning, should make what he can out of his own corner of the city, or the woods, the mountains, or the country-side that he knows. As for characters, most writers succeed best when they do not invent wholly new ones, but take people whom they know and whose actions they can anticipate. These characters may be, like the whole story, *intensified,* made simpler and clearer than nature. They may be polished and sharpened a little, without being invented as wholly new persons. Even for the plot it is well to depend upon something that the writer knows to have happened, clearing the transaction up, omitting everything confusing or unnecessary, and giving salience to its essential and significant parts. To invent a plot, however, is not so difficult or so dangerous as to invent setting or characters; if a writer knows of no suitable action performed by his characters, he can do his best to let them act one out for him.

Some Causes of Failure.—Failures with invented narratives commonly result from three causes: (1) the writer has no story to tell, gets no piece of business done; (2) the story told is not adequate for its space; (3) the story is told as it were from a distance and coldly, not as an intimate, actual experience.

Narratives of camping trips are likely to suffer from the first defect, college love stories from the second, and what students call "imaginary stories"—that is, narratives in which the writers invent the setting, such as detective stories, romantic adventures, dreams, and "The Adventures of a Silver Dollar," from the third.

IV. STRUCTURE

The Opposition of Forces.—In a narrative, a force does work of some kind, changes somebody or something in the world of physical fact or the world of ideas. A house has been built, or a heart broken, a character formed, or a weasel trapped, wages raised, or a difficult choice between alternative courses decided upon. In other words, the force has overcome a resistance. Sometimes the resistance is active, and then there is an obvious conflict to be perceived in the narrative; sometimes the resistance is merely passive, the mere inertia of things which it takes energy to change. Even in this case there is in a sense an opposition of forces. The perception of what the forces are, the opposition of which makes up the narrative, is fundamental to narrative structure.

Examples of Conflicts.—The thing done, the conflict underlying the narrative, must be big enough, heavy enough, so to speak, for the space which the writer is to fill. In a narrative of some length, the writer should deal with a conflict which is of sufficient weight to justify the space given it, and with which he is so familiar that the details giving it life arise abundantly and spontaneously before his mind. The conflicts which underlie narratives of human interest are of three sorts: conflicts between man and man, between man and circumstance, and between a man and himself—that is between one part of his nature and another. The two examples which follow illustrate a narrative of conflict between "man and man" large enough for a thousand words or so. Two girls are competing for a prize in declamation—the one being the child of parents of some means who give her the opportunity to take lessons in elocution, the other being a girl from out in the country who is carrying household burdens but possesses native talent and courage and determination. This story would fill, say, three scenes, the evening of the final contest being the climax. Or two boys are engaged with a surveying party, and each hopes to receive a permanent appointment. The events of the last day, at the end of which the chief makes his choice, would make the story. The following are examples of struggle with circumstance. An inexperienced man has gone out from the city to make his living on a farm. He has to meet unforeseen difficulties, and fails. Or a youngster in a town where there is no high school resolves to get an education. He goes to a town near by, does odd jobs to pay his way, succeeds well in his studies (his teachers have to doctor his reports somewhat, for they find he is unmercifully thrashed at home if he ever gets below ninety in any subject), goes on to a university, and becomes established as a prosperous lawyer. His career has a great effect in the little town from which he came, whence a train of other boys follow after him. The following is a conflict between a man and himself. A young fellow tries honestly to do his best, but fails in one thing after another, grows discouraged, and drifts from one menial occupation to a lower and still a lower one. He meets an old friend, gets a fresh inspiration, and comes up from his troubles—or falls back anew and more deeply.

The Sequence of Incidents.—The narrative, whatever its subject, should march by steps, should be a sequence of scenes or incidents, all tending to one end. In simple "one-line" narratives, this sequence is almost inevitable, for the mere succession of events determines it, as is explained in the first chapter.

The Unity of a Complex Process.—Now suppose a writer undertakes a more complicated problem. Suppose he endeavors to follow the working of several distinct processes, all in the end combining to produce a single result. How can he make the single line of progress followed by language serve to represent two or five or ten converging lines of progress, such as events nearly always follow in the real world? It is plain that the things which go on separately side by side must be taken up successively. How or on what principles may this be done? Suppose that there are just two main elements or lines of progress which must be followed. Suppose, for instance, we were following the course of two competitors for a prize in declamation. Each has to make his way past a throng of rivals in a series of preliminary contests, until at last the two meet in the final deciding contest. One,—let us call him Jones,—is victorious; the other, Robinson, comes off second-best. Now it would be absurd to leave Jones in a crowded hall in the middle of an evening waiting for his turn to speak, and to begin on the story of Robinson's preliminary trial held the same night. We should get through with Jones's first preliminary contest and see him declared winner before we begin with Robinson's contest. We should tell, if we were going into such detail, how the beautiful delivery of one competitor, and the energetic action of another, almost caused Jones to lose his place in the group of those chosen for the next round of the long struggle. Then, when that step had been

taken, we would go to Robinson and tell the story of his
first stadium in the race; then back to Jones, and so on,
until the two were pitted against each other in the
finals.

Consider now a somewhat less mechanical example of
the same kind of narrative. Suppose we had to tell
the story of the Battle of Bunker Hill,—an example
chosen because of the simplicity of the conflict. We
would follow the British actions up to a climax and
into relation with the Americans (say from the rein-
forcement of Boston up to the preparations to fortify
Dorchester Heights); then we would go back if necessary, to bring the American story up to a similar climax
and point of interaction (say from the organization of
the army under General Ward up to the completion of
the works on Bunker Hill); then the interaction of the
two would be told as one story (as in the first two attacks and repulses). Then would come the story of the
English preparations for the last attack; then the account of how the American reinforcements and powder
failed to reach the firing line in time. Again the two
elements would come together at the last, the successful
assault, and again would separate as the story would
be told how the British officers were surprised and disappointed to find that the colonials could hold their
own against the regular army; and the narrative would
end with the spread of confidence and determination
among the Americans as the report of the battle was
carried from town to town among the colonies.

Shakespeare, in the *Merchant of Venice,* plays with
at least four stories,—separates them, twists them together, tosses them up and catches them again, keeps
them in a stream of movement like a juggler, and to do

this he tells the casket story, and the pound of flesh
story, has Lorenzo and Jessica elope and lets Portia
play her trick upon Bassanio. He completes one main
transaction—the happy union of Portia and Bassanio.
One story advances to a stopping place, another takes
its turn, and so on until a point is reached when all
the stories are brought together. Bassanio opens his
plans; Antonio is pledged, one lover after another fails
with the caskets, Lorenzo runs away with Jessica, Bassanio chooses the right casket, and almost on the instant
a messenger comes to Portia's house, bringing with him
Lorenzo and Jessica, and also the news of Antonio's danger. The narratives of the rescue of Antonio and of
Portia's trick upon her husband are first separated and
then united; and the play ends with good news concluding the stories of Bassanio and of each of his friends.
The example illustrates the principles of structure in
the most complicated forms. Conceive of the whole
process as composed of distinct parallel processes, and
follow each one separately through its progress up to the
completion of a stadium of advance, proceeding then to
another of the subordinate processes, and tracing the
processes where they interact as a single transaction up
to a point of definite though minor completeness.

The Climax.—In every transaction there will be a
turning-point, a central or pivotal situation, at which
all the forces, as it were, meet in a focus. Here the
resistance and the moving force come into the most energetic conflict, or display themselves most effectively.
Here the tension is highest. Here the decision is
reached. To this central point all that precedes leads
up,—from it all that follows is dominated. Just what
that focus is, depends on the whole idea of the story;

and in that focus the idea is most intensely expressed. We have spoken of the Battle of Bunker Hill as a subject for a possible narrative; and the *idea* with which we have thought of telling the story is the testing of the capacity of the colonial troops to withstand the trained British regulars. The "conflict" is that between the elements which might destroy the confidence, the "morale," of the colonials, and those which support it. From this point of view the focus of the whole narrative is the first coolly withheld and terribly effective burst of rifle fire from the American breastworks. At this point the central conflict was decided: the Americans could resist—they would resist. If at this point, then, the Americans had failed to show the capacity to meet danger calmly, to hold their own against the regulars, it is not unlikely that the American Revolution would never have taken place. They stood firm; and the end was certain. What follows, however interesting in itself, is on the downward grade. The victorious force is the colonial self-confidence. But if we were telling the story of the Battle of Bunker Hill with regard to the conflict between the Americans and the British at the moment, as a mere matter of physical force, the third assault, the successful attack with the bayonet, is the central incident, for that was decisive as to the physical conflict. The victorious force in such a narrative would be the British will to occupy the heights.

Write with the Climax in Mind.—Some pivotal situation, or *climax,* of the story, will appear upon a distinct consideration of what the real transaction is. The final contest of the debate, the point when the girl who ran off to the dance met her father, Mother's hearing me say the naughty word that I picked up from the kindly milkman who took me for a ride, each of these is the climax of our story. For vigor and singleness of effect, write from the first with the climax in mind. Let that which comes before prepare for it, let that which follows show what the climax meant—how thenceforward the consequence was sure, though it seemed uncertain, and though it came slowly.

The Climax Emphasized by Contrast.—Of the means by which the climax is prepared for, the first is bringing out into action each of the contending forces the conflict of which makes up the story. The fine voice and dramatic talent of one of the two contending speakers, against the steady logic and sober weight of earnestness of the other can be shown by an incident illustrating each. The American frontiersman's soldierly qualifications, his self-reliant initiative, his hardy laboriousness, his markmanship, together with his lack of training and discipline, the confusion of his military organization, on the one hand, the fine qualities of the trained British soldiery, their steadfast courage and military steadiness, together with their fatal arrogance and the sluggishness of their leadership on the other hand, appear in the narrative not as ideas illustrated by facts, but as facts themselves, being shown in the very steps of the transaction. This contrasting of the two forces gives emphasis and vitality to the point of their final and most intense conflict.

The Climax Emphasized by Suspense.—Likewise, the playing off of one force against the other—or against the many that it must overcome—leaving the reader from moment to moment uncertain as to the result, *suspending* the course of the action as has been explained already, prepares for and gives force to the climax. This suspense may be ever present as to the result of each incident, and also as to the result of the whole conflict. Will the men hold back their fire? Will the powder come up? Will the reinforcements be in time? Will the flank be turned? Each single subsidiary part of the whole has its own problem, its own transaction in which the event comes as a discovery. And on the whole, the great climax, the central exhibition of the central idea, in preparation for which the whole development of both sides has been carried on, comes as the turning point of the conflict between two forces, either of which might have been victorious. The absolute end of the story may be and often is foreseen, but on the way there should be some tension continually kept up, some sense that the other side is at work, now in this way, now in that way, and that it may at least score if not win in the contest. In the very best of stories, each new incident comes as something not of course, with a shock not altogether of surprise, for it is natural, but at least of discovery. Gissing's *Christopherson*, Kipling's *Cupid's Arrows*, and Stephenson's *Markheim,* illustrate each in its own way this quality of tension, a continual swaying back and forth between opposing forces maintained to the very end of the narrative.

The Main Force Emphasized by Proportion.—In the course of a narrative, those elements which are central —the significant forces—naturally are developed with the greatest amount of space and attention; the central *scene* may be short, but the central *force* or *idea* will be fully presented. We shall see more of the hero than of any one else in the story, and we shall become fully acquainted with those of his traits which decided his

case. The story of the conflict between my bulldog Bill
and the grocer's boy will amplify Bill's sense of responsibility and ownership, his determination, the grip
of his teeth, if the dog's action is the central idea of my
tale. If the grocer's boy is central, I will tell all about
how his ways were such as naturally to excite a dog's
suspicions, how he regarded Bill, how his duty forced
him to go to the side door,—in brief, the main ideas are
emphasized by proportion.

The Unity of Concentration.—A narrative, then, is
most effective when it has strenuous unity,—unity of
transaction, with a central single contest, reaching a
central single climax,—a climax made salient by contrast of the central forces with other forces, by suspense as to the outcome of the alternating movement of
the conflict, and by a proper distribution of the space
among the forces of the narratives.

Autobiographies.—An exercise occasionally set for
college students is the writing of an autobiography, intended to show what forces have affected their powers
of expression, both as regards the material which they
have at command, and their mastery of language. In
the first division come the things which the writer has
seen and done, and the things that have affected his
ways of thought. Has he traveled? Has he earned his
own living? What part of the world does he come from?
What has he seen of the world of nature and of man?
Has he taken everything for granted? Has he been interested in thinking something out? In the second division are included the influences of his surroundings—
his family, the language of the communities in which
he has lived, his practice in writing, in school or pri-
vately, and his training in foreign languages, as it affects

his English. Is he of Norwegian parentage? Was the high-school course thorough? Did he write many exercises, and were they thoroughly corrected? Would the use of correct English have made him disliked by his comrades, and those with whom he did business? Here are many elements, all working to one end—the determination of his present capacity to write. Some of the matters are in some cases so insignificant that they may be neglected; others are the really important ones. Has there been any very significant influence or experience? Make that central. Perhaps it was the influence of a particular teacher, perhaps it was working six months in a factory, perhaps it was a trip abroad, perhaps it was a very good or a very bad system in the schools; whatever it is, it is central. And in the central division, there is sure to be some high point,—some incident either deciding the case, or making the whole trend of the matter clear above every other incident, something symbolic of the whole—some particular conversation with the teacher; some sight in Italy, some observation or incident at the factory, some decision at home, was the central thing. That is the climax. The order of the parts must naturally in a broad way be the order of time,—infancy, childhood, youth, for example,—and within each of the large sections the types of activity will be separated,—the family, the school, the outside experiences; or my town, my school, my reading, my adventures. Each part of the whole matter will be treated summarily, except that a typical incident may be led up to, and the central division with its main incident will receive the greater space. From the climax on the narrative proceeds, following the line marked out for it by the decisive incident, and the story closes perhaps with a retrospect showing the point to which as to provision of thought and knowledge, and as to command of expression, the process—the experience outlined—has brought the writer. Suspense—uncertainty of action and counteraction—in such a narrative will probably be strong only at the climax points; but the method of proceeding by clear-cut sections, up to a definite result will help to give unity and interest to this fairly difficult exercise.

Transition.—As to continuity in narratives it is seldom desirable to indicate formal transition from part to part by connectives. A natural sequence of events is in itself a connected thing, and if each section ends and begins sharply, the effect of decision and progress is greater than if the story passes from section to section with formal words of transition. The effect of the latter is to make the movement slow and often clumsy.

The Narrative Paragraph.—On the same principle, "topic sentences" and formal conclusions are usually out of place in the narrative paragraph. If the paragraph completes its allotted stage in the advance, its purport and relation to the rest of the composition may safely be left to the reader.

The Narrative Sentence.—The narrative sentence contributes its part to the forward movement of the whole. Hence much subordination of predication and much suspense of structure in narrative sentences,—effects which hold the attention at a stand upon one idea, until it is fully presented with its modifications,—are not so appropriate in narration as in more abstractly intellectual types of composition. The excited portions of narratives often tend to short independent predications; but in general well constructed loose sentences are the most suitable type—loose, not rambling; made up of predications clearly marked and firmly linked, not of insecurely attached tags, or sentences with no center and no single effect.

RECAPITULATION

Narration has been spoken of as the most natural form of discourse and for most people the easiest in which to make a beginning of serious effort towards improving their powers of expression; but the reader who has had the patience to make his way through this chapter may well say, "You call narration easy; but the elaborate directions given seem to imply that it does not quite come by nature." That is true; anything beyond the mere beginning in the art of story telling is of the highest difficulty. Yet the reader should not get the impression that he has been receiving cautions and suggestions which will guard him against error on every side, that he should fear perpetual pitfalls and must go forward haltingly. Nearly all the suggestions have to do not with the mere writing out of a narrative, or even with the steps to be taken after the writing is begun, but are mainly concerned with getting ready for writing, with the fundamental brain-work of preparation. First of all comes the logical backbone of the narrative; the writer should get a clear view of his narrative in advance—should find its fundamental transaction, should see the steps by which the road is to be traversed and the end reached, should think of the whole as a schemed and ordered thing. All this should be known as an experience, vivid before the mind, worked out into detail, round to the touch, distinct to the eye, sounding in the ear, odorous, having weight, having reality. The unity of the impression produced by the story should be enhanced by the omission of every disturbing or weakening element, by the selection of vital and significant details, and by the arrangement of the work so that it culminates in a single climax, the point of decisive meeting of the opposing forces, the conflict of which is the essence of the narrative. The climax may be emphasized by the contrast between those forces, and by a constantly maintained suspense in the major and minor conflicts of the narrative. The major force receives the emphasis of fuller space and greater prominence. In a story so ordered, formal transition will generally be unnecessary, the paragraphs will not generally require a formal introduction of their topics, and the sentences will generally be loose.

CHAPTER X

DESCRIPTION

If a narrative is a journey, proceeding step by step from a starting point to a terminus, then a description is a sweep of the eye, passing at one flight over a whole landscape. Narratives are concerned with the workings of things which effect or undergo change. Descriptions are concerned with the look and sound and smell of objects, with their feel, with their warmth and coldness, with all their physical characteristics. The subject of a narrative is the process of an action; the subject of a description is the state of an object.

Scientific and Practical Descriptions.—The simplest descriptions, like the simplest narratives, record bare facts—present the physical characteristics of the object dealth with, as matters of information. A physician records the events in the progress of the case, but he also notes the expression, the appearance of the skin, and the temperature of his patients; the civil engineer describes the size and shape and physical properties of the cutting where he plans to build a dam. Geography and geology must describe particular land surfaces, rocks, and rivers; botany and zoölogy the features of particular specimens; in brief every science rests on the accurate record of the observation of particular things; and what is true of science is likewise true of practical arts. A

242

man does not know angling unless he can judge the look
of a particular piece of water under the sky at a particular time; a man does not understand farming unless he knows the look and the texture of the soil in a
particular plot of ground; a man does not know men unless he knows the look, the lines in the face, the gestures
of particular men. The powers and practices that are
especially the province of description are fundamental in
all intellectual and practical activities.

Descriptions which Suggest Impresssions.—As narratives are generally something more than the mere records
of data and possess a human interest, so descriptions
are not generally mere enumerations of appearances,
but communicate a feeling about the things observed,
and suggest to the reader the peculiar impression which
the things observed have produced upon the writer.
The following examples will make clear the nature of
the two types of description.

On the southeast corner of the larger island are extensive
hot springs and steam jets, covering perhaps thirty acres of
land and extending into the lake. This portion of the island
is of hard, black basalt, with some scoriae and cinders, which
materials form the eastern end of the island, the western side
being made up of stratified ashes, more or less indurated. The
steam and hot gases escape from hundreds of vents, and often
with considerable noise. About the orifices of many of these
fumaroles there are thin red incrustations which appear to
consist of chloride of iron. There is but little smell of sulphur
and no deposit of this material. Some of these springs furnish
a copious supply of boiling water, and large quantities of it
come out at the edge of the lake, raising its temperature very
perceptibly for many rods from the shore. In one place a
large fissure occurs, caused by the falling in of a portion of
the crust, and this must have taken place at quite a recent
period, since the bushes which grew on the sunken portion are
still to be seen in the rubbish at bottom. Much steam and hot
gases issue from this cavity. There are two well-defined

craters, now filled with water, on the northeastern part of the island, in the midst of the hard, black basalt.

Whitney, J. D., in the *Geological Survey of California.*

From the hermitage we crossed another vast stream of lava, and then went on foot up the cone—this is the only part of the ascent in which there is any difficulty, and that difficulty has been much exaggerated. It is composed of rocks of lava, and declivities of ashes; by ascending the former and descending the latter, there is very little fatigue. On the summit is a kind of irregular plain, the most horrible chaos that can be imagined; riven into ghastly chasms, and heaped up with tumuli of great stones and cinders, and enormous rocks black-ened and calcined, which had been thrown from the volcano upon one another in terrible confusion. In the midst stands the conical hill from which volumes of smoke, and the foun-tains of liquid fire, are rolled forth forever. The mountain is at present in a slight state of eruption; and a thick heavy white smoke is perpetually rolled out, interrupted by enormous columns of an impenetrable black bituminous vapour, which is hurled up, fold after fold, into the sky with a deep hollow sound, and fiery stones are rained down from its darkness, and a black shower of ashes fell even where we sat. The lava, like the glacier, creeps on perpetually, with a crackling sound as of suppressed fire. There are several springs of lava; and in one place it gushes precipitously over a high crag, rolling down the half-molten rocks and its own overhanging waves; a cata-ract of quivering fire.

Shelley, *Letters.*

The Two Types not Wholly Opposite.—The two classes of description are not essentially opposed to each other; both rest on a solid basis of real and abundant observation, and follow much the same principles of de-velopment. Add to accuracy and order an awakened spirit, a delight in the "goings on" of what is contem-plated, and scientific description becomes imaginative literature. The business of Dr. Coues, the ornithologist, is mainly to inform; yet he is touched by and com-municates a feeling when he speaks of the veery's song, —"when its clear bell-like notes, resonant, distinct, yet soft and of an indescribable sadness, fall upon the ear as we press through the tangled undergrowth beneath the shade of stately trees." On the other hand when Mr. Kipling, the novelist, says, "We were sitting in the veranda in the dead, hot, close air, gasping and praying that the black-blue clouds would let down and bring the cool. Very, very far away, there was a faint whisper. It was the roar of the Rain breaking over the river,"— when he says this his main object is to give the reader the feeling that affected his characters, but at the same time he wants his readers to get the fact of the situation. Only in the extreme of both types are the two kinds of description radically unlike.

II. THE MATERIAL OF DESCRIPTION

Concrete Detail.—It is apparent that the first requisite of effective description is the possession by the writer of an abundance of concrete detail, from which he draws that which suits his purpose. Consider the following examples.

A veery's nest, which I found near Pembina, Dakota, on the Red River of the North, was placed on a little heap of decaying leaves caught at the foot of a bush; resting on these, it was settled firmly in the crotch formed by several stems diverging at once from the root. The base of the nest was quite damp, but the floor was sufficiently thick to keep the interior dry. The nest was built of various slender weed-stems, grass-stalks, and fibrous strips of bark, compactly woven and mixed with dried leaves; the latter formed the lining of the base inside. The cavity is rather small, considering the bulkiness of the whole nest, measuring only about two inches and a half across by less than two in depth. The whole is as large as an infant's head, and of irregular contour, fitting the crotch in which it was placed, and bearing deep impress of the ascending stems of the bush. This nest contained four eggs, fresh (June 9); they measured, on an average, 0.86 by 0.66, and were pale greenish-blue, without spots. The female, scared from her nest by my approach, flew silently off to a little distance, where she rested to observe my actions.

Coues, Elliot, *Birds of the Northwest.*

The soft autumn sunshine, shorn of summer glare, lights up with colour the fern, the fronds of which are yellow and brown, the leaves, the gray grass, and hawthorn sprays already turned. It seems as if the early morning's mists have the power of tinting leaf and fern, for so soon as they commence the green hues begin to disappear. There are swathes of fern yonder, cut down like grass or corn, the harvest of the forest. It will be used for litter and for thatching sheds. The yellow stalks—the stubble—will turn brown and wither through the winter, till the strong spring shoot comes up and the anemones flower. Though the sunbeams reach the ground here, half the green glade is in shadow, and for one step that you walk in sunlight ten are in shade. Thus, partly concealed in full day, the forest always contains a mystery. The idea that there may be something in the dim arches held up by the round columns of the beeches lures the footsteps onwards. Something must have been lately in the circle under the oak where the fern and bushes remain at a distance and wall in a lawn of green. There is nothing on the grass but the upheld leaves that have dropped, no mark of any creature, but this is not decisive; if there are no physical signs, there is a feeling that the shadow is not vacant. In the thickets, perhaps—the shadowy thickets with front of thorn—it has taken refuge and eluded us. Still onward the shadows lead us in vain but pleasant chase.

Jeffries, Richard, *apud* Besant, W., *The Eulogy of Richard Jeffries.*

Is it not plain that the strength of each of these passages is to be found in the author's supply of exactly observed, definite, separate realities? his stock of actual impressions of sense? This richness of physical impressions is fundamental, and to acquire it two things are necessary: the one, vigorous and healthy physical senses, the other the habit of attending to the experience of the senses and discriminating among them,—observation developed by practice and discipline.

It is on the foundation of this learning of the senses, so real, so valuable, and so little valued, that the most effective thought, as well as the most effective writing, must be built up. And in description especially, good writing depends on a supply of genuinely experienced sense expressions, stored up in the mind and drawn upon as they are needed. Abundance of vital and concrete detail, then, is the first requisite for all types of description.

III. THE POINT OF VIEW

The Fixed Point of View.—Secondly, the effective description, like the effective narrative, has a clean distinctness and singleness of outline, which is dependent, first, upon the definiteness with which the material is contemplated, secondly, upon the orderliness of arrangement, and thirdly, upon the concentration of attention on the vital points. In other words, in the first place both narratives and descriptions must each have a definite point of view. In the description, this is an actual physical fact, which must never be left in doubt, and must never be changed except with conscious intent. The more clearly fixed and the more stable the point of view, the more likely it is that the description will have the forward movement necessary to clearness and interest. Observe how in the following descriptions the indication and maintenance of the point of view contribute to vividness and movement in the objects presented to the senses.

Shelley, by taking his station on the rock, makes the water stream the more swiftly by.

Stand upon the brink of the platform of cliff which is directly opposite. You see the evermoving water stream down. It comes in thick and tawny folds, flaking off like solid snow

gliding down a mountain. It does not seem hollow within, but
without it is unequal, like the folding of linen thrown carelessly down; your eye follows it, and it is lost below; not in
the black rocks which gird it around, but in its own foam and
spray, in the cloudlike vapour boiling up from below, which
is not like rain, nor mist, nor spray, nor foam, but water, in a
shape wholly unlike anything I ever saw before. It is as
white as snow, but thick and impenetrable to the eye. The
very imagination is bewildered in it. A thunder comes up
from the abyss wonderful to hear; for, though it ever sounds,
it is never the same, but, modulated by the changing motion,
rises and falls intermittingly; we passed half an hour in one
spot looking at it, and thought but a few minutes had gone by.
                                   Shelley, P. B., *Letters*.

Conrad, by setting Mr. Jukes in his cabin at the
table, makes the apparent motion of the stars as the vessel rolls, the more sweeping and swinging.

Sprawling over the table with arrested pen he glanced out
of the door, and in that frame of his vision he saw all the
stars flying upwards between the teakwood jambs on a black
sky. The whole lot took flight together and disappeared, leaving only a blackness flecked with white flashes, for the sea was
as black as the sky and speckled with foam afar. The stars
had flown to the roll and came back on the return of the ship,
rushing downwards in a swarming glitter not of fiery points
but enlarged to tiny discs, brilliant with a clear, wet sheen.
He watched the flying big stars for a moment, and then
wrote: "8 P. M. Swell increasing. Ship labouring and taking water on her decks. Battened down the coolies for the
night. Barometer still falling."
                                   Conrad, J., *Typhoon*.

A Moving Point of View.—Occasionally a writer employs a moving point of view so as to see the object from
several aspects. Sometimes by this method not a single
description but several are written, forming a sort of
panorama. Sometimes the method gives a greater fix-
ture, a greater passivity, to the things described. In
both cases, all that keeps the parts together is the com-

mon spirit, the *tone* of the whole. The description from a moving point of view is, therefore, more difficult than that from a fixed point of view. Examples of both types of description from the moving point of view are as follows:

The old-fashioned, low wainscoting went round the rooms, and up the staircase with carved balusters and shadowy angles, landing half-way up at a broad window, with a swallow's nest below the sill, and the blossom of an old pear-tree showing across it in late April, against the blue, below which the perfumed juice of the find of fallen fruit in autumn was so fresh. At the next turning came the closet which held on its deep shelves the best china. Little angel faces and reedy flutings stood out round the fireplace of the children's room. And on the top of the house, above the large attic, where the white mice ran in the twilight—an infinite, unexplored wonderland of childish treasures, glass beads, empty scent-bottles still sweet, thrum of coloured silks, among its lumber—a flat space of roof, railed round, gave a view of the neighbouring steeples; for the house, as I said, stood near a great city, which sent up heavenwards, over the twisting weather-vanes, not seldom, its beds of rolling cloud and smoke, touched with storm or sunshine. But the child of whom I am writing did not hate the fog because of the crimson lights which fell from it sometimes upon the chimneys, and the whites which gleamed through its openings, on summer mornings, on turret or pavement.

Pater, *The Child in the House.*

The lama never raised his eyes. He did not see the money-lender on his goose-rumped pony, hastening along to collect his cruel interest; or the long-shouting, deep-voiced little mob—still in military formation—of native soldiers on leave, rejoicing to be rid of their breeches and puttees, and saying the most outrageous things to the most respectable women in sight. Even the seller of Ganges-water he did not see, and Kim expected that he would at least buy a bottle of that precious stuff. He looked steadily at the ground, and strode as steadily hour after hour, his soul busied elsewhere. But Kim was in the seventh heaven of joy. The Grand Trunk [the great main road] at this point was built on an embankment to guard against winter floods from the foothills, so that one walked, as it were, a little above the country, along a stately corridor, seeing all India spread out to left and right. It was beautiful to behold the many-yoked grain and cotton wagons crawling over the country roads; one could hear their axles, complaining a mile away, coming nearer, till with shouts and yells and bad words they climbed up the steep incline and plunged on to the hard main road, carter reviling driver. It was equally beautiful to watch the people, little clumps of red and blue and pink and white and saffron, turning aside to go to their own villages, dispersing and growing small by twos and threes across the level plain. Kim felt these things, though he could not give tongue to his feelings, and so contented himself with buying peeled sugar-cane and spitting the pith generously about the path.

Kipling, Kim.

Inconsistency in the Point of View.—A writer who speaks of seeing from a given point of view details which could not be perceived from there is of course convicted of insincerity or of a lack of imagination. Even Sir Walter Scott, as Goethe says, sometimes lapses in this way. When the palmer Ivanhoe comes into the half lighted room at Cedric's, he describes him down to the thongs on his sandals, which would have been out of sight behind the table.

In the following description, it is plain to any one that an observer in the Visitor's Gallery could not hear what the girls were saying. Moreover, any one who is acquainted with the Visitor's Gallery in question knows that it is above the delivery desk and the door, so that a spectator could not see a student draw a book and go out. The writer, then, is false and inconsistent in the point of view.

From the visitor's gallery the Library Reading Room seems to be full of great green eyes, ever vigilant of the pursuits that go on beneath their glare—and what a range of activities is seen! Here at the left are two "co-eds," each with a bulky reference book opened before her. Their hands, however, are busied tucking in the strands of hair which have strayed from the parental hair-net; their thoughts, far from Gibbon's *Decline and Fall,* are intent on wondering which one of them the handsome man across the table is looking at, and their tongues are clacking an uninterrupted stream about "the thrillingest man I met last night."

In front of certain shelves a listless freshman is trying to select a book by which he may fulfill the outside reading requirement with the least possible mental effort.—Finally he returns the first book he looked at, and with a sigh as of Atlas with the weight of the world on his shoulders, he has it charged at the desks and drags himself from the room.

IV.   SEQUENCE

The Narrative Order.—The order or method of progress in a description is in a broad way like that of narrative. The natural order of description in nearly all cases is the order in which the data presented become evident to the observer—the order of description is the order of discovery.

Such a method of progress may even make a sort of story of what is observed. This is the method followed in the description of Dover Cliff, in *King Lear.* Edgar narrates to the blinded Gloster in succession what he sees as his eye travels down the cliff to the water.

> Come on, sir, here's the place!—stand still.—How fearful
> And dizzy 't is, to cast one's eyes so low!
> The crows and choughs that wing the midway air
> Show scarce so gross as beetles; half way down
> Hangs one that gathers samphire; dreadful trade!
> Methinks he seems no bigger than his head:
> The fishermen that walk upon the beach
> Appear like mice; and yond tall anchoring bark
> Diminished to her cock; her cock a buoy
> Almost too small for sight: the murmuring surge
> That on the unnumber'd idle pebbles chafes,
> Cannot be heard so high.   I'll look no more,
> Lest my brain turn, and the deficient sight
> Topple down headlong.

As a beginning in description, this story method, utilizing especially elements that approach the special kind of interest aroused in narrative, is the easiest by which to gain an effect. Such are all elements involving change, especially sudden change,—most of all motion, then light, particularly flashing and changing light, color (coming and going), and sound (alternating with silence). The purpose of such description differs from that of narrative in that it aims to create the feeling aroused by the phenomena observed, not to follow the action as a process.

Then silence follows—the silence that is full of the night noises of a great city. A stringed instrument of some kind is just, and only just, audible. High overhead some one throws open a window, and the rattle of the wood-work echoes down the empty street. On one of the roofs a hookah is in full blast; and the men are softly talking as the pipe gutters. A little farther on, the noise of conversation is more distinct. A slit of light shows itself between the sliding shutters of a shop. Inside, a stubble-bearded, weary-eyed trader is balancing his account-books among the bales of cotton prints that surround him. Three sheeted figures bear him company, and throw in a remark from time to time. First he makes an entry, then a remark; then passes the back of his hand across his steaming forehead. The heat of the built-in street is fearful. Inside the shops it must be almost unendurable. But the work goes on steadily; entry, guttural growl, and uplifted hand-stroke succeeding each other with the precision of clockwork.

Kipling, In Black and White.

Progressive Discovery in Static Material.—A writer has made a great step forward when he is not compelled to use such bustling means of effect and when he can give to things which do not change the interest of progressive discovery. For example, in the following passage the boy comes to be observed and known step by step, little by little.

One April evening, near Wells, I was sauntering along a road separated from a copse by an old moss-grown stone wall, when I noticed a boy moving cautiously about in the deep shadows of the trees, and watching me suspiciously.

"Found any nests?" I called out suddenly to him. He very quickly replied that he was not looking for nests, and had seen none; then he added that he was looking for primroses. Now he had no primroses in his hands, and as a matter of fact none grew in that particular copse; but I did not point this out to him, being desirous of engaging him in conversation. He was a singular-looking boy, about fourteen to fifteen years old; very thin, with long legs, small head, and sharp round face, and was dressed in earth-coloured, threadbare clothes much too small for him. With that small sharp face and those shifty eyes under his little grey cap, he looked curiously like some furred creature, rat or vole, with perhaps a dash of stoat in his composition, and if his nose had been longer I might have added that there was even a touch of the shrew-mouse in his appearance.

Hudson, W. H., *Nature in Downland;* by permission of Longmans, Green, and Company.

The following description carries out the same process on a large scale and with great elaboration.

Through the heavy door whose bronze network closes the place of his rest, let us enter the church itself. It is lost in still deeper twilight, to which the eye must be accustomed for some moments before the form of the building can be traced; and then there opens before us a vast cave, hewn out into the form of a Cross, and divided into shadowy aisles by many pillars. Round the domes of its roof the light enters only through narrow apertures like large stars; and here and there a ray or two from some far-away casement wanders into the darkness, and casts a narrow phosphoric stream upon the waves of marble that heave and fall in a thousand colors along the floor. What else there is of light is from torches, or silver lamps, burning ceaselessly in the recesses of the chapels; the roof sheeted with gold, and the polished walls covered with alabaster, give back at every curve and angle some feeble gleaming to the flames; and the glories round the heads of the sculptured saints flash out upon us as we pass them, and sink again into the gloom. Under foot and over head a continual succession of crowded imagery, one picture passing into another, as in a dream; forms beautiful and terrible mixed together; dragons and serpents, and ravening beasts of prey, and graceful birds that in the midst of them drink from running fountains and feed from vases of crystal: the passions and the pleasures of human life symbolized together, and the mystery of its redemption; for the mazes of interwoven lines and changeful pictures lead always at last to the Cross, lifted and carved in every place and upon every stone; sometimes with the serpent of eternity wrapt round it, sometimes with doves beneath its arms, and sweet herbage growing forth from its feet; but conspicuous most of all on the great rood that crosses the church before the altar, raised in bright blazonry against the shadow of the apse. And although in the recesses of the aisle and chapels, when the mist of the incense hangs heavily, we may see continually a figure traced in faint lines upon their marble, a woman standing with her eyes raised to heaven, and the inscription above her, "Mother of God," she is not here the presiding deity. It is the Cross that is first seen, and always, burning in the center of the temple; and every dome and hollow of its roof has the figure of Christ in the utmost height of it, raised in power, or returning in judgment.

Ruskin, *The Stones of Venice.*

From the Vague to the Definite.—One special form of discovery is the progress from the larger and vaguer features of the object described to the smaller and more definite ones, as in the following example:

The wide pampa rough with long grass; a vast level disc now growing dark, the horizon encircling it with a ring as faultless as that made by a pebble dropped into smooth water; above it the clear sky of June, wintry and pale, still showing in the west the saffron hues of the afterglow tinged with vapoury violet and grey. In the centre of the disc a large low rancho thatched with yellow rushes, a few stunted trees and cattle enclosures grouped about it; and dimly seen in the shadows, cattle and sheep reposing. At the gate stands Gregory Gorostiaga, lord of house, lands and ruminating herds, leisurely unsaddling his horse; for whatsoever Gregory does is done leisurely.

Hudson, W. H., *South American Sketches.*

From the General to the Specific.—Similarly the description may go from the general impression to the discovery of the details which taken all together contribute to the impression.

A cornfield in July is a sultry place. The soil is hot and dry; the wind comes across the lazily murmuring leaves laden with a warm, sickening smell drawn from the rapidly growing, broad-flung banners of the corn. The sun, nearly vertical, drops a flood of dazzling light upon the field over which the cool shadows run, only to make the heat seem the more intense.

Garland, *Main-Travelled Roads.*

The Fundamental Image.—There is one noteworthy descriptive method which at least seems to contravene the principle of arranging details in the order of discovery. This is the method of beginning by laying out or planning the ground to be covered by a diagram in words, usually expressed by a comparison of some kind. Such a method of description is termed the method of the "fundamental image." Thus Hugo begins his famous description of the field of Waterloo by comparing it to a capital A, and telling us what was at every point and along every line of the letter. In like manner Carlyle compares the plateau of Bohemia to the palm of the left hand well outspread, while Stevenson follows General Sherman in comparing the peninsula of Monterey to a fish hook. Now in all these cases the perception of the shape did not come first but last, from the making up of a literal or imaginary map of the region. Such a view is in ordinary life never seen at all; it is an idea or vision such as a bird or a traveler by aeroplane might get directly or a map-reader indirectly. Such descriptions may best be developed by the imaginary or real study of the map, the order being that of discovery from the map and not from the surface of the ground.

> The main building, regarded in its entirety, was a juxtaposition of hybrid constructions, which, looked at from a balloon, would very exactly form a gallows laid on the ground. The long arm of the gallows occupied the whole of the Rue Droit-Mur, comprised between the Little Rue Picpus and the Rue Polonceau; while the shorter arm was a tall, gray, stern, grated façade, looking on the Little Rue Picpus, of which the carriage entrance, No. 62, was the extremity. Toward the center of this façade dust and ashes whitened an old, low-arched gate, where the spiders made their webs, and which was only opened for an hour or two on Sundays, and on the rare occasions when the coffin of a nun left the convent; this was the public entrance to the church. The elbow of the gallows was a square room, used as an office, and which the nuns called the "buttery." In the long arm were the cells of the mothers, sisters, and novices; in the short one the kitchens, the refectory, along which a cloister ran, and the church. Between No. 62 and the corner of Aumarais Lane was the school, which could not be seen from the exterior.
>
> Hugo, *Les Misérables.*

Salient Detail.—All the methods of description hitherto enumerated consider an object as a whole, and follow through a systematic development. But frequently what we notice first and most strongly when we come upon an object is not what it is as a whole but what is singular and outstanding about it. It is not a man's general appearance that we see first of all, but his big nose or his glass eye. Again we notice nothing but what our experience has prepared us to see—the things that concern our business, or affect our way of thought, or fit into our affair of the moment. A farmer notices in my collie a good farm dog, my daughter his wagging tail and affectionate eyes, a chauffeur his hysterical barking, my neighbor's children his enthusiastic leaping in a game, the timid postman his threatening teeth and brist-

ling hair, and a dog fancier his black back and the form
of his muzzle indicating an admixture of foreign blood.
Every one sees my dog ''according to his business and
desire.'' So the order of discovery in many cases goes
by leaps, straight to the few salient things of consequence for the purpose or spirit of the instant—perhaps to the surprising or significant single detail, or perhaps to a few such details, seldom to many. Everything else is suppressed, the description proceeding
from the more to the less obvious, from the bigger to the
littler, but always from the less significant to the more
significant. In such descriptions, every general impression is omitted, and every detail is overlooked which has
no value for the special end in view. A sharp, strong,
clear impression is aimed at, no matter how one-sided.

V. EMOTIONAL SUGGESTION

Emotional Effect.—The principles thus far laid down
apply to descriptions of both types, the informative and
the imaginative,—touch the most accurate description
with feeling, and it becomes full of suggestion. The intellectual element in both types of description is the
same. The special means by which the emotional
quality is communicated remain 'to be considered.

The emotional effect of a description depends upon
its power of *suggestion;* words cannot in fact communicate with any precision the real impressions on the senses
produced by any object. I show you a bit of painted
wood; you recognize its tint as a very definite thing,
unlike any other—an opaque ivory white, with just so
much yellow in it and no more, and with just such a
gloss on the surface and no other. Even if I could de-

fine all that in words, you would find it hard to follow me; the abundance of detail would be cumbrous, and to define every tint thus would be absolutely impossible. And the same thing is true of every line and light and shadow, and of every variation of pitch and volume and quality in every sound, and so on through every sense. But in actually seeing and hearing we get all these details directly, exactly, and in effect instantaneously. A diagram or picture will give you in an instant and with precision what no words can tell. Therefore there is no such thing as a word-picture. There are only hints and appeals to emotion. Words can give information, can make a reader understand in a rough way the few points about the object necessary to deal with it and can give you by their power over your feeling the peculiar mood excited by the object in the mind of the author, sometimes even more strongly than the object itself.

It is not usually effective for the writer to express his own feeling about a scene. Such expressions as: "One of the most beautiful scenes which it has been my good fortune to witness"—"I shall never forget"—"The most sublime of all the"—add little directly; and indirectly they challenge the description, for if it does not live up to the specifications of the introductory words the reader is disappointed and is inclined to think even less of the description than if he had read it for itself merely on its own merits. A safe principle is to avoid inferences; to record not what one knows to be true, but what one gets actually through the senses. The writer, fixing his point of view, should record a few central really experienced facts of sense, with the most exact words possible.

Oak raised his head and listlessly surveyed the scene. By the outer margin of the pit was an oval pond, and over it hung the attenuated skeleton of a chrome-yellow moon, which had only a few days to last—the morning star dogging her on the right hand. The pool glittered like a dead man's eye, and as the world awoke a breeze blew, shaking and elongating the deflection of the moon without breaking it, and turning the image of the star to a phosphoric streak upon the water.

Hardy, *Far from the Madding Crowd.*

Marty South erected one of the young pines into its hole, and held up her finger; the soft musical breathing instantly set in, which was not to cease night or day till the grown tree should be felled—probably long after the two planters had been felled themselves.

Hardy, *The Woodlanders.*

An ugly reef is this of the Dhu Heartach; no pleasant assemblage of shelves, and pools, and creeks, about which a child might play for a whole summer without weariness, like the Bell-Rock or the Skerryvore, but one oval nodule of black-trap, sparsely bedabbled with an inconspicuous fucus, and alive in every crevice with a dingy insect between a slater and a bug. No other life was there but that of sea-birds, and of the sea itself, that here ran like a mill-race, and growled about the outer reef for ever, and ever and again, in the calmest weather, roared and spouted on the rock itself.

Stevenson, *Memories and Portraits.*

Strengthen the Nouns and Verbs.—Ordinarily, writers in their first efforts in description endeavor to add effect by applied modifiers, adjectives and adverbs. They will do well to try to make their nouns and verbs more exact and significant—not that the noun and the verb have some virtue not in the adjective and adverb, but because of the tendency to neglect the latter, and also because a bare noun or verb can sometimes be made to carry the full meaning of a noun or verb modified and thus economy and energy are increased.

The following examples are drawn from Mr. Cyril Falls's *Critical Study of Kipling.*

The Great Snake Kaa seems to *pour* himself along the ground.

"I saw a sword *lick out* past Crook's ear, an' the Pathan was tuk in the apple av of his throat like a pig at Droomeen Fair."

[An object, seen through the shimmering air of summer] *reeled* in the haze.

Other examples are:

She would *arrive like a whirlwind* and pervade the house with an *atmosphere of hello!*

Wells, Tono-Bungay.

The lamp *wriggled* in the gimbals, the loosened books *toppled* from side to side on the shelf, the long barometer *swung* in jerky circles.

Conrad, Typhoon.

The Sound of Words.—In conclusion, attention should be called to the effects of the sound of words in description. It is by the sound, tone and action of words, that humanly we express our feelings in speech. A special rhythm belongs to every emotion, and the writer who most adequately expresses the emotional element of his subject does so by the sound of his words. In general, this is an instinctive tendency, but like most such tendencies, it may be highly developed or practically repressed. A discontinuous, jerky, jolting, uncentered way of writing makes a description sound as if the writer took no interest in it. Consider the following examples, in which the sound is appropriate to the feeing.

Before he had quite sunken away, however, *the sharp and peevish tinkle of the shop-bell* made itself audible.

Hawthorne, The House of Seven Gables.

[At home, at twilight.] The music of a marriage procession came to the roof above the gentle hum of the city, and a string of flying foxes crossed the face of the low moon.

Kipling, Without Benefit of Clergy.

It was near noon when we set out; a dark day with clouds and the sun shining upon little patches. The sea was very deep and still, and had scarce a wave upon it; so that I must put the water to my lips before I could believe it to be truly salt. *The mountains on either side were high, rough and barren, very black and gloomy in the shadow of the clouds, but all silver-laced with little water-courses where the sun shone upon them.*

Stevenson, Kidnapped.

With regard to all these emotional means of effect, it should be said that they are not to be neglected; but for most writers it is best to be conscious and assiduous only in removing what is inappropriate, in avoiding false notes, in considering scrupulously exactness and propriety. Positive effort to manufacture the right metaphors or to employ the right rhythm almost inevitably produces the appearance of study and consciousness, and often betrays insincerity. The writer is safe who faithfully and genuinely aims to make his words fit his thoughts and feelings and who has no aim at decoration for its own sake.

VI. DESCRIPTION A SUBORDINATE FORM OF COMPOSITION

Description seldom stands alone as the main purpose of the book. A whole book written as one description of a great organic whole would be a monstrous thing. Some books, for example books of travel, are made up very largely of successive separate descriptions, but one vast description as such worked out like a great plot, is unthinkable. The mind could not bear to stand still so long, or to be so long concerned with the outside of things. Moreover, the moods which objects produce and which descriptions are meant to communicate are necessarily transient, and one description must give place to another, as the mood changes. Descriptions are parts, indispensable and vital parts, of other compositions. Narratives, in particular, could not be written without some description, and often they owe their chief interest to the abundance of descriptive effect which they carry along with them. Most effective of all are incidental short descriptive passages, a word, a phrase, a line or two at most. The fiction of the last fifty years abounds in descriptive passages of this kind.

That evening, to cheer our souls, Learoyd, Ortheris, and I went into the waste to smoke out a porcupine. All the dogs attended, but even their clamor—and they began to discuss the shortcomings of porcupines before they left cantonments—could not take us out of ourselves. A large, low moon turned the tops of the plume grass to silver, and the stunted camel thorn bushes and sour tamarisks into the likenesses of trooping devils. The smell of the sun had not left the earth, and little aimless winds blowing across the rose gardens to the southward brought the scent of dried roses and water. Our fire once started, and the dogs craftily disposed to wait the dash of the porcupine, we climbed to the top of a rain-scarred hillock of earth, and looked across the scrub seamed with cattle paths, white with the long grass, and dotted with spots of level pond-bottom, where the snipe would gather in winter.

"This," said Ortheris, with a sigh, as he took in the unkempt desolation of it all, "this is sanguinary. This is unusual sanguinary. Sort o' mad country. Like a grate when the fire's put out by the sun."

Kipling, *Soldiers Three.*

Some seven hours' incessant, hard travelling brought us early in the morning to the end of a range of mountains. In front of us there lay a piece of low, broken, desert land, which we must now cross. The sun was not long up, and shone straight in our eyes; a little, thin mist went up from the face of the moorland like a smoke; so that (as Alan said) there might have been twenty squadron of dragoons there and we none the wiser.

Stevenson, R. L., *Kidnapped.*

In Allan Water, near by where it falls into the Forth, we found a little sandy islet, overgrown with burdock, butterbur and the like low plants, that would just cover us if we lay flat. Here it was we made our camp, within plain view of Stirling Castle, whence we could hear the drums beat as some part of the garrison paraded. Shearers worked all day in a field on one side of the river, and we could hear the stones going on the hooks and the voices and even the words of the men talking. It behooved to lie close and keep silent.

Ibid.

[Cherry blossoms]—a white gust of blossoms above the wall.
Edith Wharton, *The Valley of Decision.*

A little harp-shaped ear, bedded in dark ruffles.

Ibid.

Two old ladies, presences of black and purple silk and fur and shining dark things.

Wells, *Tono-Bungay.*

RECAPITULATION

Description deals, like narration, with concrete objects, but unlike narration it deals with their appeal to the senses, not with the processes in which they take part. Descriptions are of two types, as they are intended primarily to carry information or to suggest impressions. Good descriptions rest upon an abundance of accurately observed material, have a consistent and clearly marked point of view, and follow an orderly development. In general the order of description is the order of discovery, sometimes of an actual succession of details, sometimes of details as they gradually reveal themselves to the observer. These descriptions tend to proceed from the vague to the definite, or from the general to the specific—or it may be that the attention is fixed instantly upon the salient details. The method of the "fundamental image" follows, as it were, the discovery of a map-reader. Emotional effect depends mainly upon the choice of salient details, the suggestive power of words, and effects of the sound of language. Description appears mainly as an element in works which belong to some other form of discourse; but it is not on that account to be neglected, since descriptive power is essential to force and reality in all writing.

CHAPTER XI

EXPOSITION

I.   EXPOSITION BASED UPON CLASSIFICATION

Exposition Defined.—Third of the forms of discourse is exposition. An exposition differs from a narrative and a description in that the narrative and description, in fact or imagination, deal with things as directly experienced, while exposition deals with ideas about things, which arise when the things are contemplated by the mind. If I tell you that Abraham Lincoln was a very tall man, with a lean, worn face, rugged features, eyes somewhat misted with weariness, but manifesting the utmost variety of expression, from the most delicate sympathy to flashing indignation, I am trying to describe him to you, to record and in some degree to reproduce some aspects of his physical presence as it comes before my imagination. If I tell you that Lincoln was a man who grew gradually to his greatness, being never alien to the life about him, but developing as it developed; that he was extraordinarily receptive and slow to take the shape of a permanent mold; that he was therefore more representative of the West of his day than any other man, I am expounding ideas about him, putting forth reflections that arise as I meditate upon Lincoln in connection with his associates.

Ideas Come from Classification.—These ideas or reflections are the result of comparisons, of the finding of resemblances and differences between one thing and another. I can get an impression of Lincoln just by seeing his statue; I get ideas about him by comparing him with other men; with his opponents, with the members of his Cabinet, with statesmen of other times and places, with the great men of the world. If I were to see a chair for the first time I could make out its form, I could pick it up and feel its weight; I know what it is because it is like some other chairs and unlike some. I *place* it by comparing it with other chairs, as of one kind or another—an arm-chair or a dentist's chair—I understand it and can apply it effectively to its purpose because I put it into some class; thus my ideas come from comparisons, which establish resemblances and differences.

I know this chair as it is like and unlike other chairs. I put it in a class. I know Lincoln as an Illinoisan, a statesman, a great man, one of the stars of humanity both by his likeness and his unlikeness to the rest of his class.

Comparison and the perception of likeness and difference underlie every general idea. If I say, for example, "Intemperance causes misery," I have first got the notion of intemperance by comparing and contrasting one man's act or one man's way of life with another, and thus have made classes of temperate and intemperate acts and ways; and *intemperance* is a character which I know as common to all the members of one of these classes. In the same manner I get the notion of *misery;* and by further comparison I bring these two ideas together.

More or Less Inclusive Classes.—It is plain, then, that in forming classes the mind proceeds by perceiving resemblances and differences. In dealing with the same kind of things, attention may be centered upon a few points of resemblance, making an inclusive class, or upon more and more points of resemblance, limiting at each step the inclusiveness of the class thought of. I see in my dining-room chair so many points of resemblance to the rest of the set, in shape, size, color, weight, in everything, that I can hardly tell one from the other. But if I look at my neighbor's dining-room chairs, the number of points of resemblance is much smaller—a general likeness in shape and size and function alone can be seen. So if I look at a Morris chair and an office chair, I see fewer resemblances still. Thus if I make a class, *my dining-room chairs*, it is less inclusive, but more full of characteristics than the class of *dining-room chairs,* and this class again includes fewer members but has more common characteristics than the class of *chairs;* and this class again is less inclusive but more characterizing than the class *seats;* and this than the class *objects of furniture;* and this than *manufactured objects;* and so on.

The Importance of Good Classification.—By effective classification the superior mind is shown. An inferior mind classifies little; is not clear in its divison of classes; does not make classes that have a value for the purpose in hand; overlooks vital resemblances; is led astray by superficial likenesses; cannot maintain a line of classification systematically to an end; and fails to perceive the essential distinctions which mark off a less inclusive class from the more inclusive class of which it is a part. The poor mind sees the world as a cluttered lumber-room, an unmanageable place; the good mind puts it to some extent in order, finds each experience not new but related to other experiences, sees into it, and thus lives in a comparatively systematic world and knows what to do with it. Sound classification is the source of sensible practice, as well as of intellectual progress.

Use the Test of Classification.—A good classification, to use a common phrase, "gets you somewhere"; it is not pointless or formal, but is directed to an object which the maker of the classification sees to be of importance. This importance depends upon the purpose, the mind, of the man who has to deal with the matter in hand. If my business with a whale is to consider him as a whaler might, a whale is a *fish*, a swift shuttle-shaped creature, inhabiting the ocean, and to be caught with a line from a boat. If my business with a whale is to understand his ways of living, a whale is not a fish, but a *mammal*, a warm-blooded animal which suckles its young. As a source of oil, a whale is in one class; as a source of food, in another class. Each class is as true as another and as good as another if it fits the object in view.

A British railway-guard—what corresponds roughly to an American brakeman—saw a lady with a parrot.

"You'll have to put that parrot in the luggage-van, mem; rules of the Company."

"I don't see why. The sign up there says dogs must be put in the luggage-van; but it does n't say anything about parrots. Besides, you are not disturbing that boy with the turtle."

"Yes, mem, it has to go. It says *dogs;* and cats is dogs, and parrots is dogs; but turtles is insex."

The classification was good if somewhat inartificially named, for it served the true purpose of the rule and made a genuine and sensible line of distinction.

Use is the true test of the principle of classification.

Resemblance and Difference.—Sometimes it is of importance to make very large classes, to find the few resemblances which group a multitude of things together. To find a book in a library, you are likely to have to think of it as a member of a large class. You will not find a list of books on *amusements in small towns,* but will have to look under *recreations,* or perhaps *social science.* Sir Isaac Newton made the whole physical world from the remotest star to the bones of our bodies and the sand at our feet manageable, by classifying all matter as having weight, as under the law of gravitation.

Here it was large relations and inclusive classes that were of consequence.

At other times it is little differences and exact definitions that are of use. If two mushrooms, one edible and one poisonous, are much alike, it is somewhat important to know the likeness, but it may be a matter of life and death to know the difference. Between the two extremes any degree of inclusiveness or of narrowness may be useful and significant. If I were to buy an automobile, I should need to know both the general characteristics of automobiles, and the peculiarities of the car that I bought. A good classification may be either fine or broad, but whether fine or broad, the classification *makes a difference,* has consequences worth attending to.

Illustrations.—No matter how broad or how narrow the scope of the class formed, I can myself understand it best, and make it clearest to others, if I think of the principle which underlies the class as acting in individual cases. Thus Sir Isaac Newton, in expounding the application of his law to the heavenly bodies, showed how an object shot far enough up from the earth would keep continually falling round it in a regular orbit; and Jesus laid down the doctrine of universal benevolence by the parable of the Good Samaritan.

II. EXPOSITION OF THE RESEMBLANCES COMMON TO A CLASS

Expositions, then, may concern themselves mainly with the points of resemblance between the ideas expounded and other ideas, or mainly with the points of difference, or in varying degrees with both resemblances and differences. Of whatever type they may be and in whatever field they lie, they nearly always require concrete illustration to be made fully clear and vivid. Further, they may seek to elucidate primarily the nature of the class considered by itself and may view only the members of that class, or they may look for wider relations and broader outlines, in order to bring out the significance of the class in comparison with more inclusive conceptions. Let us consider first those expositions which treat the class by itself, without looking beyond it. And let us begin with the simplest cases we can find.

Generalized Narratives.—Probably the simplest form of exposition is that dealing with processes, in which the elements common to a number of transactions are considered. The following is a brief example.

As typical of the ordinary flame illuminants we may consider the case of the ordinary paraffin candle. In the candle the flame melts the wax at the foot of the wick, forming a cup there. The melted wax is sucked up the wick by capillary attraction and vaporised and burned as a vapour in the flame. The upward draught of air to the flame keeps the sides of the candle cool and prevents the edge from melting. The wax of course prevents the flame from burning too far down the wick. The top of the wick bends over into the edge of the flame and is consumed there.

Houstoun, R. A., A Treatise on Light.

To recur to our illustration of the chemical experiment, I report my experience as a story; but the important thing about it is that every time the same results will follow, so that instead of telling a story of my adventures with potassium permanganate in a florence flask, the useful thing for me to do is to neglect the peculiarities, the mistakes or misfortunes of my experiment, and to tell what everybody's experience is—to make a class of transactions—in other words to conceive of the report of the process as generalized narrative. Thus there is a kind of exposition in which the steps of a process are recounted not as individual but as typical;—how to do something, simple or complicated,—how to build a flat-bottomed row boat, or a house with a balloon frame, or to make pie crust, or to smelt zinc,—in brief to recount the essential steps common to all the examples of the process under consideration. The writing of such an exposition is in general a relatively simple problem; it is simply telling a story without individual features. The exposition differs from an ordinary narrative chiefly in one point, that conscious effort should be made to discover and express the fundamental idea or the purpose of the whole course of events. Why roll pie-crust? What is the ultimate reason for the complicated system of valves in a locomotive engine? What is the underlying idea of the whole business? If there are secondary purposes, connected with special steps in the process, they too should be made clear. For it is the purpose which is the most fundamental element of the process; the steps are determined by the purpose, and if the same purpose can be achieved by steps differing in detail, the process may vary somewhat, though it is essentially the same in nature. A good treatise on metallurgy will not only tell correctly what are the ordinary steps to be taken in smelting metallic oxides, but will explain that most metallic oxides when heated will part with their oxygen to carbon if any be present, leaving the metal more manageable and nearer purity than before. A good treatise on cookery will have something to say about the principles of the union of fat, fluid, and flour in pastry, and will not only direct that pie-crust should be cold, and should be rolled, but will tell why. A good account of the process of uplift by which some types of mountains are formed will not be satisfied with merely recounting the phenomena, such as earthquakes and eruptions, but will try to reach the more fundamental elements, the slip or dislocation of the deeper parts of the surface of the earth along lines of weakness.

What has been said applies to expositions which are addressed to an intelligent general public, not specially familiar with the subject treated. It would be a waste of time to present general principles for the benefit of those to whom they are already well known. An engineer looking at a new type of locomotive does not care to go back to the beginning of engine-making; he wishes to know the features characteristic of this engine and the special peculiarities of the method of running it. A cook wants to know what is *new* in a new recipe, not what is old. But for practice it is best to address oneself to a public of educated and intelligent people, not specialists. The following passage illustrates the combination of somewhat technical ideas with untechnical language, in a generalized narrative.

In the torrid zone, the ordinary succession of weather from day to day is remarkably constant. The range of temperature, the faint double oscillation of the barometer, the periodic increase and decrease of cloudiness all show a regularity of recurrence that is unknown in our latitudes. If in such a region the barometer is noticed to rise unusually high, or to stand stationary when its diurnal fall is expected, this may be often on land the first sign of a coming cyclone; but at sea, the faint rise of the barometer is preceded by the arrival of a long rolling swell that swings rapidly out from the storm on all sides, so as to herald its coming even three or four days before its arrival.

The faint rise of the barometer is felt on nearly all sides of the storm area, and it therefore marks what may be called the pericyclonic ring. When its highest pressure is reached, the wind commonly fails. Then fine plumiform cirrus clouds are seen spreading over the sky from the quarter towards the storm center, which may then be one or two hundred miles away in the direction of the doldrums; and about the time of the appearance of these clouds the barometer slowly falls and the calm is succeeded by a gentle breeze. The air becomes sultry, and the sunsets take on lurid colors. When first felt, the breeze generally blows five or six points to the right (in the northern hemisphere) of the direction leading to the storm center. All these signs become more marked as the cyclone draws near; the cirrus clouds thicken and become matted together in cirro-stratus form, veiling the blue of the sky; the refraction of sunlight through the ice crystals of the clouds forms halos around the sun or moon, with the orange or red color on the inner and the blue on the outer side of the circle. Later, the mass of clouds become so thick as to obscure the sun, and leave the upper air evenly overcast. The winds have freshened by this time, and blow to the right of a low and distant mass of dark cloud; isolated patches of cloud are seen to form at one side, increase in size, and flow in to join the central nimbus mass.

The wind increases to a gale, the waves rise on the sea, the dark clouds approach, thickening as they come, and rain begins to fall from them. The storm center may be then fifty or more miles away, advancing slowly with the whole system of whirling winds at a rate of eight, ten, or twelve miles an hour. The barometer continually [sinks], and at last falls rapidly; with this the roaring wind increases to full hurricane strength, the low scud clouds fly before its blasts, the lightning flashes, the rain descends in drenching torrents, cooling the sultry air.

Before the law of storms was learned, many a ship was borne before such a hurricane, with all sails furled or blown away, helpless in the violence of the winds and waves; and when the vessel was at last about to founder, the wind has suddenly weakened to a calm in the eye of the storm; falling from its greatest violence to an almost perfect repose in fifteen minutes or less. The rain ceases, even the clouds break away, showing the blue sky by day and the stars by night; but the waves still roll and toss, and in even more dreaded form than their regular heaving before the hurricane; for in the eye of the storm they swing in from all sides, and pitch and heave tumultuously, forming irregular pits and peaks of water which strain a vessel violently, even to leaking and sinking. A few careful records made in the calm storm center while passing over a land station show a peculiar change in the temperature and humidity of the air. Underneath the surrounding heavy clouds, the air is somewhat cooled and held close to its dewpoint by the rainfall; yet the air within the calm center has been found to be comparatively dry with a temperature unduly high; but it is not yet known if these features always prevail. The diameter of the calm space may be ten, twenty, or thirty miles, perhaps a tenth or a fifteenth of the diameter of the whole storm; and its duration in passing a given point may vary from half an hour to two hours: the barometer reading in the center may be even less than 27 inches.

As the hurricane on the further side of the central calm approaches the observer, its moaning can be heard in the distance, rising in a portentous roar as it comes near, and then breaking suddenly with as great a fury as the hurricane which died away before, but its direction is now the reverse of that of the winds by which the calm was preceded. All the elements of the cyclone reappear; the blasts of the wind beat up the waves to their greatest height, the clouds hang low and heavy over the darkened sea, the rain falls again in torrents; and then as the storm gradually moves away, all these signs of its activity weaken. In the course of a day or two, the barometer rises nearly to its usual height, the wind dies down, the waves fall to a long low swell, the lower clouds recede, the lofty cirrus plumes retreat after them, and the sky is left in its accustomed clearness.

Davis, W. M., *Elementary Meteorology;* by permission of Ginn and Company.

Generalized Descriptions.—As narration may thus be generalized and become expository, so may description. My own dog or cat interests me most because it is itself, and is after all not like any other creature of its kind; and if I write about it I may write somewhat indeed of its cattiness or doggishness,—of the cat's fitness for domestic ornament and charm without losing a certain independence in the midst of civilized life,—but I also write of its special behavior,—of how it comes down the street to meet me as a dog would. I tell not alone of the dog's pathetic devotion and dependence but how the dog dislikes the postman and likes the grocer's boy, for no reason that I can see. But if I become interested in kinds and classes of cats and dogs I neglect the specialties of the individual, and try to learn and communicate general truths about the structure and appearance and habits of the animals. In this way I build up an exposition depending upon the observation of physical resemblances. I find out if I can what features are common to all dogs. I discriminate between the high-built long-muzzled swift type of dog, which fights by leaping and slashing, and the stocky, short-muzzled, heavy type, which fights by gripping and tugging. A generalized description is not so simple as a generalized narrative, both because it is not so easy to decide upon the order of the parts, and because it is not so often possible to perceive a clearly defined purpose or general law which gives a reason for the existence of the other characteristics. If such a principle can be perceived, then of course, it becomes central in the generalized description. Otherwise, the order and emphasis of descriptive exposition commonly follow the method of proceeding systematically from the general to the particular with a conclusion accentuating the general result of the discussion. Dr. Elliott Coues writes a descriptive exposition of the mode of flight of the short-tailed grouse.

The mode of flight of this species is not peculiar; it rises with a startling whirr from the ground, till it attains a certain elevation—its straight, steady course, performed with great velocity by alternate sailing and flapping, are points it shares with its relatives. The wing-beats are rapid and energetic, giving it an impulse that enables it to sail long distances, when the wings are held stiffly expanded to their full extent, somewhat decurved, and with the points of the quill-feathers separated. The bird's voice is highly characteristic. It is so almost invariably uttered during flight, at particular moments with reference to the delivery of the wing-strokes, that for some time after my first acquaintance with the birds I was in doubt whether the sound were mechanical or vocal; nor was the uncertainty removed until I had heard it from the birds at rest. The ordinary note of alarm is almost invariably sounded just before the bird takes wing, whether from the ground or from a tree, and is usually repeated with each succeeding set of wing-beats, seeming to be jerked out of the bird by its muscular efforts. But we hear it also when, the bird being at rest, it becomes alarmed, yet not sufficiently to fly away; and when a bird is passing at full speed, sufficiently near, we may clearly distinguish the mechanical whirring sound of its wings, as well as, sometimes, the creaking rustle of its tail-feathers as it turns its flight. When roosting at ease among the trees, and probably at other times, the grouse have a different set of notes—a sociable cackling or clucking, with which they entertain each other.

Coues, Elliott, *Birds of the Middle West.*

Structures.—From these types of exposition it is natural to proceed to a more abstract type, which follows the same method—a type which mainly deals with the characteristics common to a group of things, but which concerns itself not primarily with physical phenomena, but with conceptions of the mind. Even in discussing elm-trees and pie-crust the attention naturally turns somewhat to ideas, purposes, and principles of construction. The following passage illustrates the bringing out of the central idea of a structure.

I have here in my hand one of the simplest possible examples of the union of the graphic and constructive powers,—one of my breakfast plates. Since all the finely architectural arts, we said, began in the shaping of the cup and the platter, we will begin, ourselves, with the platter.

Why has it been made round? For two structural reasons: first, that the greatest holding surface may be gathered into the smallest space; and secondly, that in being pushed past other things on the table, it may come into least contact with them.

Next, why has it a rim? For two other structural reasons: first, that it is convenient to put salt or mustard upon; but secondly, and chiefly, that the plate may be easily laid hold of. The rim is the simplest form of continuous handle.

Farther, to keep it from soiling the cloth, it will be wise to put this ridge beneath, round the bottom; for as the rim is the simplest possible form of continuous handle, so this is the simplest form of continuous leg. And we get the section given beneath the figure for the essential one of a rightly made platter.

Ruskin, *Aratra Pentelici.*

Types of People.—Likewise in the treatment of classes of people, such as The Village Gossip, or The City Banker, though appearance and demeanor are not neglected, character and ideas are more central and more important.

Nature has stamped the Indian with a hard and stern physiognomy. Ambition, revenge, envy, jealousy, are his ruling passions; and his cold temperament is little exposed to those effeminate vices which are the bane of milder races. With him revenge is an overpowering instinct; nay, more, it is a point of honor and a duty. His pride sets all language at defiance. He loathes the thought of coercion; and few of his race have ever stooped to discharge a menial office. A wild love of liberty, an utter intolerance of control, lie at the basis of his character, and fire his whole existence. Yet, in spite of this haughty independence, he is a devout hero-worshipper; and high achievement in war or policy touches a chord to which his nature never fails to respond. He looks up with admiring reverence to the sages and heroes of his tribe; and it is this principle, joined to the respect for age springing from the patriarchal element in his social system, which, beyond all others, contributes union and harmony to the erratic members of an Indian community. With him the love of glory kindles into a burning passion; and to allay its cravings, he will dare cold and famine, fire, tempest, torture, and death itself.

These generous traits are overcast by much that is dark, cold, and sinister, by sleepless distrust, and rankling jealousy. Treacherous himself, he is always suspicious of treachery in others. Brave as he is,—and few of mankind are braver,—he will vent his passion by a secret stab rather than an open blow. His warfare is full of ambuscade and stratagem; and he never rushes into battle with that joyous self-abandonment, with which the warriors of the Gothic races flung themselves into the ranks of their enemies. In his feasts and his drinking bouts we find none of that robust and full-toned mirth, which reigned at the rude carousals of our barbaric ancestry. He is never jovial in his cups, and maudlin sorrow or maniacal rage is the sole result of his potations.

Over all emotion he throws the veil of an iron self-control, originating in a peculiar form of pride, and fostered by rigorous discipline from childhood upward. He is trained to conceal passion, and not to subdue it. The inscrutable warrior is aptly imaged by the hackneyed figure of a volcano covered with snow; and no man can say when or where the wild-fire will burst forth. This shallow self-mastery serves to give dignity to public deliberation, and harmony to social life. Wrangling and quarreling are strangers to an Indian dwelling; and while an assembly of the ancient Gauls was as garrulous as a convocation of magpies, a Roman senate might have taken a lesson from the grave solemnity of an Indian council. In the midst of his family and friends, he hides affections, by nature none of the most tender, under a mask of icy coldness; and in the torturing fires of his enemy, the haughty sufferer maintains to the last his look of grim defiance.

Parkman, F., *The Conspiracy of Pontiac;* by permission of Little, Brown, and Company.

Analysis of General Ideas.—But the process of analysis may deal with matters still more abstract. What do I mean, for example, by a *law*—in other words, what is the common element in all the rules issued by cities, counties, states, governments of all types? They are commands; obedience to them is enforced by penalties; they are the will of the recognized rulers of organized society in its political aspect. What are the duties of a tenant? What is a medium of exchange? In such expositions, the process involved is the perception of common features, grouped about the most fundamental and general idea of all. In these more abstract expositions the relation of cause and effect must be considered even more carefully than in generalized narrations and descriptions, and concrete illustrations are often essential to make clear the application of the ideas discussed.

If you will carefully consider what it is that you have done most often during this day, I think you can hardly avoid being drawn to this conclusion: that you have really done nothing else from morning to night but *change your mind.* You began by waking up. Now that act of waking is itself a passage of the mind from an unconscious to a conscious state, which is about the greatest change that the mind can undergo. Your first idea upon waking was probably that you were going to rest for some time longer; but this rapidly passed away, and was changed into a desire for action, which again transformed itself into a volition, and produced the physical act of getting up. From this arose a series of new sensations; that is to say, a change of mind from the state of not perceiving or feeling these things to the state of feeling them. And so afterwards. Did you perform any deliberate action? There was the change of mind from indecision to decision, from decided desire to

volition, from volition to act. Did you perform an impulsive
action? Here there is the more sudden and conspicuous change
marked by the word *impulsive;* as if your mind was a shuttlecock, which has its entire state of motion suddenly changed by
the *impulse* of the battledore: conceive the shuttlecock descending quite regularly with a gentle corkscrew motion—the battledore intervenes—instantaneously the shuttlecock flies off in
a totally unexpected direction, having apparently no relation to
its previous motion; and you will see how very apt and expressive a simile you use when you speak of certain people
as having an *impulsive temperament.* Have you felt happy
or miserable? It was a change in your way of looking at
things in general; a transition, as Spinoza says, from a lower
to a higher state of perfection, or *vice versa.* In a word, whatever you have done, or felt, or thought, you will find upon
reflection that you could not possibly be conscious of anything
else than a change of mind.

Clifford, W. K., *Lectures and Essays;* by permission of
the Macmillan Company.

Resemblance in Spite of Difference.—All the forms of
exposition discussed depend upon the enumeration of
resemblances among the members of a class. These
resemblances are the more significant and interesting
the greater the difference among the members of the
class.

It is those resemblances which exist in spite of differences which have the most meaning. Huxley, for
example, intends in the following passage to insist upon
the resemblance in fundamental aspects of the substance
of all living creatures; and he looks first to the differences between them, thus making the class idea predominate over the individual idea.

In order to make the title of this discourse generally intelligible, I have translated the term "Protoplasm," which is the
scientific name of the substance of which I am about to speak,
by the words "the physical basis of life." I suppose that, to
many, the idea that there is such a thing as a physical basis,
or matter, of life may be novel—so widely spread is the con-

ception of life as a something which works through matter, but is independent of it; and even those who are aware that matter and life are inseparably connected, may not be prepared for the conclusion plainly suggested by the phrase, "the physical basis or matter of life," that there is some one kind of matter which is common to all living beings, and that their endless diversities are bound together by a physical, as well as an ideal, unity. In fact, when first apprehended, such a doctrine as this appears almost shocking to common sense.

What, truly, can seem to be more obviously different from one another, in faculty, in form, and in substance, than the various kinds of living beings? What community of faculty can there be between the bright-coloured lichen, which so nearly resembles a mere mineral incrustation of the bare rock on which it grows, and the painter, to whom it is instinct with beauty, or the botanist, whom it feeds with knowledge?

Again, think of the microscopic fungus—a mere infinitesimal ovoid particle, which finds space and duration enough to multiply into countless millions in the body of a living fly; and then of the wealth of foliage, the luxuriance of flower and fruit, which lies between this bald sketch of a plant and the giant pine of California, towering to the dimensions of a cathedral spire, or the Indian fig, which covers acres with its profound shadow, and endures while nations and empires come and go around its vast circumference. Or, turning to the other half of the world of life, picture to yourselves the great Finner whale, hugest of beasts that live, or have lived, disporting his eighty or ninety feet of bone, muscle and blubber, with easy roll, among waves in which the stoutest ship that ever left dockyard would flounder hopelessly; and contrast him with the invisible animalcules—mere gelatinous specks, multitudes of which could, in fact, dance upon the point of a needle with the same ease as the angels of the Schoolmen could, in imagination. With these images before your minds, you may well ask, what community of form, or structure, is there between the animalcule and the whale; or between the fungus and the fig-tree? And, *a fortiori*, between all four?

Finally, if we regard substance, or material composition, what hidden bond can connect the flower which a girl wears in her hair and the blood which courses through her youthful veins; or, what is there in common between the dense and resisting mass of the oak, or the strong fabric of the tortoise, and those broad disks of glassy jelly which may be seen pulsating through the waters of a calm sea, but which drain away to mere films in the hand which raises them out of their element?

Such objections as these must, I think, arise in the mind of every one who ponders, for the first time, upon the conception of a single physical basis of life underlying all the diversities of vital existence; but I propose to demonstrate to you that, notwithstanding these apparent difficulties, a threefold unity— namely, a unity of power or faculty, a unity of form, and a unity of substantial composition—does pervade the whole living world.

                    Huxley, *The Physical Basis of Life.*

III.   EXPOSITION OF A CLASS BY DISTINCTION FROM RELATED CLASSES

Now it is difficult in the treatment of such topics as have been suggested for the writer to confine himself to the characteristics of the class which he is directly treating, and to avoid making clear its nature by insisting upon its difference from other classes. Often, as has been suggested, it is the difference which is of consequence. The provisions of the civil law, the rules of social conventions and the principles of morality are alike; all are commands given for the regulation of human conduct, all are cherished and enforced by a social sanction, the infraction of each brings a penalty. What is the distinction that makes law *law?* A conception is made clear by considering what it is not and why it is unlike other conceptions, as well as by considering what it is and why it is like other conceptions.

A difference has no point except as between things which have some resemblances, as a resemblance is most interesting and instructive when it exists in spite of differences. It is a commonplace, for example, that a white-oak tree and a scrubby little bush are different; but if the little bush turns out to be a chinquapin, also a species of oak, the fact that being botanically alike in flower and fruit the two plants are so different in habit, or that being so different they turn out to be of the same botanical family—the likeness in spite of unlikeness, and the unlikeness in spite of likeness are interesting.

Wherever, therefore, differences are to be insisted upon, resemblances should be found, and a class formed to include the differing things. To say of two characters in literature, Beowulf and Achilles for example, that they are unlike, that one is grave, sombre, and steady while the other is brilliant and emotional, is of little interest. But to discern that here are two heroes of epic story, both young, both favored by superhuman agencies, both princely commanders of a force of men, both doomed to a tragic end, both confident and boastful in word, brave and mighty in deed, all this gives significance to the differences, the greater variety and richness of contrast in the Greek hero as compared with the somewhat monotonous Beowulf, to the more human interest which characterizes Achilles, because though mighty he has not Beowulf's magic gifts of superhuman endurance and physical strength, while at the same time the Germanic hero is more stable and more self-sacrificing than the Greek hero. Many young writers make the mistake of failing to lay the foundation of likeness as a basis for differences and thus cause their work to be relatively pointless.

It is not easy to write a familiar style. Many people mistake a familiar for a vulgar style, and suppose that to write without affectation is to write at random. On the contrary, there is nothing that requires more precision, and, if I may so say, Purity of expression, than the style I am speaking of. It utterly rejects not only all unmeaning pomp, but all low, cant phrases, and loose, unconnected, slipshod allusions. It is not to take the first word that offers, but the best word in common use; it is not to throw words together in any combinations we please, but to follow and avail ourselves of the true idiom of the language. To write a genuinely familiar or truly English style, is to write as anyone would speak in common conversation, who had a thorough command and choice of words, or who could discourse with ease, force, and perspicuity, setting aside all pedantic and oratorical flourishes. Or to give another illustration, to write naturally is the same thing in regard to common conversation, as to read naturally is in regard to common speech. It does not follow that it is an easy thing to give the true accent and inflection to the words you utter, because you do not attempt to rise above the level of ordinary life and colloquial speaking. You do not assume indeed the solemnity of the pulpit, or the tone of stage-declamation: neither are you at liberty to gabble on at a venture, without emphasis or discretion, or to resort to vulgar dialect or clownish pronunciation. You must steer a middle course. You are tied down to a given and appropriate articulation, which is determined by the habitual associations between sense and sound, and which you can only hit by entering into the author's meaning, as you must find the proper words and style to express yourself by fixing your thoughts on the subject you have to write about. Anyone may mouth out a passage with a theatrical cadence, or get upon stilts to tell his thoughts: but to write or speak with propriety and simplicity is a more difficult task. Thus it is easy to affect a pompous style, to use a word twice as big as the thing you want to express: it is not so easy to pitch upon the very word that exactly fits it. Out of eight or ten words equally common, equally intelligible, with nearly equal pretensions, it is a matter of some nicety and discrimination to pick out the very one, the preferableness of which is scarcely perceptible, but decisive. . . . A fine tact is shown in adhering to those which are perfectly common, and yet never falling into any expressions which are debased by disgusting circumstances, or which owe their signification and point to technical or professional allusions. A truly natural or familiar style can never be quaint or vulgar, for this reason, that it is of universal force and applicability, and that quaintness and vulgarity arise out of the immediate connection of certain words with coarse and disagreeable, or with confined ideas. The last form what we understand by cant or slang phrases. To give an example of what is not very clear in the general statement I should say that the phrase *to cut with a knife,* or *to cut a piece of wood,* is perfectly free from vulgarity, because it is perfectly common; but *to cut an acquaintance* is not quite unexceptionable, because it is not perfectly common or intelligible, and has hardly yet escaped out of the limits of slang phraseology. I should hardly therefore use the word in this sense without putting it in italics as a license of expression, to be received *cum grano salis.* All provincial or bye-phrases come under the same mark of reprobation—all such as the writer transfers to the page from his fireside or a particular coterie, or that he invents for his own sole use and convenience. I conceive that words are like money, not the worse for being common, but that it is the stamp of custom alone that gives them circulation or value.

Hazlitt, W., On Familiar Style.

IV. EXPOSITION OF A CLASS BY ANALOGY WITH RELATED CLASSES

In all the cases hitherto dealt with, it is the content of the class idea within itself that has been under examination. But sometimes it may be more important to consider the class as a branch or member of a wider group governed by similar principles. If for example we write of *College Spirit,* we shall best manifest its fundamental nature by thinking of it as a *loyalty* comparable to other loyalties. It is not its peculiar characteristics as a class that are most vital but primarily the characteristics which it has in common with loyalty in general. When these are defined it becomes easy to apply the conception to the pecularities of college experience. We have loyalty to family, to country, to church, even in some sense to the business establishment in which we are employed; we have loyalty even to committees and casual assemblages. In other words we owe a loyalty to groups of human beings which we did not form, and which we did not enter of our own will, yet the mere being in which creates for us a duty. In all these cases there are a selfish and an ideal loyalty. There is a loyalty to a mere organization as it exists, and there is a loyalty to the idea which lies behind it. Thus one might proceed at length investigating the nature of loyalty as fully as possible, and then applying the conception to college spirit.

A somewhat similar method of exposition is to explain the characteristics of a class of things by comparing it to another class like it in some essential points, but simpler or more familiar. This method, known as exposition by *analogy*, is of use particularly with difficult subjects.

If I were to wet my finger and then rub it along the edge of this glass, I should no doubt persuade the glass to give out a certain musical note. So also if I were to sing to that glass the same note loud enough, I should get the glass to answer me back with a note.

I want you to remember that fact, because it is of capital importance for the argument we shall have to consider tonight. The very same note which I can get the tumbler to give out by agitating it, by rubbing the edge, that same note I can also get the tumbler to answer back to me when I sing to it. Now, remembering that, please to conceive a rather complicated thing that I am going to try to describe to you. The same property that belongs to the glass belongs also to a bell that is made out of metal. If that bell is agitated by being struck, or in any other way, it will answer back if you sing that sound to it; but if you sing a different sound to it then it will not answer.

Now suppose that I have several of these metal bells which answer to quite different notes, and that they are all fastened to a set of elastic stalks which spring out of a certain centre to which they are fastened. All these bells, then, are not only fastened to these stalks, but they are held there in such a way that they can spin round upon the points to which they are fastened.

And then the centre to which these elastic stalks are fastened or suspended, you may imagine as able to move in all manner of directions, and that the whole structure made up of these bells and stalks and centre is able to spin round any axis whatever. We must also suppose that there is surrounding this structure a certain framework. We will suppose the framework to be made of some elastic material, so that it is able to be pressed in to a certain extent. Suppose that framework is made of whalebone, if you like. The structure I am going for the present to call an "atom." I do not mean to say that there is anything in an atom which is in the shape of a bell; and I do not mean to say that there is anything analogous to an elastic stalk in it. But what I mean is this—that an atom is something that is capable of vibrating at certain definite rates; also that it is capable of other motions of its parts besides those vibrations at certain definite rates; and also that it is capable of spinning round about any axis. Now by the framework which I suppose to be that structure made out of bells and elastic stalks, I mean this—that supposing you had two such structures, then you cannot put them closer together than a certain distance, but they will begin to resist being put so close together after you have put them as near as that, and they will push each other away if you attempt to put them closer. That is all I mean then. You must only suppose that that structure is described, and that set of ideas is put together just for the sake of giving us some definite notion of a thing which has similar properties to that structure. But you must not suppose that there is any special part of an atom which has got a bell-like form, or any part like an elastic stalk made out of whalebone.

Clifford, W. K., *Lectures and Essays;* by permission of the Macmillan Company.

V. EXPOSITION BY DIVISION

In the methods just treated we as it were ascend, to obtain broader views. We may also need to descend, to obtain closer and more exact ideas. Instead of going beyond the class to be expounded in order to enlarge the range of our ideas, we may require to break it up into smaller classes, and obtain an understanding of the scope and significance of the class by observing what classes it includes. In doing this, it is best not to proceed from a very large class suddenly to a very small

class, but first to divide the inclusive class into the
largest group which can naturally be included under it,
and then to proceed systematically, subdividing as far
as may be useful under the circumstances. There would
not commonly be much point in comparing domestic
cattle with other domestic animals, such as swine, or
sheep; the more valuable knowledge is to be obtained
by dividing the class of cattle into dairy cattle, beef
cattle, and cattle adapted in a fair degree for both purposes. And of course it would be unprofitable to leap
at once from the general class of cattle to Herefords and
Jerseys. In considering public officials it is not usually
the general characteristics of the public official that are
of consequence, but the various officers and the distribution of their functions. Botanists divide up leaves,
stems, roots, flowers, fruits, all the parts of a plant, into
classes. One geologist classifies harbors as formed by
the intrusion of a water area into a land area, or the
embayment of a water area by a land mass. Of the
first class, most harbors are formed by erosion, produced
either by water or by ice, usually followed by subsidence;
the enclosing masses in the second type are, for example,
detritus carried by currents of air or water, coral, and
volcanic extrusions. Thus he divides harbors into these
ultimate classes: delta harbors, reëntrant delta harbors,
glacial or fiord harbors, mountain range harbors, glacial
moraine harbors, lagoon or sand bar harbors, sand spit
harbors, volcanic crater harbors, and coral reef harbors.

VI. EXPOSITIONS DEALING WITH INDIVIDUAL THINGS

Character Analysis.—Even an individual thing may
be the subject of an exposition, as it may be the subject
of intellectual contemplation, which expressly or im-

plicitly relates it to others of its kind. The characters of persons are thus subjects for exposition.

The enthusiasm of the disinterested and chivalrous Champlain was not the enthusiasm of La Salle; nor had he any part in the self-devoted zeal of the early Jesuit explorers. He belonged not to the age of the knight-errant and the saint, but to the modern world of practical study and practical action. He was the hero, not of a principle nor of a faith, but simply of a fixed idea and a determined purpose. As often happens with concentred and energetic characters, his purpose was to him a passion and an inspiration; and he clung to it with a certain fanaticism of devotion. It was the offspring of an ambition vast and comprehensive, yet acting in the interest both of France and of civilization. His mind rose immeasurably above the range of the mere commercial speculator; and, in all the invective and abuse of rivals and enemies, it does not appear that his personal integrity ever found a challenger.

He was capable of intrigue, but his reserve and his haughtiness were sure to rob him at last of the fruits of it. His schemes failed, partly because they were too vast, and partly because he did not conciliate the good-will of those whom he was compelled to trust. There were always traitors in his ranks, and his enemies were more in earnest than his friends. Yet he had friends; and there were times when out of his stern nature a stream of human emotion would gush, like water from the rock.

In the pursuit of his purpose, he spared no man, and least of all himself. He bore the brunt of every hardship and every danger; but he seemed to expect from all beneath him a courage and endurance equal to his own, joined with an implicit deference to his authority. Most of his disasters may be ascribed, in some measure, to himself; and Fortune and his own fault seemed always in league to ruin him.

It is easy to reckon up his defects, but it is not easy to hide from sight the Roman virtues that redeemed them. Beset by a throng of enemies, he stands, like the King of Israel, head and shoulders above them all. He was a tower of adamant, against whose invulnerable front hardship and danger, the rage of man and of the elements, the southern sun, the northern blast, fatigue, famine, and disease, delay, disappointment, and deferred hope, emptied their quivers in vain. That very pride, which, Coriolanus-like, declared itself most sternly in the thickest press of foes, has in it something to challenge admiration. Never, under the impenetrable mail of paladin or crusader, beat a heart of more intrepid mettle than within the stoic panoply that armed the breast of La Salle. To estimate aright the marvels of his patient fortitude, one must follow on his track through the vast scene of his interminable journeyings, those thousands of weary miles of forest, marsh, and river, where, again and again, in the bitterness of baffled striving, the untiring pilgrim pushed onward towards the goal he was never to attain. America owes him an enduring memory; for in this masculine figure, cast in iron, she sees the heroic pioneer who guided her to the possession of her richest heritage.

Parkman, F., *France and England in America;* by permission of Little, Brown, and Company.

Criticism.—Criticisms of books and works of art likewise, though they are founded upon classification, arise directly from the consideration of specific works.

Boswell has a little of the true Shakesperian secret. He lets his characters show themselves without obtruding unnecessary comment. He never misses the point of a story, though he does not ostentatiously call our attention to it. He gives just what is wanted to indicate character, or to explain the full meaning of a repartee. It is not till we compare his reports with those of less skilful hearers, that we can appreciate the skill with which the essence of a conversation is extracted, and the whole scene indicated by a few telling touches. We are tempted to fancy that we have heard the very same thing, and rashly infer that Boswell was simply the mechanical transmitter of the good things uttered. Any one who will try to put down the pith of a brilliant conversation in the same space, may soon satisfy himself of the absurdity of such an hypothesis, and will learn to appreciate Boswell's powers not only of memory but artistic representation. Such a feat implies not only admirable quickness of appreciation, but a rare literary faculty. Boswell's accuracy is remarkable; but it is the least part of his merit.

Stephen, L., *Johnson;* by permission of Harper and Brothers.

That the end of life is not action but contemplation—being as distinct from doing—a certain disposition of the mind: is, some shape or other, the principle of all the higher morality.

In poetry, in art, if you enter into their true spirit at all, you touch this principle, in a measure: these, by their very sterility, are a type of beholding for the mere joy of beholding. To treat life in the spirit of art, is to make life a thing in which means and ends are identified: to encourage such treatment, the true moral significance of art and poetry. Wordsworth, and other poets who have been like him in ancient or more recent times, are the masters, the experts, in this art of impassioned contemplation. Their work is, not to teach lessons, or enforce rules, or even to stimulate us to noble ends; but to withdraw the thoughts for a little while from the mere machinery of life, to fix them, with appropriate emotions, on the spectacle of those great facts in man's existence which no machinery affects, "on the great and universal passions of men, the most general and interesting of their occupations, and the entire world of nature,"—on "the operations of the elements and the appearances of the visible universe, on storm and sunshine, on the revolutions of the seasons, on cold and heat, on loss of friends and kindred, on injuries and resentments, on gratitude and hope, on fear and sorrow." To witness this spectacle with appropriate emotions is the aim of all culture; and of these emotions poetry like Wordsworth's is a great nourisher and stimulant. He sees men and women as parts of nature, passionate, excited, in strange grouping and connexion with the grandeur and beauty of the natural world:—images, in his own words, "of man suffering, amid awful forms and powers."

Pater, Walter, *Wordsworth.*

Ideas Arising from the Contemplation of Concrete Things.—Likewise there may be an exposition founded on any concrete fact; the ideas which arise about the Great Wall of China, or the River Tiber, for instance.

At last we came to Icolmkill [the site of the monastery of St. Columba, the apostle of northern Scotland], but found no convenience for landing. Our boat could not be forced very near the dry ground, and our Highlanders carried us over the water.

We were now treading that illustrious island, which was once the luminary of the Caledonian regions, whence savage clans and roving barbarians derived the benefits of knowledge, and the blessings of religion. To abstract the mind from all local emotion would be impossible, if it were endeavored, and would be foolish, if it were possible. Whatever withdraws us from the power of the senses; whatever makes the past, the distant, or the future, predominate over the present, advances us in the dignity of thinking beings. Far from me, and from my friends, be such frigid philosophy, as may conduct us indifferent and unmoved over any ground which has been dignified by wisdom, bravery, or virtue. That man is little to be envied, whose patriotism would not gain force upon the plain of Marathon, or whose piety would not grow warmer among the ruins of Iona.   Johnson, S., *Tour to the Hebrides.*

VII.   THE FORM OF EXPOSITIONS

Introductions.—An exposition may require an introduction and a conclusion. The functions of the expository introduction are mainly two: first, to enable the readers to approach the subject intelligently, and secondly, to bring the subject into some relation with them that will make it seem to them significant. The introduction should make the readers able and desirous to follow the discussion.

One or both of these ends are subserved by an account of the circumstances giving rise to the exposition. What field of thought is entered by the discussion of the theory of radio-action? What experiments led to the investigation of the subject? What is it all about?

From the earliest times, the diamond has fascinated mankind. It has been a perennial puzzle—one of the "riddles of the painful earth." Speculations as to the probable origin of the diamond have been greatly forwarded by patient research, and particularly by improved means of obtaining high temperatures, an advance which we owe principally to the researches of Professor Morrison.
          Crookes, Sir W., *The Romance of the Diamond,*
                    (*North American Review,* March, 1908).

There is more truth than poetry in giving to the era beginning with the year 1850 the name of "The Age of Steel." The metallurgical inventions and discoveries which mark abruptly that period have effected a revolution in the industry of the world. Steel is to us what iron was to our grandfathers; what bronze was to the armies that sat in league before Troy; what stone was to the naked savages that dwelt in the caves of Gaul before the beginning of history. The very web and woof of modern civilization is woven out of steel. The production of steel in 1882 was as great as the crude iron product of 1850. The metal is omnipresent; it has replaced iron, wood, brass, and copper. The rails, ships, cannon, and machinery of the world are steel. The best definition yet given of man is that he is a tool-using animal; his tools are steel, and the tools wherewith he makes his tools are steel.

> From the *St. Louis Globe-Democrat,* in Bird's *Modern Science Reader;* by permission of the Macmillan Company.

Passages bringing the matter to be discussed into relation with the reader's experience are often effective as introductions:

If a well were sunk at our feet in the midst of the City of Norwich, the diggers would very soon find themselves at work in that white substance almost too soft to be called rock, with which we are all familiar as "chalk."

Not only here, but over the whole county of Norfolk, the well-sinker might carry his shaft down many hundred feet without coming to the end of the chalk; and, on the sea-coast, where the waves have pared away the face of the land which breasts them, the scarped faces of the high cliffs are often wholly formed of the same material. Northward, the chalk may be followed as far as Yorkshire; on the south coast it appears abruptly in the picturesque western bays of Dorset, and breaks into the Needles of the Isle of Wight; while on the shores of Kent it supplies that long line of white cliffs to which England owes her name of Albion.

> Huxley, *On a Piece of Chalk.*

A direct explanation, a little essay in itself explaining the importance of the matter to be taken up, and its bearing upon something already seen to be important by the reader, is sometimes useful as an introduction.

It may have occurred (and very naturally too) to such as have the curiosity to read the title of this lecture [*On the*

Aims and Instruments of Scientific Thought], that it must necessarily be a very dry and difficult subject; interesting to very few, intelligible to still fewer, and, above all, utterly incapable of adequate treatment within the limits of a discourse like this. It is quite true that a complete setting-forth of my subject would require a comprehensive treatise on logic, with an incidental discussion of the main question of metaphysics; that it would deal with ideas demanding close study for their apprehension, and investigation requiring a peculiar taste to relish them. It is not my intention now to present you with such a treatise.

The British Association, like the world in general, contains three classes of persons. In the first place, it contains scientific thinkers; that is to say, persons whose thoughts have very frequently the characters which I shall presently describe. Secondly it contains persons who are engaged in work upon what are called scientific subjects, but who in general do not, and are not expected to, think about these subjects in a scientific manner. Lastly, it contains persons who suppose that their work and their thoughts are unscientific, but who would like to know about the business of the other two classes aforesaid. Now, to anyone who belonging to one of these classes considers either of the other two, it will be apparent that there is a certain gulf between him and them; and that an opportunity for sympathy and comradeship is lost through this want of understanding. It is this gulf that I desire to bridge over, to the best of my power. That the scientific thinker may consider his business in relation to the great life of mankind; that the noble army of practical workers may recognize their fellowship with the outer world, and the spirit which must guide both; that this so-called outer world may see in the work of science only the putting in evidence of all that is excellent in its own work,—may feel that the kingdom of science is within it: these are the objects of the present discourse. And they compel me to choose such portions of my vast subject as shall be intelligible to all, while they ought at least to command an interest universal, personal, and profound.

Clifford, W. K., *Lectures and Essays;* by permission of the Macmillan Company.

The introduction should in a word interest the reader in the discussion and prepare him for it. It should be a vital part of the composition, and not merely a conventional performance. Young writers sometimes begin, for example, by "histories" of the matter to be treated, usually very commonplace, and taken uncritically from unauthoritative sources. For instance, an exposition of the proper way to make a tennis court will begin with the history of the game of tennis, back to antiquity. Now anybody who has occasion to concern himself about laying out a tennis court has no use for a history of the game. In such a case a reasonable introduction would be a statement of the central idea of the theme.

"I propose, in the following paper, to consider only the ordinary requirements for a satisfactory clay tennis court in California."

"The making of a good tennis court is an elaborate and somewhat expensive operation. No one should undertake it without being prepared to wait long enough for the ground to be put in order, and to spend enough to insure thorough work."

Conclusions.—The conclusion should do whatever is necessary to draw the whole thing into one and to give it point. The unity of the whole as a mere piece of logical analysis may be brought out by a summary, though this is usually the tamest and least effective type of conclusion. If a summary is used it should emphasize the main ideas, and not attempt to embody the subordinate divisions of the exposition. Better than a summary is a conclusion which applies the results of the analysis, indicating the consequences of the ideas presented, or commenting upon some special aspect of the subject. If a writer has expounded the method of making window glass, he may call attention to the fact that only men of powerful physique and very special training can become successful blowers of the large cylinders. Men so qualified were to be found in large numbers before the war only in Belgium, which was the center of the window-glass industry for the whole world. It will be interesting to see whether or no the industry will return to its ancient seat. Or a writer, after expounding Gresham's law, that poor money drives out good money, may call attention to the fact that a rise in the price of silver makes it hard to keep ten-cent pieces in circulation, and may result in the issue of paper in less denominations than a dollar—"shin-plasters," as they used to be called. Or a writer may wind up a disquisition on a landlord's troubles, by the advice not to become a landlord. In a word, a conclusion which points the exposition as directed to some end, or views it as a whole, is better than a mere recital of its main points.

Transitions—Transitions require more care in exposition than in narrative and description. Above all, each section should be brought to an adequate and complete close, leaving no doubt that an end has been reached, and each section should begin decisively and distinctly. So far as may be, the mere order of the parts and the statement of the topics should make the course of thought clear, but wherever necessary, words, phrases, sentences, or even paragraphs of transition should be employed.

In particular the reader should never enter a new and important subject without being made aware that a new start has been made.

He should not be left in doubt whether the new idea is a further step in the same direction as that which precedes, a modification, a concession, the meeting of an objection, or in general what its relation is to the whole proposition and to the adjacent parts.

Topical Outlines.—Every piece of writing, as was said at the beginning, consists of large sections or stages of advance, each composed of subsidiary stages, which may again become divided. The maintenance of the proper relations between the parts requires more conscious adjustment in an exposition than in a narrative or description. To make sure in advance that an exposition has been well-planned, it is usually helpful to draw up a topical outline, presenting in a diagrammatic way the relation of the sections. Though such an outline should follow the general form of the elaborate outlines given in the chapter on the *Consultation of Authorities,* it ought usually to be much briefer than they and more of a preliminary sketch than a fully developed analysis.

The Expository Sentence and Paragraph.—As regards both sentences and paragraphs, the exposition differs naturally from the narrative and description in style. The paragraphs more often require a distinct enunciation of the topic at the beginning, and a clear indication of the main contents at the close. The sentences, also, tend to introduce more modifying expressions, to be longer, to be more suspended, and to subordinate predication to a greater degree. In brief, the purely logical aspects of style receive greater emphasis in exposition than in narration. The diction is naturally more abstract, though a good expositor will do his utmost to give a concrete form to his ideas. Abstract thought in concrete terms is the ideal to be held up for exposition.

VIII. INFORMAL EXPOSITIONS

In the treatment of narrative and description, two types of each were distinguished—the informational and the emotional. Obviously all that has been said about exposition has to do with an informational and impersonal type of writing. Is there such a thing as emotional and imaginative exposition? Consider such paragraphs as the following from Stevenson, Charles Lamb, and Hazlitt. These writers expound—set forth ideas based upon classifications—as when Charles Lamb divides mankind into the two great divisions of borrowers and lenders, and presents the magnificent qualities of the great race of borrowers, who lay tax and tribute on the meaner men who earn a living and lend. Hazlitt discusses *Going a Journey,* and Stevenson, *Talk and Talkers,* not with cold impersonality but with warm fancy and feeling. This irregular essay, not systematically developing a subject, but touching upon only those aspects of it, especially the less obvious and familiar, which excite the fancy of the writer, bears somewhat the same relation to serious exposition of a formal type which the imaginative narrative or description bears to the purely practical report of facts and observations.

The human species, according to the best theory I can form of it, is composed of two distinct races, *the men who borrow,* and *the men who lend.* To these two original diversities may be reduced all those impertinent classifications of Gothic and Celtic tribes, white men, black men, red men. All the dwellers upon earth, "Parthians, and Medes, and Elamites," flock hither, and do naturally fall in with one or other of these primary distinctions. The infinite superiority of the former, which I choose to designate as the *great race,* is discernible in their figure, port, and a certain instinctive superiority. The latter are born degraded. "He shall serve his brethren." There is something in the air of one of this cast, lean and suspicious; contrasting with the open, trusting, generous manners of the other.

Observe who have been the greatest borrowers of all ages— Alcibiades—Falstaff—Sir Richard Steele—our late incomparable Brinsley—what a family likeness in all four!

What a careless, even deportment hath your borrower! what rosy gills! what a beautiful reliance on Providence doth he manifest,—taking no more thought than lilies! What contempt for money,—counting it (yours and mine especially) no better than dross! What a liberal confounding of those pedantic distinctions of *meum* and *tuum;* or rather, what a noble simplification of language (beyond Tooke), resolving these supposed opposites into one clear, intelligible compound adjective!—What near approaches doth he make to the primitive *community,*—to the extent of one half of the principle at least!—

Lamb, The Two Races of Men.

Instead of a friend in a post-chaise or in a tilbury, to exchange good things with and vary the same stale topics over again, for once let me have a truce with impertinence. Give me the clear blue sky over my head, and the green turf beneath my feet, a winding road before me, and a three hours' march to dinner—and then to thinking! It is hard if I cannot start some game on these lone heaths. I laugh, I run, I leap, I sing for joy. From the point of yonder rolling cloud, I plunge into my past being and revel there, as the sun-burnt Indian plunges headlong into the wave that wafts him to his native shore. Then long-forgotten things, like "sunken wrack and sumless treasuries," burst upon my eager sight, and I begin to feel, think, and be myself again. Instead of an awkward silence, broken by attempts at wit or dull common-places, mine is that undisturbed silence of the heart which alone is perfect eloquence. No one likes puns, alliterations, antitheses, argument, and analysis better than I do; but I sometimes had rather be without them. "Leave, oh, leave me to my repose!" I have just now other business in hand, which would seem idle to you, but is with me "very stuff of the conscience." Is not this wild rose sweet without a comment? Does not this daisy leap to my heart set in its coat of emerald? Yet if I were to explain to you the circumstance that has so endeared it to me, you would only smile. Had I not better then keep it to myself, and let it serve me to brood over, from here to yonder craggy point, and from thence onward to the far-distant horizon? I should be but bad company all that way, and therefore prefer being alone. I have heard it said that you may, when the moody fit comes on, walk or ride on by yourself and indulge your reveries. But this looks like a breach of manners, a neglect of others, and you are thinking all the time that you ought to rejoin your party. "Out upon such half-faced fellowship," say I. I like to be either entirely to myself, or entirely at the disposal of others; to talk or be silent, to walk or sit still, to be sociable or solitary.   Hazlitt, *On Going a Journey.*

Talk should proceed by instances; by the apposite, not the expository. It should keep close along the lines of humanity, near the bosoms and business of men, at the level where history, fiction, and experience intersect and illuminate each other. I am I, and You are You, with all my heart; but conceive how these lean propositions change and brighten when, instead of words, the actual you and I sit cheek by jowl, the spirit housed in the live body, and the very clothes uttering voices to corroborate the story in the face. Not less surprising is the change when we leave off to speak of generalities—the bad, the good, the miser, and all the characters of Theophrastus—and call up other men, by anecdote or instance, in their very trick and feature; or trading on a common knowledge, toss each other famous names, still glowing with the hues of life. Communication is no longer by words, but by the instancing of whole biographies, epics, systems of philosophy, and epochs of history, in bulk. That which is understood excels that which is spoken in quantity and quality alike; ideas thus figured and personified, change hands, as we may say, like coin; and the speakers imply without effort the most obscure and intricate thoughts. Strangers who have a large common ground of reading will, for this reason, come the sooner to the grapple of genuine converse. If they know Othello and Napoleon, Consuelo and Clarissa Harlowe, Vautrin and Steenie Steenson, they can leave generalities and begin at once to speak by figures.

Stevenson, *Memories and Portraits;* by permission of C. Scribner's Sons.

RECAPITULATION

Exposition is concerned with the ideas which arise upon the contemplation of experiences, and these ideas depend upon the formation of classes by the mind. Classes are good in so far as they serve some purpose, practically or intellectually of some significance. Classes vary in extent inversely to their fulness of characterization. Expositions may deal with classes according to the resemblances among their members, or the differences, or may bring out difference in spite of resemblance, or resemblance in spite of difference; they may distinguish a class from related classes, or be concerned with its analogies with related classes. Expositions may also divide a class into its subordinate classes. Expositions may take their origin from the reflections suggested by individual things, though the intent to classify or to find general ideas is always present in such cases. Expositions require a certain formal clearness of outline, by means of introductions, conclusions, and distinct transitions. They tend to have their paragraphs developed from topic sentences, and their sentences characterized by suspense and the subordination of predication, more than do narratives and descriptions. There is an informal and emotional type of exposition as well as a logical and analytic type. In all forms of exposition, concrete illustrations add to both clearness and interest.

CHAPTER XII

ARGUMENT

I. PROPOSITION AND ISSUE

Argument Defined.—An argument is intended to cause its hearers or readers to "make up their minds" —to induce them to believe or to do as the proponent of the argument desires. An argument, like an exposition, is concerned not with direct experiences of the physical senses, but with ideas, and involves classification and the perception of likeness and difference; in brief it is prepared for and has its foundation laid in exposition. It differs from exposition in that the ideas which are merely contemplated and considered in an exposition are in an argument accepted or rejected as things valid as a basis of action, whether they are at the time acted on or not.

The Proposition.—The direct object of an argument is always to establish a *proposition*,—to produce an affirmation which cannot be expressed except by a complete predication. You cannot argue a *house* or the *Egyptian language* or the *League of Nations* or *social justice*, though you may contemplate and expound the ideas connected with them. You can argue, *I ought (or ought not) to buy a house*, or, *The Egyptian language is (or is not) related to the Hebrew*, or, *The League of Nations will (or will not) be stable*, or, *Social Justice is (or is not) more nearly attained now than one*

302

hundred years ago. These are propositions; they can be
accepted or rejected by the mind and acted upon.
First of all, in argument the disputant should frame
a clear statement of his proposition. The writer himself ought to know clearly what he is driving at, even
if he does not reveal it clearly at the outset. In drawing up an argument, the first step is to frame the
proposition as a complete sentence.

Thus Alexander Hamilton concludes his introduction
to the series of papers in which he with others urged
the citizens of New York to adopt the Constitution
of the United States, then before them for ratification,
with an emphatic statement of his proposition.

In the course of the preceding observations I have had an
eye, my Fellow-Citizens, to putting you upon your guard
against all attempts, from whatever quarter, to influence your
decision in a matter of the utmost moment to your welfare by
any impressions other than those which may result from the
evidence of truth. You will, no doubt, at the same time, have
collected from the general scope of them that they proceed
from a source not unfriendly to the new Constitution. Yes,
my Countrymen, I owe to you, that, after having given it an
attentive consideration, I am clearly of opinion, it is your
interest to adopt it. I am convinced, that this is the safest
course for your liberty, your dignity, and your happiness.

A proposition should be so framed as to cover the
exact purpose of the argument, no more and no less.
It is in this aspect of the work that the common error
of endeavoring to cover too broad a subject is likely to
be shown. If you believe in some large proposition, but
have not the space or time in which to treat it, frame
the proposition of your argument so as to cover only
that part or branch of the subject which you treat.
Suppose yourself to be arguing in favor of bonding your
town for a new school-house and to have one minute in

which to speak. Do not talk about the blessings of a
good education. You have time to deliver say a hundred and fifty words. Decide whether you will treat
the need, or the feasibility, or the legality of the step.
If it is the need which you will discuss, decide whether
the special aspect of the need which you will treat is the
overcrowding, or the insanitary condition of the school,
or the lack of space for modern equipment. Then
frame your proposition;—*We ought to relieve the overcrowding, by building a new school-house.* If you are
arguing for or against the suffrage amendment and
have five hundred words in which to present your ideas,
decide what ideas you can present effectively in your
space and do not go outside of them. Contend, for
example, that the great body of intelligent women do
(or do not) wish the suffrage. If you are urging a
friend to come to your college, and have not space or
time to treat all the advantages of the institution, show
him one thing thoroughly. Expound to him the opportunities of study in the field that most interests him,
—the excellence and the reputation of the instructors,
the admirable equipment of the laboratory, the riches
of the library, the enthusiastic group of co-workers.
In a word, fit the scope of your argument to your space,
and fit your proposition to the scope of your argument.

Defining the Issue.—Usually, persons who differ
about the truth of a proposition agree about many points
connected with it, but fail to reach the same conclusion
because of some definite divergence along the line of the
reasoning. ''I agree that it would be a good thing to
have a new school-house, but we cannot afford it'';—
''I agree that we need a new school-house, but not so
large a one as is planned, because I do not believe in

all these newfangled studies for which space is demanded'';—''I agree that there is need for more space; but we can obtain it by putting up an addition to the old building.'' The point at which opponents differ, the point where the saying *yes* of one, and the saying *no* of the other determines the judgment, is called the issue. Strive, after deciding upon, limiting, and exactly phrasing your proposition, to ascertain whether there is any body of agreement between you and your opponent and where he and you part company. Reserve the agreement for your introduction, and frame your decision upon the issue as a new proposition.

It is in deciding where the issue lies that sagacity is shown. The man who habitually sees the issue solves the questions that others ineffectually blunder around. He ''hits the nail on the head''; he ''does the trick.''

The issue may arise from any aspect of a case or any kind of thing that people differ about. Youngsters sometimes argue as school exercises such questions as whether city life or country life is preferable. One side tells all about the advantages of the city and the disadvantages of the country, and the other all about the advantages of the country and the disadvantages of the city, but each side might admit all that the other had brought forward, and still be justified in holding to its view undisturbed. The issue is, which of the two bodies of advantage taken all together, with all the disadvantages on both sides, is on the whole the more important in determining the best place of residence for normal human beings. The question is one of relative values for normal people. When one sees that, he sees that the question is practically impossible of solution, for the estimate of human values is one of the most delicate, uncertain, and profound of problems, and it is doubtful whether there is any such thing as a standard of normal humanity. Yet it is by the settlement of this issue that the question if determined at all must be determined.

Perhaps the issue is a question of fact. In a discussion of the eight-hour day, one issue might be, is it or is it not true that in the long run—not for short exceptional periods but month in and month out—the product of industrial activity under ordinary conditions is greater on an eight-hour basis than on a ten-hour basis.

Perhaps the issue is a question of moral judgment. "He did ride to Chicago on the blind baggage; what of it?" Perhaps it is a matter of inference. "I know there was a little tadpole in the milk bottle; but I think that rascally Tom Jones put it there." Whatever the issue is, it should be found and must be met. Only a cowardly or insincere person will refuse to be pinned down to an issue on a real question which another person has a right to discuss with him. You owe it to yourself alike to avoid quibbles and evasions and unrealities in your statement of your case, and to resist the attempt of an opponent to take refuge in quibbles and evasions and unrealities in his statement of his case. Abraham Lincoln owed much of the persuasive force of his speeches to his insight in fixing and his fairness in stating the issue. His famous Cooper Union speech, delivered in 1860, begins as follows:

Mr. President and Fellow-citizens of New York: The facts with which I shall deal this evening are mainly old and familiar; nor is there anything new in the general use I shall make of them. If there shall be any novelty, it will be in the mode of presenting the facts, and the inferences and observations following that presentation. In his speech last autumn at Columbus, Ohio, as reported in the *New-York Times,* Senator Douglas said:

Our fathers, when they framed the government under which we live, understood this question just as well, and even better, than we do now.

I fully indorse this, and I adopt it as a text for this discourse. I so adopt it because it furnishes a precise and an agreed starting-point for a discussion between Republicans and that wing of the Democracy headed by Senator Douglas. It simply leaves the inquiry: What was the understanding those fathers had of the question mentioned?

What is the frame of government under which we live? The answer must be, "The Constitution of the United States." That Constitution consists of the original, framed in 1787, and under which the present government first went into operation, and twelve subsequently framed amendments, the first ten of which were framed in 1789.

Who were our fathers that framed the Constitution? I suppose the "thirty-nine" who signed the original instrument may be fairly called our fathers who framed that part of the present government. It is almost exactly true to say they framed it, and it is altogether true to say they fairly represented the opinion and sentiment of the whole nation at that time. Their names, being familiar to nearly all, and accessible to quite all, need not now be repeated.

I take these "thirty-nine," for the present, as being "our fathers who framed the government under which we live." What is the question which, according to the text, those fathers understood "just as well, and even better, than we do now"?

It is this: Does the proper division of local from Federal authority, or anything in the Constitution, forbid our Federal Government to control as to slavery in our Federal Territories?

Upon this, Senator Douglas holds the affirmative, and Republicans the negative. This affirmation and denial form an issue; and this issue—this question—is precisely what the text declares our fathers understood "better than we."

Horace Mann devoted his great abilities and his marvelous energy to the cause of public common schools. In his day the support of free public schools was not universally accepted as a duty of the state. Why? he asks; and he finds the answer in the divergence of views

as to the right of government to lay taxes for the purpose. Here then is the issue.

And yet, notwithstanding these views have been presented
a thousand times with irrefutable logic, and with a divine eloquence of truth which it would seem that nothing but combined
stolidity and depravity could resist, there is not at the present
time (1845), with the exception of the States of New England
and a few small communities elsewhere, a country or a state
in Christendom which maintains a system of free schools for
the education of its children.

I believe that this amazing dereliction from duty, especially
in our own country, originates more in the false notions which
men entertain respecting the nature of their right to property
than in anything else. In the district school meeting, in the
town meeting, in legislative halls, everywhere, the advocates for
a more generous education could carry their respective audi-
ences with them in behalf of increased privileges for our
children, were it not instinctively foreseen that increased privileges must be followed by increased taxation. Against this
obstacle, argument falls dead. The rich man who has no children declares that the exaction of a contribution from him to
educate the children of his neighbor is an invasion of his rights
of property. The man who has reared and educated a family
of children denounces it as a double tax when he is called upon
to assist in educating the children of others also; or, if he has
reared his own children without educating them, he thinks it peculiarly oppressive to be obliged to do for others what he re-
frained from doing even for himself. Another, having children, but disdaining to educate them with the common mass,
withdraws them from the public school, puts them under what
he calls "selecter influences," and then thinks it a grievance to
be obliged to support a school which he contemns. Or, if these
different parties so far yield to the force of traditionary sentiment and usage, and to the public opinion around them, as to
consent to do something for the cause, they soon reach the limit
of expense at which their admitted obligation or their alleged
charity terminates.

It seems not irrelevant, therefore, in this connection, and for
the purpose of strengthening the foundation on which our free-
school system reposes, to inquire into the nature of a man's
right to the property he possesses, and to satisfy ourselves
respecting the question whether any man has such an inde-
feasible title to his estates or such an absolute ownership of

them as renders it unjust in the government to assess upon him his share of the expenses of educating the children of the community up to such a point as the nature of the institutions under which he lives, and the well-being of society, require.

II. THE DEVELOPMENT OF THE ARGUMENT

To Whom is the Argument Addressed?—The issue once stated, the next thing is to develop the argument. To whom is your argument addressed? To those who already agree with it? or to those who do not? There might be legitimate reasons for addressing either group, the one to confirm them in their faith, to excite their devotion to the cause, to cause them to reprobate the opposite opinions, and to give them greater boldness and determination in following out the line of action to which their ideas commit them; the other to win your opponents over to your side, or if that be impossible to make them understand your position and respect it, and to gain at least the support of openminded seekers after truth. The highest achievement is to persuade some who have declared against you; the rational and decent end is as a fair-minded man to lead other fair-minded men along the path you have found to the goal you have reached. It is a lower aim to appeal to those already persuaded. From this point of view the highest praise was given to Lincoln's Cooper Union Speech, the beginning of which has been quoted, when it was characterized as not the most eloquent of political addresses, but the one which would persuade its audience more completely to the orator's point of view than any other which had ever been delivered in America.

The method to be followed differs widely according as the argument is addressed to stimulating those already in agreement with it or to persuading those on the other side. Confident assertion, ugly nicknames, bold claims quite unsupported by reasoning may satisfy the group already on your side; but real reasons, civility and candor to opponents, and cautious avoidance of overstatement may persuade an occasional person on the other side, and will weigh much more strongly with the unprejudiced. Young writers often enjoy asserting themselves more than they think of converting their adversaries, and hence they easily fall into rude or at least tactless treatment of those who happen to differ from them in opinion, and resent the necessity of giving chapter and verse for the statements which they confidently utter without any ground except their own enthusiasm. A disputant then should lay the foundation for his argument in a real study of the subject, should have some deliberation in taking sides, should candidly scrutinize and seriously weigh what seem to be the sound arguments for both positions. One who has thus prepared himself is not likely to shut his eyes to the fact there is something to be said for the other side, though he thinks the grounds for his position the better. He will not despise or ridicule his opponent, unless his opponent energetically provokes ridicule, and even then he will be cautious and will not "prove too much,"—that is heedlessly overstate the grounds of his position.

Look for Causes or Effects of the Proposition.—The types of reasoning upon which argument is based have been classified and analyzed very thoroughly by theorists. For our purpose it is enough to say that in considering any proposition one should look for possible causes or effects of the proposition in order to test its truth. I see a result; I know some cause must have produced it, and I affirm the existence of the most prob-able cause;—"Where there is smoke there is fire." I see a live fish; and I declare that it cannot have been long out of water. Likewise I perceive the existence of a phenomenon that is regularly succeeded by a result, and I affirm the probable existence of the result. I see lightning and I expect thunder. I see a tree chopped into on both sides until it sways; and I expect it to fall.

To be sure, my judgment may prove false. The cause which produced the effect may not have been what I believed it to be. The scratches on the window-sill which look so like the marks of a boot heel *may* have been made by nails in a piece of wood; the typhoid fever may have come from infected milk, and not from an infected water supply. The tree may catch in an-other tree; the storm may be further away than I think, so that I do not hear the thunder. Reasoning from cause to effect and from effect to cause may then vary from practical certainty to a very slight shadow of prob-ability.

Benjamin Franklin at one time supported a proposal to change the proprietary government of Philadelphia to the form of a royal colony. He contends: (1) that the effects show proprietary governments to be in fact bad; and (2) that there are causes which naturally result in making such governments bad.

It is remarkable, that disputes of the same kind have arisen in all proprietary governments, and subsisted till their dissolu-tion. All were made unhappy by them, and found no relief but in recurring finally to the immediate government of the crown. Pennsylvania and Maryland are the only two of the kind remaining, and both at this instant agitated by the same contentions between proprietary interest and power, and popu-lar liberty. Through these contentions the good people of that province are rendered equally unhappy with ourselves, and their proprietary, perhaps, more so than ours; for he has no Quakers in his assembly to saddle with the blame of those contentions, nor can he justify himself with the pretence, that turning to the church has made his people his enemies.

Pennsylvania had scarce been settled twenty years, when these disputes began between the first proprietor and the original settlers; they continued, with some intermissions, during his whole life; his widow took them up, and continued them after his death. Her sons resumed them very early, and they still subsist. Mischievous and distressing as they have been found to both proprietors and people, it does not appear that there is any prospect of their being extinguished, till either the proprietary purse is unable to support them, or the spirit of the people so broken, that they shall be willing to submit to anything, rather than continue them. The first is not very likely to happen, as that immense estate goes on increasing.

Considering all circumstances, I am at length inclined to think, that the cause of these miserable contentions is not to be sought for merely in the depravity and selfishness of human minds. For, though it is not unlikely that in these, as well as in other disputes, there are faults on both sides, every glowing coal being apt to inflame its opposite; yet I see no reason to suppose that all proprietary rulers are worse men than other rulers, nor that all people in proprietary governments are worse people than those in other governments. I suspect, therefore, that the cause is radical, interwoven in the constitution, and so become the very nature, of proprietary governments; and will therefore produce its effects, as long as such governments continue. And, as some physicians say, every animal body brings into the world among its original stamina the seeds of that disease that shall finally produce its dissolution; so the political body of a proprietary government, contains those convulsive principles that will at length destroy it.

I may not be philosopher enough to develop these principles, nor would this letter afford me room, if I had abilities, for such a discussion. The fact seems sufficient for our purpose, and the fact is notorious, that such contentions have been in all proprietary governments, and have brought, or are now bringing, them all to a conclusion. I will only mention one particular common to them all. Proprietaries must have a multitude of private accounts and dealings with almost all the people of their provinces, either for purchase money or quit-rents. Dealings often occasion differences, and differences produce mutual opinions of injustice. If proprietaries do not insist on small rights, they must on the whole lose large sums; and, if they do insist on small rights, they seem to descend, their dignity suffers in the opinion of the people, and with it the respect necessary to keep up the authority of government. The people, who think themselves injured in point of property, are discontented with the government, and grow turbulent; and the proprietaries' using their powers of government to procure for themselves what they think justice in their points of property, renders those powers odious. I suspect this has had no small share in producing the confusion incident to those governments. They appear, however, to be, of all others, the most unhappy.

For and Because.—The words expressing the connection of cause and effect are *for* and *because;* and we can test and control the conduct of our intellect in adhering to a course of reasoning, if we can sensibly connect our final proposition by the words *for* or *because* with the propositions which support it, and connect these with others in the same way, until we reach ultimate propositions that seem to us to stand firm.

Tests of the Argument from Effect to Cause.—Arguments by which the existence of an effect is made use of to prove the existence of a state of facts which caused the effect are subject to the following tests: (1) Does the effect really exist? (2) Is the cause adequate—that is, would the result have followed if the condition existed? (3) Would some other state of facts equally well account for the effect?

Does the Effect Exist?—I say: "I heard thunder; there must have been lightning somewhere." I may be answered, "Are you sure it was thunder? Perhaps what you heard was a wagon rolling along the street." That is; *are you sure of the effect which you declare to exist?*

There is a well-known story that King Charles II

sent to the newly founded Royal Society a query why a bowl of water with a fish in it weighed no more than the bowl without the fish. Theorists began to dispute; but a careful investigator quickly showed that if no water was removed from the bowl when the fish was put in, the exact weight of the fish was added to that of the bowl of water.

When a package of rare plants from the Orient was unwrapped in the study of Professor Asa Gray, the botanist, the peculiar string in which the package was tied up attracted the attention of one of the group of young men of science present. Several others looked at it, turned it over, tested its strength. What remarkable twine! How strong and lustrous! It cannot be silk. What can such string be made of?

They were all busy conjecturing; but Professor Gray burned a trifle, smelled the end of the burned string, and chuckled a little. "It *is* silk."

Is the Alleged Cause Adequate?—I say: "There must be a terrible amount of profiteering to produce such high prices." I may be answered: "Profiteering by itself is not sufficient to account for the rise in prices." That is; *the result exists; but the cause alleged, whether it exists or not, is inadequate to the result.*

Sir Charles Lyell, in his *Principles of Geology*, endeavors to refute such an argument. He contends that it is not necessary to believe that past changes in the animate and inanimate world were produced by catastrophes, or to suppose that forces of greater energy than those which at present exist have been at work previously on the surface of the earth. Present forces are adequate if allowed sufficient duration.

If we could behold in one view all the volcanic cones thrown up in Iceland, Italy, Sicily, and other parts of Europe, during the last five thousand years, and could see the lavas which have flowed during the same period; the dislocations, subsidences, and elevations caused during earthquakes; the lands added to various deltas, or devoured by the sea, together with the effects of devastation by floods, and imagine that all these events had happened in one year, we must form most exalted ideas of the activity of the agents, and the suddenness of the revolutions. Were an equal amount of change to pass before our eyes in the next year, could we avoid the conclusion that some great crisis of nature was at hand? If geologists, therefore, have misinterpreted the signs of a succession of events, so as to conclude that centuries were implied where the characters imported thousands of years, and thousands of years where the language of Nature signified millions, they could not, if they reasoned logically from such false premises, come to any other conclusion than that the system of the natural world had undergone a complete revolution.

Lyell's opponents declare that present causes are inadequate; he asserts, give them time, and they are adequate.

Do Other Causes Account for the Effect?—Again I might say: "The telephone company must have taken on a lot of new girls; the service is very slow." I might be answered: "That is not the trouble; they have just made some alterations in the arrangements of the office, and the operators have not got used to them yet." That is, *the effects exist, and the cause suggested is adequate to produce them; but other known causes sufficiently account for the facts.*

Thus, a man has killed another, and is charged with murder—that is with slaying the dead man deliberately and with the intention to do a wrong. He is defended as insane. The act is admitted, and the cause suggested is adequate, but in point of fact another cause really impelled him to do the deed.

The Existence of Facts Proved by Their Effects.— Generally speaking, the existence of facts must be proved by their effects. A fact produces results, and it should be possible to reason back from the results to the cause which produced them. Thus Horace Binney argued that Stephen Girard, the founder of Girard College, was not a hard man without natural feelings, because the effects which would have flowed from such a state of affairs did not in fact exist.

There were not wanting persons of that large class who are liberal with other men's money, and equally liberal of their censures to such as will not permit them to dispose of it, who thought proper to think and speak of him while he lived as of a man in whom the love of money had deadened all the kindly affections. They did not know him. There were many proofs to the contrary during his life. His death has published an irrefragable proof to the contrary in his will. To the Pennsylvania Hospital, the institution of the deaf and dumb, the orphan asylum, the comptrollers of the public schools, the poor house-keepers and room-keepers in the city, whose provision for fuel in the winter is the severest tax upon their small resources, his brethren of the society of Free Masons, the poor children in the township in which his country seat was situated, the captains of his ships, his apprentices, his house-keepers, the members of their family, his old negro slave, all are remembered, and remembered in such a way as to show the acuteness of his mind, as well as the strength of his feelings, in the kind of provision he makes for them. It is a striking, and to myself personally a most grateful, evidence of the tenacity of his regard to those who deserved well of him, that he gives a liberal annuity for life to the venerable widow of his faithful counselor and friend, my honored master, Mr. Ingersoll, who had departed many years before him. A memory so retentive of good offices could not have been the companion of an insensible heart. The amount of these legacies, including the value of life annuities, does not fall short of one hundred and seventy thousand dollars, all of them tokens of regard, and of the most provident concern for the welfare of the legatees.

Testimony.—There is one form of the argument from effect to cause which demands special consideration, namely the argument from testimony. The fact that a person testifies to the existence of a certain condition of affairs is a natural effect of the existence of the condition. Testimony is subject to the same tests as other forms of the argument from effect to cause. Of course the adequacy of the cause does not come into question, for the truth of the statement is an adequate cause for its being made. Thus the first question that arises is this, is it true that the testimony is actually given? Dr. Jones says there is a case of leprosy in the town of Albion. We say, "Are you sure that he says so? Is he not wrongly reported?" Again the question may be raised whether some other cause than the truth of the statement was the reason for its being made. We say: "Dr. Jones does n't know what he is talking about"; or, "Dr. Jones is a liar." The causes which produce false or inaccurate evidence are then two: (1) the lack of adequate observation and careful discrimination, causing the witness unconsciously to misrepresent the facts; or (2) some cause working to produce conscious falsification on the part of him who testifies. In citing testimony, for example, the testimony of a "source" in history, it is proper first to scrutinize the exact words of the witness, and then to consider with care the circumstances which may throw light upon the question whether the witness is in a position to know and judge the facts, and thirdly to consider whether any motive may have been at work causing him to misrepresent the truth. Thus Webster discusses the testimony of a witness in the White murder case.

As to the testimony of Leighton, as far as manner of testifying goes, he is a bad witness; but it does not follow from this that he is not to be believed. There are some strange things about him. It is strange that he should make up a story against Captain Knapp, the person with whom he lived; that he never voluntarily told anything,—all that he has said was screwed out of him. But the story could not have been invented by him; his character for truth is unimpeached; and he intimated to another witness, soon after the murder happened, that he knew something he should not tell. There is not the least contradiction in his testimony, though he gives a poor account of withholding it. He says that he was extremely bothered by those who questioned him. In the main story that he relates he is entirely consistent with himself. Some things are for him, and some against him. Examine the intrinsic probability of what he says. See if some allowance is not to be made for him on account of his ignorance of things of this kind. It is said to be extraordinary that he should have heard just so much of the conversation, and no more; that he should have heard just what was necessary to be proved, and nothing else. Admit that this is extraordinary; still, this does not prove it untrue. It is extraordinary that you twelve gentlemen should be called upon, out of all the men in the county, to decide this case. No one could have foretold this three weeks since. It is extraordinary that the first clew to this conspiracy should have been derived from information given by the father of the prisoner at the bar. And in every case that comes to trial there are many things extraordinary. The murder itself is a most extraordinary one; but still we do not doubt its reality.

It is argued that this conversation between Joseph and Frank could not have been as Leighton has testified, because they had been together for several hours before; this subject must have been uppermost in their minds, whereas this appears to have been the commencement of their conversation upon it. Now this depends altogether upon the tone and manner of the expression; upon the particular word in the sentence which was emphatically spoken. If he had said, "When did you *see* Dick, Frank?" this would not seem to be the beginning of the conversation. With what emphasis it was uttered it is not possible to learn, and therefore nothing can be made of this argument. If this boy's testimony stood alone, it should be received with caution. And the same may be said of the

testimony of Palmer. But they do not stand alone. They
furnish a clew to numerous other circumstances, which when
known, mutually confirm what would have been received with
caution without such corroboration. How could Leighton have
made up this conversation? "When did you see Dick?" "I
saw him this morning." "When is he going to kill the old
man?" "I don't know." "Tell him, if he don't do it soon, I
won't pay him." Here is a vast amount in a few words. Had
he wit enough to invent this? There is nothing so powerful
as truth, and often nothing so strange. It is not even suggested that the story was made for him. There is nothing so
extraordinary in the whole matter as it would have been for this
ignorant country boy to invent this story.

Authority.—In the argument from authority, an
eminent person is cited not to prove a fact to which he
testifies, but to support an opinion which he shares
with the proponent of the argument. I believe that
Mars is inhabited; and I am supported by the authority
of some eminent astronomers, Professor Percival Lowell,
for example.

Such an argument has little weight as direct proof in
a controverted case; it is of value in proving that an
opinion is not silly, but is really worth considering seriously. The arguments which convince the eminent
authorities are in themselves just as strong without the
names of their supporters as with them. So authority
may entitle a case to a hearing, but can hardly decide
it. Authority, like testimony, is an effect. I argue,
the cause of this belief is the truth of it; if the belief
were not sound such eminent men would not hold it.
The tests of authority are similar to those of testimony.
Is it true that the authorities cited do actually hold
these opinions? Are they entitled to consideration:
(1) because of thorough familiarity with the question,
(2) because of skill and capacity to reason justly on

the matter, (3) because of desire and ability to report their conclusions accurately?

Some of the opponents of Professor Lowell allege that his observations are inaccurate, and that the continuity of the canals is an optical illusion; others regard his arguments as unsound.

If all the great body of the specially qualified in any field agree, the "layman" is entitled to regard their consensus as probably true. There is a tendency, however, to exaggerate the value of authority, to call in authority upon questions with reference to which disputants can reason perfectly well, to set name against name, and in general to avoid the real investigation of the subject by hiding behind specialists.

Tests of the Argument from Cause to Effect.—The argument from a cause known or alleged to an effect expected is subject to tests similar to those applicable to the argument from effects to cause; (1) does the cause exist? (2) is it adequate to produce the effect? (3) is it certain that nothing will interfere to prevent the cause from resulting in the effect expected?

"The streetcar company has adopted a five-minute schedule, and I think we can get down to the Square, without having to spend so long on the corner."

"Are you sure the schedule was adopted? I understand the plan fell through."

That is; *the cause does not certainly exist.*

"I have started a fire in the furnace, and the house will get warm pretty soon."

"Are you sure that furnace will heat the house? It looks pretty small to me."

That is; *the cause in itself is not adequate to produce the effect.*

"I hope that dog will learn not to bark at automobiles; I have certainly punished him enough."

"Yes; but Tom gets him on the sly and excites the poor beast to rush after them whenever he sees them."

The cause is adequate in itself but other causes operate against it.

Arguments as to What Ought to be Done.—Arguments as to what ought to be done are usually based upon reasoning from cause to effect. Consider the following examples, taken from the debates as to the adoption of the Federal Constitution. Mr. Madison argued that physical conditions were such as to cause it to be reasonable to unite the American territories under one government.

It has often given me pleasure to observe, that Independent America was not composed of detached and distant territories, but that one connected, fertile, wide-spreading country was the portion of our western sons of liberty. Providence has in a particular manner blessed it with a variety of soils and productions, and watered it with innumerable streams, for the delight and accommodation of its inhabitants. A succession of navigable waters forms a kind of chain round its borders, as if to bind it together; while the most noble rivers in the world, running at convenient distances, present them with highways for the easy communication of friendly aids, and the mutual transportation and exchange of their various commodities.

Mr. Mason argued that the physical conditions were such that only by the establishment of a despotism could so large a country as America be held together.

Mr. Chairman, Whether the Constitution be good or bad, the present clause clearly discovers that it is a national government, and no longer a Confederation. I mean that clause which gives the first hint of the general government laying direct taxes. The assumption of this power of laying direct taxes does, of itself, entirely change the confederation of the states into one consolidated government. This power, being at discretion, unconfined, and without any kind of control, must carry everything before it. The very idea of converting what was formerly a confederation to a consolidated government, is totally subversive of every principle which has hitherto governed us. This power is calculated to annihilate totally the state governments. Will the people of this great community submit to be individually taxed by two different and distinct powers? Will they suffer themselves to be doubly harassed? These two concurrent powers cannot exist long together; the one will destroy the other: the general government being paramount to, and in every respect more powerful than the state governments, the latter must give way to the former. Is it to be supposed that one national government will suit so extensive a country, embracing so many climates, and containing inhabitants so very different in manners, habits, and customs? It is ascertained, by history, that there never was a government over a very extensive country without destroying the liberties of the people: history also, supported by the opinions of the best writers, shows us that monarchy may suit a large territory, and despotic governments ever so extensive a country, but that popular governments can only exist in small territories. Is there a single example, on the face of the earth, to support a contrary opinion? Where is there one exception to this general rule? Was there ever an instance of a general national government extending over so extensive a country, abounding in such a variety of climates, &c., where the people retained their liberty?

The Relation of the Steps in an Argument.—An argument in which proposition is connected with proposition by the words *for* and *because* moves downwards towards the foundation; each new point lays a foundation for the proposition which it supports. Every new point made may raise a new issue; and thus each step in an argument is a little argument, complete in itself, but dependent upon another argument or group of arguments. Sooner or later, all arguments must rest upon the common experience of mankind, about which in general it is foolish to debate.

III.   THE STRUCTURE OF AN ARGUMENT

The Order of Parts in an Argument.—With regard to the order in an argument, the suggestions already made about exposition are in place. Arguments naturally divide into three sections, the introduction, the body, and the conclusion. The introduction should include all the preliminary explanation requisite to clear up the issue, to exhibit the reasons for raising the question at all, and to put the statement of the case in such light that those to whom it is addressed will listen willingly. In brief the introduction should enable the readers to approach the subject intelligently, with interest, and with a candid mind. It includes all that precedes the statement of the issue. With the statement of the issue begins the real conflict, and problems of arrangement are generally to be met with in what now follows, namely, the body of the argument. As was suggested in discussing the arrangement of exposition, the number of divisions should be few,—if practical not more than five, and three is better. Nobody can keep before his mind seventeen separate points, still less one hundred and twenty-five good reasons; but one can remember three groups, one of two heads with three points under one and four under another, and two others of five points each. The ultimate argument should be grouped under more inclusive propositions, these latter again being grouped in a systematic way so that the tendency of the whole argument and the bearing of each step taken shall be clear. Put last the strongest and most striking group, and in general, put last in each group the strongest argument of that group. Put first a strong and striking argument, especially one which is easily understood and which raises on the face of it a presumption in favor of the conclusion put forward. Put between first and last the less convincing or striking arguments, arranging at least the last part of each group in the order of a climax. Do not end with a refutation; end positively; and do not begin with a refutation unless compelled to do so by the necessity of removing a strong prejudice.

In the conclusion state the proposition again, and state it if possible in a fresh way, as modified by the experience of going through the argument; do not be satisfied with a mere summary, but if possible apply the proposition in some practical way, exhibit its bearings and scope, and drive it home as a thing not only proved but significant and valuable.

Outlines.—These principles will be made more clear by the study of skeleton arguments arranged as outlines or topical summaries, bringing out the line of reasoning to be followed in the completed argument. As an exercise in reasoning, and for the purpose of making the course of thought obvious to the writer of the argument and to a critic of it, the outline is best constructed by linking every proposition in the body of the argument with the propositions which support it by expressions which show that a reason is being given: *for, because, for the reason that, since.* This type of connection should be confined to the body of the argument; a *therefore* in the body is evidence of an inverted order; a *for* or *because* in the introduction suggests that the author has failed to define his issue exactly.

OUTLINE OF THE SPEECH OF SENATOR BEVERIDGE IN THE
SENATE OF THE UNITED STATES, JANUARY 9, 1900, ON THE
PHILIPPINE QUESTION.

Introduction:

I speak in response to invitations and in order to refute
hurtful speeches made here, which are costing the lives
of our soldiers.

Body:

Proposition. WE SHOULD HOLD AND GOVERN THE PHILIP-
PINES, for—

A. Our commercial advantage demands it, for—

  I. Through them we shall get wealth from China, because

    a. Holding them will enable us to control the Pacific
strategically and commercially, and

    b. Our greatest future trade will be with China, for—

      1. Chinese commerce is multiplying rapidly.

      2. The value of this trade is shown by the fact that
other countries are trying to control it.

  II. The islands are very valuable in themselves, for—

    a. Their products are valuable, in—

      1. Tropical and temperate agricultural produce;

      2. timber;

      3. mineral wealth.

    b. Their territory is comparable to that of great
states; their cities to other great cities.

    c. British experience in Hong-Kong shows this, for—

      1. Hong-Kong is very valuable, and—

      2. The climate of the islands is superior to that of
Hong-Kong.

B. The nature of the people makes this policy the only
feasible one, for—

  I. The people are incapable of self-government, for—

    a. They are barbarians, modified by association with
a decadent race, without leaders of a high type,
for—

      1. The testimony of all classes proves this;—

        a. professional men,

        b. business men,

        c. planters,

        d. men of all races.

C. The policy of conquest is our duty, for—

   I. Complete conquest alone can lay the foundation of a proper settlement, for—

      a. It is not true that the military results of our campaign give grounds for abandonment, for—

         1. The force has been insufficient, and the policy indecisive.

         2. A sufficient force and a decisive policy will be effective.

      b. Our kindness has been excessive, for—

         1. The facts prove that we have been kind.

         2. Our kindness has not been understood.

         3. Orientals cannot understand it.

         4. We have tried conciliation ineffectively.

      c. American opposition to the war is the chief factor in prolonging it, for—

         1. It has encouraged ignorant Filipinos, since—

            a. They do not understand our freedom of speech.

D. The United States should rule the islands with a strong and simple government, for—

   I. The attempt to apply self-government is absurd, for—

      a. The Filipinos are incapable of self-government, for—

         1. They are children.

         2. They have been perverted by bad government.

         3. Their racial traits unfit them.

   II. Extending American control over them will not create economic danger, for—

      a. The Filipinos will not compete with American labor, for—

         1. They will not come to America.

         2. The problem in the islands is to get labor.

         3. The experience of other states proves this.

   III. The standard of government must be that fitted for the most backward races, since—

      a. Some races can never be civilized, and

      b. The government must be uniform throughout the islands, for—

         1. Otherwise there will be discontent.

   IV. The only practicable method is American control, for—

      a. The Dutch and English method of operating

through hereditary chieftains is impossible, for—
1. There are none.
  b. A protectorate is undesirable, for—
    1. It will be either weak or meddlesome.
    2. It will be of no advantage to us.
V. The necessary type of administrators can be found, for—
  a. American politicians will not interfere.
  b. Such men are already found.
VI. Effective government in the islands will react beneficially at home.

E. The plan is not un-American, for—
  I. The future of America now depends upon administration and the development of other lands—not on self-government and internal development.
  II. The plan is not contrary to precedent, for—
    a. The treatment of the Indian is an example.
  III. The plan is not contrary to the Declaration of Independence, for—
    a. The consent of the governed is simply a means to life, liberty, and the pursuit of happiness, for—
      1. Otherwise our government could recognize only democratic governments.
  IV. The government of our territories as we please is constitutional, for—
    a. Precedent supports it, for—
      1. Florida, Louisiana, Alaska are precedents.
      2. Contiguity of territory is not essential.
    b. The Constitution expressly recognizes the right.
    c. It necessarily implies the right.

F. A high destiny calls us, for—
  I. The history of our race makes it natural.
  II. We are among the peoples chosen by God to do the duty of organizers.
  III. For the imperial destiny of the flag it is glorious to spend money, or to give up life.

Conclusion:

The announcement of this policy will stop bloodshed and make possible the beginning of our beneficent work in the government of the Philippines.

OUTLINE OF MR. W. J. BRYAN'S SPEECH OF AUGUST 8, 1900, ON ACCEPTING THE DEMOCRATIC NOMINATION FOR THE PRESIDENCY.

Introduction:

1. The Republican party in the present campaign is attempting to shift the issue from questions of human rights to questions of economic policy.
2. But the vital issue is the Philippine Question.

Body:

Proposition. THE PHILIPPINES SHOULD BY ACT OF CONGRESS BE RECOGNIZED AS INDEPENDENT, WITH A GUARANTEE OF PROTECTION, AS IN THE CASE OF CUBA, for—

A. The attempts to excite prejudice against those who urge this course are not warranted, for—
   I. It is not true that it is inconsistent to urge this course after accepting the treaty.
   II. It is not just to charge the responsibility for the resistance of the Filipinos upon those who support this course, for—
      a. Their resistance is natural.
      b. Those who condemn sympathy with their aspirations must condemn all our greatest American patriots.

B. The imperialist policy is fundamentally un-American, for—
   I. A colonial imperialist policy weakens the principle of self-government at home, for—
      a. Our course in the Boer War proves this.
   II. The previous policy of territorial expansion does not support it, for—
      a. The Philippines are not contiguous with the United States.
      b. The Philippines are not habitable by Americans.
   III. An imperialist policy means militarism, for—
      a. It makes requisite a large standing army.
   IV. A Filipino can be neither a citizen nor a subject of the United States, for—
      a. If he is a citizen he endangers our civilization.
      b. If he is a subject, the fundamental conceptions of our government are contravened.

C. A colonial policy is unjust to the Filipinos, for—

  I. The Republicans will not relieve the Filipinos from vassalage, for—

    a. Their course with Porto Rico proves this.

  II. The democratic theory of our government refuses to recognize men as possessions.

  III. Having accepted the services of the Filipinos in fighting against Spain, we are bound to grant them independence.

D. The minor reasons adduced in support of the imperialistic policy are insufficient, for—

  I. It is not our duty to control the Philippines, for—
    a. It is our duty to respect their right of self-government.
    b. We owe to the rest of the world no duty to control the Filipinos.

  II. It is not true that the Filipinos are incapable of self-government.

  III. The flag that floats over our dead should be hauled down, if keeping it aloft is to the injury of both the United States and the Philippines.

  IV. The question is not whether we can govern colonies, but whether we can govern colonies without incurring the penalties of violating human rights.

  V. It is not true that we shall improve Philippine education.

E. The main arguments in favor of imperialism are not sound, for—

  I. It is not true that we must hold the Philippines in order to become a world-power, because—
    a. The United States is already the greatest world power.

  II. The argument from commercial interest is not valid, because—
    a. If it were true it would be wrong to extend trade by means of war, and—
    b. It is not true.

  III. The religious argument has no validity, because—
    a. To spread religion by force is un-Christian.

    IV. It is not true that there is no honorable retreat, for—
        a. There was an honorable retreat from Cuba.
        b. The Democratic policy of a protectorate similar to
           that in Cuba is honorable.
    V. The argument from destiny is cowardly and im-
      moral, for—
        a. Destiny is to be achieved.

Conclusion:

    The ideal to be held before the American people is the
achievement of a republic founded upon justice and the
rights of man, which by its success may become the supreme moral factor in the government of the world.

Transitions.—As regards the conclusion of one section
and the beginning of the next, all that has been said
upon the subject with reference to exposition is even
more applicable to argument. The steps in an argument must be consciously marked off and indicated.
Each section should lead to a definite though subordinate conclusion, which must be stated in such a way as
to let the reader know beyond a doubt the point which
has been reached. The indications of relation should,
if possible, not be formal; the argument is most vigorous if the mere presentation of the subject makes the
relation clear; but it is better to be formal than obscure.
Leave no doubt, then, when a new step is taken and
whither it is tending, whether it is a reason, an inference, an abatement, or a supplement to what has been
said.

Introductions.—Something should be said with reference to the substance and expression of the introduction
and the conclusion. Young writers are often unreal
and conventional in their introductions. It is well to
take hold as promptly as possible. The writer should
ask himself, what is necessary to make my readers feel

an interest in this matter, why does the topic concern them, why is it worth discussing? Where does it lead? How did it arise? What is necessary to remove prejudice and to awaken goodwill, so that my message will be listened to? Must any false impressions be removed, or can any spring of favorable emotion be touched?

I am about to write an article in favor of the system of consolidating several small rural school districts, and of providing transportation to the new schoolhouse. I plan to contribute it to a periodical of general circulation, addressing an intelligent public, who do not know anything about the system which I support. I begin by making clear the present system, and this I do by the most vivid description I can write of a tiny child ploughing three miles along the snowy road to school, or kept at home for days because of inclement weather. I describe the ungraded rural school,—the teacher's crowded schedule, the inadequacy of the instruction, the lack of proper janitor service, the lack of equipment, the narrowness of outlook. Then I explain the general system proposed, and having reached the issue I enter upon the reasons which caused me to support the plan. But if I were arguing before a citizens' meeting called to discuss the plan of consolidating a particular district it would be absurd to begin so far away from the immediate issue. Perhaps no introduction would be necessary, perhaps an account of the official steps taken to call the meeting together would be appropriate; perhaps a comparison of this district with others, intended to bring about the feeling that the plan was not an untried one.

In dealing with an historical topic on the other hand, say the question whether Aaron Burr was a traitor or

not, the introduction would be quite different. It
would be in place to deal with the fascination of Burr's
character, and with the interest which even now gathers
about all matters connected with him. It would be
necessary to narrate the story of his expedition, leading
to the issue: what was Burr's motive? was it to invade
Mexico? or was it to carve out a principality in the
United States? or was it simply to exercise pressure upon
government officials in support of his own personal am-
bitions?

Every argument requires an introduction to its particular subject, and not a mere formal set of phrases
having no distinct relation to the topic under consideration.

Conclusions.—The conclusion, likewise, is a part of
the argument and not a mere annex to it. A mere
restatement of the proposition may be enough. "In
the light of this evidence, Burr's treason can hardly be
doubted;"—or "The charge that Burr was traitorous
falls to the ground." Or a more energetic appeal may
be in place. A director arguing in favor of an addition
to an industrial plant may urge the unfortunate results
which he expects if his project is not carried out. A
scientist may point with solemn enthusiasm to the profound cosmic importance of the consequences which follow from the view which he maintains with regard to
the constitution of matter. A prosecuting attorney in
ending his argument for the conviction of a man charged
with crime may urge with all the power of his mind and
heart the dangers to home and family of letting crime
go unpunished. In a word, the circumstances and the
nature of the argument decide the character of the conclusion which is appropriate to it.

IV. PERSUASION

It is not necessary to point out that the principles of argument are again nothing but the general principles of composition applied to the special objects of this form of discourse. Arguments, finally, like other types of composition, may be addressed to the intellect or may be colored by an emotional and esthetic quality. Indeed the type of argument which reaches beyond mere intellectual conviction and is intended to arouse the motives which affect the will, exciting the passions and setting the whole nature into action has received a separate name, *persuasion,* and is often treated as a separate form of discourse. Persuasion, however, is related to conviction, as purely logical argument is called, in the same way in which each of the other emotional types of writing is related to its purely intellectual and matter-of-fact analogue.

It is, on the whole, the fault of most young writers in American schools rather to write with a dry indifference to the emotional side of their expression than to be guilty of excessive verbal finery or insincere decoration. But it is as truly insincere, though not so disgustingly so, to neglect and repress the eager workings of the soul as it is to counterfeit emotion which one does not feel. Concentrate your attention energetically on the purpose of your writing, analyze it with the most abstract coldness, but do not be afraid of saying with energy what you think and feel. There is more to be hoped from the young writer who is guilty of some generous mistakes of exuberance, than from one who writes with timid correctness, or the dryly pragmatic writer who never rises to a figure of speech and cultivates a lack of openness to every impulsive and imaginative turn of style and thought.

In writing an argument, frame the proposition to be proved with care and definiteness. Determine the issue, the point on which the decision turns, and state it with fairness. Support your side of the issue by reasons, framed as subordinate propositions, and these by other similar reasons, carrying the process down as far as it seems needful. In general, strive to find in your reasoning some ground based on the relation of cause and effect, reasoning from cause to effect or from effect to cause as the case may require. Arguments as to fact generally are supported by reasoning from effect to cause. The main tests of such arguments are: does the effect exist? is the alleged cause adequate? do other causes as well account for the effect? The argument from testimony is from effect to cause. In such arguments the fact that the testimony is given should be determined, and then the causes why it should be given: is the witness able to tell the truth? does he wish to tell the truth? The argument from authority is similar. Does the authority give his support? is he qualified as an authority? is he free from bias and intent to mislead? Arguments from cause to effect are subject to tests analogous to those applicable to the argument from effect to cause: does the cause exist? is it adequate? do other causes intervene to modify its action? Arguments as to right and wrong are usually arguments from cause to effect.

Arguments should be constructed in sections, and usually require an introduction, a body, in which the real work of the argument is done, and a conclusion. In the arrangement of the body, a strong argument should be put first, and in general the strongest argument last, the less important matter, including the refutation, in less conspicuous places. A similar system should be followed in the subordinate steps of the argument. Clearness of connection is of great importance in an argument, and logical orderliness is often assisted by the drafting of an outline argument in which each proposition is linked to those which support it by a causal conjunction. Arguments may like the other forms of discourse be touched with emotion, and elevated by beauty. Without some such elements an argument cannot have the highest degree of power over those to whom it is addressed.

CHAPTER XIII

THE USE OF AUTHORITIES

I. TWO WAYS OF USING AUTHORITIES

Books and other authorities may be made the basis of
two sorts of written compositions. In the one, the ideas
of the authority are simply restated, usually in shorter
form; in the other, the authority is used as raw material, is assimilated by the writer, and worked into
something substantially new, which bears the impress
of the writer's mind. Each form of exercise is valuable
in its own way, but the two are essentially different, and
should not be confused. The first form is primarily an
exercise in reporting, and the completed work is of use
to readers only as information about the authority, or
as a guide in following his thought. The second exercise is a genuine exercise in original composition, and
has the use of communicating the writer's own thought,
—his own, though others before him may have had the
same idea as he. In such writing the knowledge drawn
from books becomes a part of his own mind as completely
as the knowledge drawn from his own direct observation
and experience, and is used in the same way. For clearness in his own mind as well as for honesty in his dealings with others, a writer should know and should let
others know just how much use and what kind of use
he is making of his sources.

II.   SUMMARIES, OUTLINES AND NOTES

Analytic Reading.—The reporting of what is in an authority takes these main forms: the topical outline; the connected summary; and notes.   All three, however, depend upon the same methods of work and should produce substantially the same result as to their content and the relations of their parts.   They should present the essential idea of the matter reported, clearly and with due emphasis, proportion, and logical connection, but divested of the amplification, the illustration, the concrete fulness, of the original.   To accomplish this end, the writer of a report should master the central idea and the course of thought of that which he reports. He should be sure that he knows the main purpose of his author, that he can divide the work into its main sections, that if necessary he can further subdivide these sections, and that he follows the logical connection binding one part to another.   The practice of alert reading of this sort begun by careful and slow preparation steadily becomes habitual, and more and more easy, and in the long run saves a great deal of time.   Inexpert readers endeavor to take their author's meaning *en masse,* do not distinguish between what is fundamental and what is subsidiary, and tend to substitute their own thoughts for what they read, often failing utterly with an author of intellectual energy and power to take advantage of the opportunity to enlarge their own range of ideas.   Such a superficial method may easily do more harm than good, by concealing from the reader his lazy and superficial habits, and making him believe that he is studying when he is only muddling his own mind. But by practice and habitual attention to the central ideas of the whole and of each part, the power of rapid and at the same time accurate perception becomes developed to an extraordinary degree, so that a trained listener can grasp the course even of a very complicated spoken address without difficulty, and may be able to restate the substance of a speech which he has just heard without hesitation and without omission. This is the ideal toward which we should aim—to be able with one reading or at one hearing to grasp and to express the author's meaning with accuracy and reasonable fulness in adequate language.

The Preliminary View.—The steps which lead to this skill are indicated in the following suggestions. At the beginning of such practice it will be found that a general view of the whole is requisite in order to apprehend the significance of the parts. After a time it becomes possible for a reader to sense the tendency of the whole as he goes along, but at first the attention to details obscures the meaning of the whole. A preliminary reading or survey, then, should be made, from which the general meaning is deduced. This first view is likely to be vague, but that does no harm, for further analysis will develop it and make it definite; but—what is really unfortunate—it is often incorrect. Even so it helps to give a standard or point of reference as to details, and can in turn be corrected by the observation of the details and their bearing on each other.

For example, the general drift of Senator Beveridge's argument on the Philippine question is to support an imperialistic policy on the grounds of its practical advantage to the United States; of Mr. Bryan's argument to oppose that policy on grounds of its fundamental immorality and danger to the higher American ideals. So the main idea of Huxley's address on a liberal education is that English education should be reformed from top to bottom on the basis of adjusting those who are being educated to the laws of nature. The main idea of a narrative may likewise be perceived and stated. *The Pilgrim's Progress* compares the course of the Christian life to a dangerous and adventurous journey through a mainly hostile region. Kipling's *Jungle Books* deal with the theme of a human being, brought up from infancy by the wild creatures of the jungle, and adding to human resource and adaptation the instinct and truth of wild nature.

Building up from Paragraph Topics.—To complete the analysis of any work, it is possible to begin from the largest elements and to work downward to the smallest subdivision or to begin with the smaller elements, and to build up the whole. With difficult material it is usually best to proceed in the latter way, though it is usually the case that the mind cannot systematically hold strictly to this method step by step but will leap to an understanding of the main divisions from the massing of a few of the smaller elements. In practice, it is best after catching the bearing of the whole, however dimly, to begin with the paragraphs, restating with neat brevity the content of each, but not hesitating, as soon as any larger section relatively complete within itself is detected, to mark it off as separate. The statement of the content of the larger sections, however, is usually best left until the paragraphs are summarized. Thus several paragraphs will build up a section, and several sections will build up a larger section, and several of these again combine, until the whole is apprehended not merely as the sum of all its parts, but as organically composed of related members.

Topical Outlines.—The graphic representation of these relations helps to make them clear to most minds; and hence the value of the topical outline, especially in the earlier stages of the training in analytic study.

For example, consider the sequence of thought in the following sonnet of Shakespeare.

A.

> That time of year thou mayst in me behold
>   When yellow leaves, or none, or few, do hang
> Upon those boughs which shake against the cold—
>   Bare ruin'd choirs, where late the sweet birds sang.
>
> In me thou see'st the twilight of such day
>   As after sunset fadeth in the west;
> Which by-and-by black night doth take away,
>   Death's second self, that seals up all in rest.
>
> In me thou see'st the glowing of such fire,
>   That on the ashes of his youth doth lie,
> As the death-bed whereon it must expire,
>   Consum'd with that which it was nourish'd by.

B.

> This thou perceiv'st, which makes thy love more strong,
> To love that well which thou must leave ere long.

The general meaning of the poem is to the effect, "My life is drawing to its end, and therefore thy love is the more tender and intense."

Stanza 1. I am like autumn with its leafless trees.
Stanza 2. I am like the fading day, drawing toward night.
Stanza 3. I am like a fire, dying in its ashes.

These three parallel comparisons evidently build up a section of thought—"My life is fading"—upon which as a whole the last two lines make a comment,—''hence thy love is all the stronger.'' A topical outline exhibits this structure of thought, which the grammatical structure of the poem accentuates.

> A. My life is in the period just before its end:
>   1. like autumn coming to winter,
>   2. like twilight drawing to night,
>   3. like fire burning to ashes;
> B. Hence thy love is the more intense.

Observe that as to thought, there is a real parallelism among the coördinate elements (the three comparisons; the two statements), and that as to form, the syntax is parallel where the thought is parallel (three similar phrases; two distinct predications).

The Method of Analysis Applied.—We now proceed to apply the same method to a typical example in prose. A prose writer who takes great pains to indicate the relations of his ideas, and who constructs his expositions very symmetrically is Professor Huxley. A topical outline of one of his addresses is comparatively easy to draw up.

Topical Outline of Huxley's *A Liberal Education*

A. Introduction: the importance of defining *a liberal education*.
  I. Education is a profoundly important subject.
  II. Education is a subject now discussed much, but in a confused way.
    a. There is no agreement as to the grounds for popular education.
    1. It is agreed that popular education is necessary.
    2. All kinds of reasons are given for this idea.
    3. None of these reasons are satisfactory: not
      a. the politician's.
      b. the clergyman's,
      c. the manufacturer's.

        b. There is no agreement on practical suggestions:
           1. as to including theology;
           2. as to the extent of the curriculum.
   III. It is fundamentally necessary to define what the nature of the best education is.

B. A liberal education is that education which most completely produces harmony with nature.
    I. Education is: intellectually, instruction in the knowledge of the laws of nature; morally, discipline in harmonious adjustment to those laws.
        a. If life were a game of chess, learning the laws of the game would be fundamental to education.
        b. Life is analogous to such a game.
        c. Education is learning the laws of nature and learning to obey them.
    II. Experience provides education, but this education is harsh and wasteful.
        a. Experience would educate a lonely man in the laws of external nature.
        b. Experience would teach a social man the laws of human nature.
        c. Experience is always thus teaching all of us, but harshly and wastefully.
   III. A liberal education anticipates experience, providing the highest form of perfect adjustment to nature.

C. This kind of education does not now exist anywhere in England.
    I. It is not found in the primary schools.
        a. The teaching is inadequate in the most important matters, and stresses the less important.
        b. The teaching has no relation to actual life.
           1. Moral teaching lacks a proper foundation and adaptation to modern life.
           2. Nothing is taught of modern history and government.
           3. Nothing is taught of science.
        c. Such an education lacks the fundamental requisite of leading to wisdom.
    II. It is not found in the higher schools.
        a. They are ineffective in what they do teach and wholly neglect all modern culture and all science.

      b. How extraordinarily ill adjusted to all the conditions of modern English life!

      c. The classics if taught well would not make the best basis of modern education.

      d. In fact they are taught badly.

   III. It is not found in the universities.

      a. Universities need thoroughgoing reform.

        1. Good testimony shows this.

        2. English leaders in science and letters are not in universities.

        3. Universities do not recognize their leaders.

        4. English universities do not bear comparison with German universities.

D. There is a great opportunity for the South London Working-Men's College to establish a truly liberal education, if properly supported.

   I. What it does and what it looks forward to doing.

Let us now undertake a more difficult task. Let us take up a section of Emerson's *Essay on Self-Reliance,* complete within itself, though the part omitted would somewhat modify and explain it. Emerson is difficult since he has no "topic sentences," and leaves it to the reader to make out the sequence of his thought. The general tendency of the passage is obviously to urge reliance upon one's own genuinely native intuitions, because they are in consonance with the law of nature as a whole. There are twenty-five paragraphs, which may be summarized as follows:

1. The genuinely original works of others call upon us to be frankly reliant upon our deep intuitive convictions.

2. Only by courageous and obedient realization of our special nature can we do the special things we were made to do.

3. Only by acting with confidence in the special conditions in which we are placed can we do any worthy work.

4. Like children, like youths among their natural associates, let a man be of individual mind.

5. A man should, like a frank boy, be undisturbed by self-consciousness.

6. Of this independence society is the enemy, demanding conformity.

7. But conformity to anything not true to your inmost nature is radically sinful.

8. It is not virtuous action, which may be external, but the whole man, that has real worth.

9. My duty is to my essential self.

10. Conformity to that which is not in vital consonance with a man's own nature makes him weak, false, and foolish.

11. A neglect of the ill-will of others earned by truth to one's self requires a deep and magnanimous faith.

12. An enemy of self-trust is the fear of inconsistency.

13. Why fear to be inconsistent?

14. Speak out, being true to your conception, and fearing not inconsistency though you should be misunderstood.

15. Your character has unity, no matter what your actions as to particular things.

16. A succession of actions true to yourself with no thought but of the immediate will build up a consistent character.

17. The true measure of things is not consistency or conformity, but individual manhood.

18. The study of art tends to produce subservience to convention. All famous works of men are made for every man, that he may command them, not they him.

19. Likewise, the study of history tends to blind the eyes by over-emphasis on the acts of those in illustrious place.

20. Yet in this reverence for the great there is a symbol of the reverence due from man to man as such.

21. The ground for this reliance on a man's intuitions is that they are a part of the one great universe, and move inevitably in accordance with its nature.

22. Since God, the spirit of this universe, gives perpetually renewed and immediate revelations, creating the world anew, for the open mind and obedient soul the past is not sacred but is useful only in subordination to the present.

23. Like the things of nature which fulfil their whole nature in every movement of their being, a man should live his whole life at one with his nature and with the nature of the universe, complete in each present instant.

24. When a man so lives, his own expression of himself needs no traditional sacred words but will have the charm and power of natural things.

25. The deep reality of intuitive perceptions is mysterious; it is a vision of tranquillity, something above all human passion.

It is obvious on the face of the paragraphs that there is a section (¶ ¶ 6–11) on conformity, a section (¶ ¶ 12–16) on consistency, and a section (¶ ¶ 21–24, or 21–25) on intuition. Will further consideration reveal other groups of paragraphs falling under single heads? The first five paragraphs, it can be seen upon reëxamination, are all a development of the general idea, *Trust thyself,* and the portion between paragraphs 17 and 20 again urges reverence for and dependence upon individual manhood. There are, then, five sections, or groups of paragraphs plainly distinguishable; and a further consideration shows that the middle three, the second, third and fourth, all deal with practical applications of the general proposition. The last paragraph of all causes some difficulty. Is it the conclusion only of its own section, or has it weight and power enough to stand as the conclusion of the whole? Readers will differ. I incline to regard it as concluding the whole, and hence I make it a separate section. The complete outline, accordingly, is as follows, the topics of the paragraphs being omitted.

I. Introduction—Have confidence in your deepest self (¶¶ 1–5).
II. Practical applications of the injunction, trust thyself (¶¶ 6–20).
    a. Be not afraid of nonconformity (¶¶ 6–11).
    b. Be not afraid of inconsistency (¶¶ 12–16).
    c. Depend for your measure of all values upon individual manhood (¶¶ 17–20).
III. The reason for confidence in intuition is that it is consonant with the law of the universe (¶¶ 21–24).
IV. The nature of intuition is unfathomably mysterious; he

who has it possesses a tranquil vision of reality,
raising him above fear and hope, and all human
passion (¶ 25).

The Connected Summary.—A connected summary
presents the same matter as the topical outline, effect-
ing subordination and giving salience by the ordinary
means of expression. As the topical outline may be developed from the utmost degree of brevity, such as the
single main statement, up to the utmost minuteness of
division, so the connected summary may be on any scale
of development, but should always deal with the essential parts with due proportion. Each of the following
summaries is sound; but they differ in scale.

Trust thyself.

Be true to your intuitions, for they are in agreement with
universal nature.

Since the deepest intuitions of a man's own nature are but
manifestations of the spirit of the universe, he should trust
them boldly, not striving to conform to a conventional standard
external to himself, or fearing that inconsistency between the
appearance of his acts shall make him inconsistent with himself. So shall he gain that tranquil sense of truth that raises
him above passion, and space and time, and life and death.

Trust thyself. The genuinely original works of others stimulate us to be frankly reliant upon our own deep instinctive
convictions; for only by courageous and obedient realization
of our individual nature can we do the individual things we
were intended to do, and only by acting with confidence in the
special conditions in which we are placed can we do any worthy
work. Like children, like youths with their natural associates,
let men be of undivided minds. Like a frank boy, let a man be
undisturbed by self-consciousness.
Be a nonconformist. By demanding conformity, society is
the enemy of native independence; but conformity to anything
not true to our inmost nature is radically sinful. It is not
virtuous action, which may be external, but the whole man,
that has real worth. My duty is to my essential self. Con-

formity to that which is not in vital consonance with a man's own nature makes him weak, false, and foolish. A neglect of the ill-will of others caused by truth to one's self requires a deep and magnanimous faith.

Do not fear to be inconsistent. Speak out without thinking of what you once thought, and without care whether you should be misunderstood. Your character has unity, and the general tendency of your actions will have essential consistency.

The true measure of things is individual manhood. Works of art are meant to be measured by men, not to measure men. The study of history tends to conventional falsehood by over-emphasis on the acts of those in illustrious place. Yet even in this there is a symbol of the reverence due to men as men.

The ground for relying on the intuitions of our nature is that they are genuine products of the inner spirit of the universe. Since God, the spirit of the universe, gives new revelations, and makes the world anew, the past is not sacred, but is useful only with reference to the present. A man's being, like the being of natural things, should be complete and full in each instant, without reference to past or future. When a man so lives, his own expression of himself needs no traditional sacred words, but has the charm and power of natural things.

The deep reality of intuition is mysterious; it is a vision of tranquillity, something above all human passion.

Notes.—Notes are summaries, often abbreviated and incomplete in form, sketching the outline of a subject. They are best taken so as to leave adequate space between them and adequate margin to write in headings or memoranda. Following are notes on this part of Emerson's Essay, the parts in italics being added after the original notes were taken, to show connection.

Value of spontaneous originality.
   Admonition of genuinely original works—Plato, Moses, Milton. Hold to your own spontaneous impressions. Else take your own opinion from another.

Boldly adhere to and speak out your best self.
   Take yourself for better for worse. You only know what you can do and that only when you have tried. Ex-

press yourself. Only your best satisfies you. Live boldly in your own time. Trust thyself. Confide in genius of your own age. Work boldly forward in your own conditions.

Like children, like youths among their own associates, be single-minded.

Examples of children, babes, brutes. Calm self-confidence. Youth too bashful with seniors, frank with contemporaries.

Like boys be undisturbed by self-consciousness.

Boy the master of society; man pledged by reputation.

and so on.

Lectures.—Lectures afford constant practice in taking analytic notes. Sometimes, indeed, a body of detailed facts and formulas is dictated, which must be taken down at length. In general, however, lecture notes are taken down confusedly, the idea being lost in the illustrations and amplifications by which it is meant to be elucidated. Good notes should catch the main ideas, and in some manner indicate relations, so that the notes make a kind of analytic outline. The form of the Emerson notes may suggest how this can be done. Important matter can be underlined and headings written in as the lecture proceeds. Often the ideal manner of taking notes would be to listen throughout a lecture and to summarize from memory afterwards; but in some cases there may be too much of important detail to be remembered.

In brief: strive to detect in the sections of the work which make up units the centrally important matter in each unit, then to associate the units under more inclusive heads, and thus to apprehend the total as made up of related things. The practice of reporting speeches is valuable, after some proficiency has been gained with printed matter. It is an accomplishment of no small value to be able to report the words of a speaker within small compass, with due proportion and with fidelity to the original. Newspaper reports, which often distort and misrepresent the speaker grotesquely and shamefully, show how rare it is.

III.   THE CONSULTATION OF AUTHORITIES

In writing based upon authorities, there are three steps to be taken: finding the references, obtaining the material from them, and putting into written form the results of one's own study.

Test the Value of Authorities.—The first thing for the student to learn about printed works is that they differ in value. There is a natural tendency for one who has been looking up to text-books, and has been under the guidance of the printed work, to take every book as valuable, and to regard every statement in print as trustworthy. But the men who make books are only men like you and me, and are only talking with pen and ink. To be sure, they are more deliberate, and they speak to a wider public than you and I, but they are, like you and me, imperfect, sometimes prejudiced, sometimes credulous, well-informed about some things, imperfectly informed about others, unintelligent in some directions, biased, perhaps even deceitful. They get out of date, also, as we may. There are books which are no more to be relied on than the pictures on the outside of a seed catalogue. In every political campaign, there are biographies published of the chief candidates for the presidency. They are written by partisans, for partisans. They may tell the truth; but can you be sure they are telling the truth as to any particular point?

If you were trying to learn the facts about any region, you could not be sure of getting them from the circulars of a company that had land to sell in that region. You know that in such advertisements, even if everything said is true, the whole is not true, because of what it omits.

A book is thoroughly reliable if the author knows his subject well, if he has the insight to perceive the facts in the right relations, if there are no obstacles in the way of his exercising his ability, and if he has the desire to state his sincere beliefs. As to knowledge, a man knows what he sees, what he studies, what he is occupied with. A college president may be assumed to know something about colleges; he has to prove his knowledge if he writes about farm loans. A man who has made money in real estate would be likely to know something about the value of a lot; he may or may not know any more about a wise foreign policy than a peddler of vegetables. Again, a man may have grown old and forgotten the facts of his youth. There are well authenticated stories of perfectly honest general officers who told in their old age stories about battle-fields from which their own letters written at the time of the battle proved that they were miles away. As to insight a man may be a fool, even in print, as men have been fools about the pyramids of Egypt, or the Ten Tribes. Again a man may be so biased, consciously or unconsciously, that he cannot see the truth. Macaulay writes about William III to whose establishment on the throne the English Whig party looked back as its foundation, as a Whig, a thick-and-thin admirer. He condones every fault and exalts every excellence of his hero. James Boswell wrote a biography of Samuel Johnson. Bos-

well was jealous of all Johnson's friends, particularly
of Goldsmith and of Mrs. Thrale; he told some truth
about them but could not help coloring it. You may accept his statement of facts, in detail, and yet find it
necessary to study what he says about these people, in
order to form your own idea of them.

A man may conceal, or misrepresent from a conscien-
tious motive, because of devotion to a creed, or a party;
or of course he may deceive from interested motives.
As a rule, ''recognized authorities''—authorities recom-
mended and respected by specialists in their fields—are
trustworthy. The title-page of a book sometimes gives
some information about an author's standing. Some
series of works are under the direction of responsible and
careful editors; some are mere pieces of bookmaking.
All in all, the reader will do well to do what he can to
assure himself of the weight of his authority; to learn
whether his author has knowledge, ability, freedom from
bias and prejudice, and honesty.

Use Bibliographical Aids.—The second thing to learn
about printed works is that their number is overwhelm-
ing. A great library has a marvelous number of works
on most subjects, and something on nearly all. The
student then must learn how with the least waste of
time to find the best authorities on his subject.

For this purpose there are many helps in the form of
indexes. The accumulation of knowledge is so vast that
only by indexes can it be made at all manageable.

> ''. . . index learning turns no mortal pale;
> We catch the eel of knowledge by the tail.''

The Card Catalogue.—The first aid to the student is
the card catalogue of the library. In it every book in

the library is represented by at least two cards, an author card and a subject card.

The author card, on which the last name of the author is the leading or index word, the *heading* as it is called, looks like this:

BKB
.W27

       WASHBURN, Margaret Floy.
         The animal mind; a text-book of comparative psychology.　N. Y. 1908.
         (The animal behavior series.　v. 2)
         Bibliography: p. 295–323.

The author card gives the author's name, if known, the title of the book, perhaps abbreviated, the number of volumes, and the place and year of publication. It may also contain other information, in which the fact that the book contains a bibliography is of the greatest importance to the student.

The subject-card has the following appearance.

Y
.1B17

       SHORT STORY.
      Baker, Harry T.
         The contemporary short story.　Bost. [c. 1916].
         Bibliography: p. 257.

Observe in the upper left-hand corner of each card the *call-number*. This indicates the place of the book on the shelves, and should be exactly copied when the book is called for at the desk. Every symbol on it, down to each dot, has a meaning. $\frac{Y}{.2}$ M 3 4 is not the same with

$\frac{Y}{.M\ 3\ 4}$. E is not the same with .E.
2

There may be a title-card, on which the title, neg‹ lecting introductory articles, is the heading:

BKB
.W27
          ANIMAL mind.
          Washburn, Margaret F.

The subject catalogue in the nature of things cannot be quite so complete as the author catalogue. One book often treats of many subjects, and it might not be possible to make a card for every single topic in it. There may also be subjects which the catalogues have not thought of listing. The catch-word used by the cataloguer may not occur to you. What then?

Suppose you want to find out about William of Orange, the third king of England of that name. You look in the card-catalogue under *William of Orange*. You may not find any entry about your man. In a good catalogue you would find a cross-reference to William III. But even if you have not that help, you reflect that his name might be entered as William III, King of England. You look that up: you find nothing in English on this king. Consider, then, whether there is not some class to which he belongs. He was king of England. Any history of England on a fairly large scale must have something to say about his reign; and perhaps there are special histories dealing with it fully. Some such books, too, will contain a bibliography of the references to their authorities. The cards in a good card catalogue will contain a note to that effect—*e.g.*, *bibl.* If you get one book somewhere near what you want it may refer to others. So the subject index under *England: history* will give guidance; and perhaps under this heading there may be further subdivisions, such as

Stuarts, Protestant Revolution, and the like, in which you may find the books wanted.

Other Guides.—In other words, think of several ways in which the subject may be approached, and try one after another, if the first or the second does not help to the necessary title. If there is nothing in the subject catalogue about *coal,* think of *fuel, geological formations, carbon;* if there is nothing about *dress,* try *costume, fashion, textiles;* if there is nothing about *trap-shooting,* try *shooting,* or *sports.* In many cases, the information obtained in this way may be sufficient. But there are other helps. In the case of William III, the encyclopedia may save the trouble of turning over even the cards on English history. Try the *Encyclopedia Britannica* or the *New American Cyclopedia,* and look at the end of the article on William III. Here are listed those authoritative works in English chiefly concerned with William which were published before these encyclopedias were published. Have there been any of importance published since? This question leads us to the problem of ascertaining what guides to the special branch of science we are concerned with there may be. To answer such questions Miss Alice B. Kroeger's *Guide to the Use of Reference Books* is the best general aid. Look in the index of this book for *History,* turn to the pages indicated, and find the name of the index listing the publications in the field of history. If there are none, look up some larger class including history. You may even have to go to some yearly catalogues of all the books published in England or America.

For articles in general periodicals there are a series of indexes, the most important dealing with recent material being the *Readers' Guide to Periodical Literature.*

Every student should know how to use it, and understand its plan of ''cumulation''—its latest monthly issue, is quarterly cumulations, its latest yearly cumulations, its quinquennial cumulations. For earlier periodicals the main reliance will be upon *Poole's Index* and its supplements. Periodical articles in popular magazines are ordinarily somewhat hasty, as compared with books, and are meant to be entertaining rather than instructive. Magazines as a whole also differ greatly in the seriousness and trustworthiness of their articles. The writer who is searching for truth must therefore use them critically, and prefer books when he can get them.

There will also be found in a fairly extensive library several other periodical indexes of use, especially the *Readers' Guide to Periodical Literature, Supplement,* indexing periodicals not in the *Readers' Guide;* and the *Annual Magazine Subject Index,* supplementing the *Readers' Guide,* with articles not in that index, and indexed by subject only.

For information as to books published of recent years, the *Book Review Digest* is convenient, but too popular in its nature always to lead to the best authorities on serious or special subjects.

For most general subjects likely to come within the range of college freshmen, the preceding guides are likely to be sufficient. But for many special sciences, trades, or arts, there are special aids and guides—Poor's *Manual of the Railroads of the United States,* Monroe's *Cyclopedia of Education,* the *Navy Yearbook,* the *Engineering Index,* the *Experiment Station Record,*—with which the student who enters the field of special study must acquaint himself.

The Student's Duty to the Library.—In any investigation, it is the duty of the student to follow out some such line as has been suggested, and not to give up, or to ask the aid of the library attendants until he has fairly exhausted his own resources. A library is a great public benefaction, maintained at public expense; it is the monument of past coöperation, and a work of present coöperation, and intended to help those who help themselves. The readers who profit by all this coöperative help ought to coöperate in return. Library staffs are the most liberal of their aid, the most kindly, the most devoted and patient of public servants. They are always overworked and underpaid. It is an abuse of their good nature and an imposition on the public, a wholly unfair thing, to call upon them for personal assistance until you have done your best to obtain your information by the help of the printed resources placed so conveniently within your reach. It is your business to learn your business—and part of a student's business is to know how to get at books.

General References.—In addition to these bibliographical helps to the special information on your subject, there are a number of books of reference, either general or special. Everyone, of course, should use the encyclopedia, the dictionary, the gazetteer, and the atlas. *The World Almanac*, the *American Year Book*, *Who's Who in America*, and *Who's Who* (English) are very useful books of reference on recent years, the encyclopedias necessarily being far from contemporary. There are two unabridged dictionaries of good repute, *Webster's International*, and the *Standard;* there are also a dictionary including much encyclopedic information, *The Century*, and a dictionary on a great scale, commonly known as *Murray's Dictionary,* giving the full history of English words.

Small Dictionaries.—As to one's own moderate-sized dictionary, there are only three worthy of consideration for steady practical use by an American. Of abridged dictionaries the largest is *Webster's Collegiate Dictionary,* published by G. & C. Merriam Co. It is based on *Webster's New International Dictionary,* and is for most practical purposes more convenient than the full-sized dictionary, and as adequate. The *Desk Standard Dictionary* is at this moment the latest small dictionary to receive revision. This and *Webster's Secondary School Dictionary* are smaller books, based on the unabridged *Standard* and *International,* and though in the main trustworthy, they will not relieve the student of the need to consult the unabridged editions pretty often. The purchaser of a dictionary should be on his guard against fraud. Unscrupulous publishers make use of out-of-date dictionaries to get up inadequate and hastily composed books, which they bind and make up to resemble really reliable and scholarly works, printing them in fairly large type on poor paper, and being at no expense for the services of the great body of trained specialists required to create a genuine work, can afford to vend their fraudulent ware at a low price. It would be better to pick up a genuine old unabridged *Webster* at second-hand than to waste money on one of these things.

Keeping References.—As you go along with your work get the names of your references accurately, list them; do not lose one. Keep each one on a separate card or slip. The accepted method of doing this is to begin with the name of the author, last name first, to follow this with the title, and to add such other information as is necessary to identify the book without question; at least the place of publication, and the year. Sometimes other information is necessary—the edition, for example, and the number of the volume. There is no one accepted form of citation. Some italicize titles, some put dates in parentheses, some capitalize only the first word of the title. The following are standard forms:

Pope, Alexander, Poetical Works, Globe edition, Lond., 1869.

Clemens, Samuel L. (Mark Twain), *The Adventures of Tom Sawyer*, N. Y., 1917.

Dana, J. D., Manual of Geology, 4th ed., N. Y., 1895.

The same principle holds in reference to periodicals, modified to suit the case, for example:

Bourinot, J. G., Canadian Studies in Comparative Politics: Royal Society of Canada, vol. XI, sec. 2, pp. 77–94; 1893.

IV. THE USE OF AUTHORITIES

Orientation.—Either with or after the making of your list of references comes the obtaining of knowledge from them. No subject should be undertaken with regard to the relations of which to the general field in which it lies the writer is not informed,—about which he is not *oriented,* does not know where north, south, east, and west lie, and what kind of country surrounds it. Before beginning to study definitely about *The Punishment of Crime in the Days of Charlemagne,* one should know something about primitive Teutonic ideas of crime, and something about the world in Charlemagne's day.

Before treating the by-products of coal, one should know something about the main products in the form of coal and gas, and something about the chemical nature of coal-tar and ammonia. Before treating the costume of women in 1849, one should know something about women's attire in general. So be sure of a sufficient background of knowledge, and have a basis.

Limiting the Scope of Study.—Then as rapidly as possible narrow the scope and define the point of your study—write not on William III, but on his qualities as a military leader, or the reasons for his lack of popularity; not on coal, but on the special value of Pocahontas coal or the saving of ammonium sulphate; not on fashions, but on what forces decide the fashions of men's clothing; not on tractors, but on the conditions which must be fulfilled in any given case in order to make a tractor a profitable investment for a farm. The topic once clear and defined in relation to its background, strive to ascertain from each reference what it contains of value upon your chosen topic, neglecting everything else. Look in the index of a big book—using your insight and imagination to guide you as to the headings you shall refer to. Every work ought to have an index; nearly all serious books do so. When sure that you have a general knowledge of coal and its qualities, look only for Pocahontas, and closely related coals. When you know Goldsmith and Boswell fairly, look in the index of Boswell's *Life of Johnson* only for Goldsmith's name, if you are writing about Boswell's presentation of Goldsmith's character. Concentrate; go to the center; aim at the bull's eye. In taking notes, for most purposes, it is a waste of time to copy much verbatim—a few catch-words to show the tendency of the

passage is likely to be enough. But be careful to make
your references to the page or section so clear that you
can be sure of finding the passage you want, if you
should need to refer to it again, and keep each note on a
separate card or slip.

Shaping the Work.—It will often be the case that in
the mere course of collecting material and taking memoranda, the writer makes his mind up as to what he desires to say. The work in some degree takes shape almost of itself under his hands—sometimes indistinctly,
sometimes quite clearly. As it does, it may be feasible
to note on each reference card the heading or point that
it has reference to : *efficiency, cost-economy, statistics of
consumption;* or, *early years, youth, first important public works, causes of failure.*

But the writer should not hasten the action of his
mind, or crystallize too soon. After the reading is
done, and the notes are taken, the writer will have still
to consider much detail, to plan and adjust, and decide
what the climax—the central point of all is, to plan for
systematic connection, to decide what help the reader
will require at the beginning to be able to follow the
paper; in brief the evolution of the whole must be
settled. A preliminary outline, not necessarily elaborate and formal, but clear and concise, is a help to most
people in working out the actual composition.

Acknowledgment of Obligations.—The obligations to
the writer's sources will be of two kinds. Some of his
reading will have guided his mind, set him thinking,
given him suggestions as to method or general views of
his subject; the references to such works may be made at
the end of the whole paper in a list of references, or
bibliography. The form of citation should be exactly

the same as for the titles already indicated,—for books, by author's name, title, place and date of publication; for periodicals, by author's name, if known, title of article, and name, volume, page, and year of publication of the periodical.

The author may also rely upon authorities for particular facts, or small details. In such cases, the exact place from which the material is drawn should be given, by indicating the title, with the page (or other method of exact reference) so as to make it possible for the reader who desires to do so to compare the citation with what the writer says. This is best done by footnotes. If the same work is several times referred to, some short way of indicating the source may be used. When the words of the author are used, they should be enclosed in quotation marks. But the writer should have as his purpose independently presenting his material, and should never be satisfied with any presentation of matter which is not absolutely the result of his own complete assimilation and recreation of the work. It is a cheat to modify an original slightly, or even to accept the development of the ideas, still more the illustrations and method of thought of an original. What has been thought out for oneself can never take the shape or follow the lines of an authority in sequence or proportions. The evolution of the thought will be the writer's. In particular, it is not legitimate, whether in the writer's words or not, to utilize the author's illustrations or comparisons, without full acknowledgment. Be sure to acknowledge with even fastidious completeness not only the fact of indebtedness, but its extent and its nature. This is only honest; it is also a defense against criticism, for it shifts from the writer's shoulders to those of his authority the responsibility for the statements made.

Authorities may be used in two ways: as the basis of reports and as the materials of original work. Reports, which may be of three forms, topical outlines, connected summaries, and notes, involve the analysis of the work into its main divisions, of these into subdivisions, and so on as far as is desirable, with the indication of the topical relation of the parts. There results a clear understanding of the whole as organic. Frequently, indicating the topics of the individual paragraphs helps in building up the analytic outline of the whole composition. The various forms of outline may vary in scale from a bare statement of the general idea of the whole, to a very full analysis of the development of the whole through the sequence of its parts.

A writer making use of authorities as the basis of original work should strive to estimate the value of the authorities upon which he depends. He should learn how to use bibliographical aids and indexes independently, and to take notes and memoranda intelligently. In working up his material, he should follow essentially the same course as with any other original work, striving to obtain an independent point of view, and to follow out by reflection his own course of thought, assimilating his material completely and not merely following an author. It is incumbent upon him to make full acknowledgment of his indebtedness to his authorities, indicating the nature and extent of his indebtedness as well as the mere fact that he has used certain works.

INDEX